Erich B. Ries

Terrorism, Guerilla, Small-Scale Warfare, People's War

Theory and Practice

A Social and Theoretical History from its Beginnings to 1985

1st Edition 2024

Publisher: BoD · Books on Demand GmbH,

In de Tarpen 42, 22848 Norderstedt

Printed by: Libri Plureos GmbH, Friedensallee 273,

22763 Hamburg

ISBN: 978-3-7693-0251-6

Machine-translated from German

© Copyright 2024

Contents

A short foreword p. 10

Terror p. 12

People's War p. 16

Small war tactics p. 21

Methodological structure p. 24

Chapter 1

Terminology and history p. 26

Guerrilla in the 18th century p. 28

Chapter 2

Theory of guerrilla / guerrilla warfare

in the 19th century p. 34

Neidhardt von Gneisenau p. 37

Carl von Clausewitz p. 41

Chapter 3

Marxism and the revolutionary

Violence p. 43

Friedrich Engels and the guerrillas p. 55

Strategy and tactics in Friedrich Engels p. 57

Bourgeois-democratic and socialist

Revolution p. 57

Small-scale war tactics in Engels p. 65

Chapter 4

Guerrilla in the 19th century p. 72

Chapter 5

EXCURSUS: TERRORISM P. 76

Definition and manifestations

Chapter 6

Small-scale war tactics in the Russian revolutionary movement of the 19th century: Narodnaya Volya p. 86

Chapter 7

Guerilla in the 20th century

Lenin and revolutionary violence p. 99

The Russian Revolution of 1905 and Lenin's military theory p. 102

Chapter 8

The small-scale war in the 1st World War up to Beginning of the 2nd World War p. 117

Chapter 9

The Second World War p. 128

The Soviet-Russian partisan war against the German Wehrmacht

Blitzkrieg strategy p. 130

Partisan warfare in the Stalinist era

Military doctrine p. 132

The tactics p. 144

German "gang warfare" against

Russian partisans p. 148

Chapter 10

Anti-fascist liberation movements

In Europe p. 156

Chapter 11

The Chinese wars of liberation p. 165

MAO and CLAUSEWITZ p. 166

Social analysis and strategy p. 170

Partisan warfare p. 191

The "encirclement and

Extermination campaigns" of the Kuomintang

against the Communists p. 196

The fifth "encirclement and

extermination campaign" and the

"Long March" p. 201

The Sino-Japanese War p. 209

The guerrilla war against Japan

1st phase p. 210

Partisan warfare and war of movement

2nd phase p. 221

Summary p. 224

Chapter 12

Guerrillas in Latin America

Political and economic conditions of the

Guerrilla p. 232

Chapter 13

Latin America and the Left p. 240

Chapter 14

Cuba p. 245

The democratic movement p. 249

The Cuban resistance p. 258

Strategy and tactics of the

Cuban guerrillas p. 264

The tactics p. 275

Chapter 15

Cuba and the Latin American

Revolution p. 278

Chapter 16

The failure of the land guerrillas in

Latin America p. 289

Chapter 17

The urban guerrilla concept

In Latin America p. 296

a. Brazil

Organisational problems

the urban guerrilla p. 308

The tactics of the urban guerrilla p. 314

b. The Tupamaros in Uruguay p. 319

Chapter 18

Guerrillas in Latin America - Balance sheet p. 323

Chapter 19

Urban guerillas in the Federal Republic

Germany p. 333

Terrorism versus people's war p. 348

Afterword by the author p. 351

References p.358

 Summary of the content

Expert opinion by Prof Dr Fernando Mires p. 385

Expert opinion Prof. Dr Shapour Ravasani p.388

A short foreword

This work is both a historical account of the phenomena of small-scale war, terrorism, guerrilla and people's war, as well as a theoretical-historical analysis of the associated military-political issues.

The scope of the material requires both a limitation to selected examples and a limitation to the time frame: The presentation ends in the 80s of the twentieth century.

I wrote this thesis in 1986 as part of my degree in social sciences; the work was completed and **has lost nothing of its significance in terms of content, at least I hope so!**

I was tempted to update the book to include the topics of Islamist extremism and Islamist terrorism in particular, but I decided not to do so because this **would have required** an **extensive account of the history of religion and, due to the extremely large number of terrorist activities that have taken place, an extensive phenomenological account:** Mujahideen and Taliban in Afghanistan, 11 September USA, IS in Syria and so on - this would certainly have gone beyond the scope of the book, so I thought it made sense to do without it altogether!

More on this in my epilogue!

If you are interested in a brief summary and assessment of the content, I would recommend that you first read the expert opinions prepared by Dr Fernando Mires on page 416 and by Prof. Dr. Shapour Ravasani on page 419!

I hope that the readers will gain some insight from my presentation!

Erich B. Ries, Oktober 2024

TERROR

"Our task is to create a

execute a lightning-fast attack

and to render everything harmless, everything

to kill!" - "Captain Medina, my

Do you also mean women and children?" -

"I mean everything! Men, women, children,

Cats, dogs - everything!"

(from: "I loved being in Vietnam" - Leutnant

Calley reports. CALLEY, 1972:70)

Terrorism (1) is almost as old as humanity itself, and the history of the emergence of Western democracies is also written in blood: Fire and murder were natural means of the "Glorious Revolution" in Britain, guerrillas and terror also played a significant role in the American War of Independence, and that "revolutionary terrorism" was the order of the day in the great French Revolution, which had "Liberty, Equality, Fraternity" written on its banners, is common knowledge.

Nevertheless, it hardly occurs to anyone to question the democratic legitimacy of bourgeois constitutional states, which are often based on violent revolutions and revolutionary terrorism, on these grounds.

The "revolutionary creation of states" often stood at the beginning of modern states, be it within society or with the beginning of the liberation struggle against a colonial power or an imperialist annexation by foreign powers.

However, Germany is an exception here: both the Weimar Republic and the Federal Republic of Germany's democracy were the result of lost world wars, and in view of the millions and millions of fallen and murdered in the two world wars, the number of deaths from revolutions, be they "bourgeois" or "socialist", seems comparatively small: in the French Revolution, an estimated 30,000 people fell victim to the terror of the Jacobins - that is fewer than fell in a single ordinary Napoleonic battle!

And in the great Russian October Revolution of 1917, the death toll is said to have been as low as 7 or 8. (HOBSBAWM, 1982:24 ff). However, this was more of a coup against a weakened and divided bourgeois government, and the subsequent civil war battles claimed millions of victims over the course of time...

Even today (1986), terrorism plays a not insignificant role in the policy of the Western alliance, as it does in the policy of the Warsaw Pact states: In Latin America, the USA and some allies supported anti-communist terrorist guerrilla forces and terrorist groups/death squads: Be it the so-called "Contras" on Nicaragua's borders after the Sandinista revolution, dependent on US financial and arms aid, former members of the ousted US protege and dictator Anastasio Somoza, who lost their privileges through the Sandinista revolution and proceeded with similar brutality as the Green Berets in Vietnam at the time (Cf. the above quote from "I liked being in Vietnam").

The US military's support for the completely discredited government in El Salvador, which even had priests murdered by its death squads during a church service because they were too far to the "left", also falls into this category...

In return, the Soviet Union also supported various terrorist groups worldwide, if only they were directed against "US imperialism".

The most famous example is Cuba...

In my opinion, it is completely pointless to derive morality or immorality, sense or nonsense of regular wars as well as of people's wars, guerrillas and terrorism **exclusively** from their violent character.

As a "continuation of politics by other means", such political options, which all result from antagonistic political interests, can only be discussed in the context of the very political purposes to which they owe their origin!

One of the aims of these presentations is to demonstrate this connection!

Carl von Clausewitz says: "The war of a commonality - of whole peoples - (...) always starts from a political state and is only caused by a political motive. It is therefore a political act... (:21) (...) War is a mere continuation of politics by other means. (...), for the political intention is the end, war is the means, and the means can never be thought of without an end." (Clausewitz, 1963:22)

One of the intentions of this work is therefore to emphasise popular war, guerrilla warfare and terrorism for what they are: Political options whose morality or immorality, sense or nonsense can only become clear in their social context!

People´s War

"The sovereignty of a people

will not be discussed, it will be

defended with a weapon in his hand".

FSLN

In a widely used dictionary of foreign words (Textor, Das Fremdwörterlexikon), the following succinct definition can be found under the keyword "democracy": "popular rule as a form of government".

"Democracy" therefore refers to conditions in which a people determine their own policies, i.e. the people are the "sovereign". (Politics = dealing with the management of public affairs": Textor)

This leads to the reverse conclusion that we can only speak of "democracy" where there is **popular sovereignty: military occupation or control by another people therefore excludes popular sovereignty and consequently also democracy,** even if formal democratic institutions may exist. According to the motto: "Every nation has an army in its country - either a foreign one or its own!"

So to be able to speak of democracy, it has to be your own army!

Insofar as they are directed towards the goal of establishing or restoring popular sovereignty, people's wars *can* therefore be **a component of democratic movements** and sometimes a necessary, but never sufficient, means of establishing or restoring popular sovereignty and democracy.

In line with the complexity of the topic of people's war - small-scale war, this work has been limited in terms of content: although small-scale war or individual terrorist tactics have often been used as a counter-revolutionary method with varying degrees of success - the example of the failed CIA-led mercenary invasion in the Cuban Bay of Pigs may stand for many such right-wing guerrilla actions - a people's war directed **against** popular sovereignty is a contradictio in adjecto, a contradiction in terms!

The fact that I categorise the people's war in general as a moment of democratic movements does not, of course, mean that the guerrilla, which always includes terrorist methods, cannot be reduced to being a political option with democratic legitimacy from the outset, on the contrary:

It is almost always **the ruling power** that tries to bring the people to their senses by using terrorist methods and spreading fear and terror.

Violence has played a decidedly reactionary role in the majority of historical events, even if it was unable to halt social development in the long term.

Whenever social conditions became unbearable, when poverty and oppression reached such proportions that any change in conditions seemed better than the status quo, when not even a mostly artificially created enemy image against an imaginary external enemy or marginalised groups within society could form the cement that holds a centrifugal and divided society together, then it was always **naked violence** that was supposed to prevent what is ultimately inevitable: **social change.**

A fundamental mistrust of violence-orientated political options is therefore neither surprising nor wrong based on historical experience, on the contrary...

Where the social situation is characterised by a reasonably intact balance between the "common good" and the interests of the ruling power elites, violence as a form of political conflict usually plays no role: **the interference of violence in political processes characterises precisely a situation where conventional, i.e. peaceful, forms of political conflict are no longer possible, or hardly possible at all.**

It is no coincidence that all the popular wars and guerrilla movements analysed here - representing many others - are the result of such extremely antagonistic conditions, as will be shown.

Where this is not the case, i.e. where revolutionary violence is used to achieve the political goals of a minority, "revolutionary violence" has an intrinsically dysfunctional character, as will also be shown.

The terrorist violence of the "avant-garde" makes the state's counter-violence appear as a legitimate means of preserving law and order, and even those states that do not take democracy very seriously appear as the guardians of democracy. In this case, the state at least finds approval, if not active support from the majority of the population: as a "revolutionary method of intervention by generally weak revolutionary forces" (RAF), the urban guerrilla concept contributes more to the legitimisation of unchecked state violence than to its "unmasking", as the guerrillas usually intend. (see chapter 19 ff).

The topic of "people's war - small-scale war - guerrilla terrorism" dealt with in this social and theoretical history thus encompasses a broad spectrum of social movements: People's wars with a mass character (example China, Chapter 11), guerrilla movements with a class-pluralist composition and representative character (example Cuba, Chapter 14), resistance movements against a foreign occupying power, partly with a mass character (example Soviet Union, Chapter 9), partly with a representative character (example other anti-fascist resistance movements, Chapter 10), terrorist movements that act as the mouthpiece of certain social strata (example: Narodniki in pre-revolutionary Russia, Chapter 6) and finally social revolutionary movements with no or only a very small mass base, which try to compensate for this shortcoming, albeit so far unsuccessfully, through particularly radical and spectacular actions.

Small war tactics

"If the enemy advances, we move

Us back; if he stops, worry us

We beat him; when he is tired, we beat

Too; if he leaves, we pursue him."

MAO-TSE-TUNG

As different as the political objectives were and are, there are structural tactical similarities that characterise small-scale warfare (guerrilla warfare); these characteristic methods from the 19th century to the anti-imperialist people's wars of the 20th century have undergone relatively few changes in principle.

These general strategies and tactics or features that characterise small-scale warfare include

The numerical inferiority

The example of the Chinese People's War in particular makes it clear that this ratio, which is strategically very unfavourable for the guerrillas, can be largely offset by the right tactics - strategically one to ten, tactically 10 to one.

Not only does numerical inferiority almost inevitably result in the need to fragment the enemy through correct, situation-adequate manoeuvring in order to establish at least a balance of forces or, better, superiority **at the tactical level**, but also the need for comprehensive **reconnaissance** as the basis for successful and superior manoeuvring and outmanoeuvring of the enemy.

Surprise as a component of the small-scale warfare method opens up the possibility of attacking the enemy precisely at the moment when he is at his most defenceless. This is an elementary prerequisite for any victorious guerrilla in the face of an enemy that is far superior in conventional terms.

Surprise is an element of **offensive warfare**, and nowhere is the classic rule that attack is the best defence as true as in small-scale warfare: offensive warfare means constantly retaining the initiative, thereby being able to determine the aim and location of the "theatre of war".

Irregularity, another characteristic of small-scale warfare, includes two aspects: The irregularity of warfare and the irregularity of the combatants.

While irregularity in the planning and execution of actions is the conditio sine qua non of the guerrilla - a predictable guerrilla loses its dangerousness because the indispensable element of surprise is eliminated - the irregularity of the combatants is only of elementary importance where the territory of the theatre of war can be completely controlled by the enemy army.

This applies, for example, to the Western European resistance movements during the Second World War (cf. Chapter 10), but also to modern urban guerrillas and urban terrorism (cf. Chapter 15 ff).

On the other hand, Fidel Castro's "Barbudos" in the barely controllable Sierra Maestra were recognisable as combatants, as were parts of the Red Army in China - but they only became "regulars" after the seizure of power.

Although, paradoxically, the revolutionisation of warfare in the twentieth century and the development of ever greater overkill potentials seem to have contributed to the activation of the guerrilla movement, it can be said that the tactical methods and characteristics of small-scale warfare have changed only relatively little over the centuries.

From a tactical point of view, too, the particularities of each case result less from the tactics used than from the economic, social, political and cultural contexts to which the guerrilla owes its origins.

Methodological structure

Small-scale warfare has always been a component of violent conflicts, but guerrilla warfare in the context of a people's war dates back to the end of the 18th and beginning of the 19th century; the people's war guerrilla has its origins in the age of bourgeois revolutions and the constitution of nation states.

On the one hand, people's wars are "individual" phenomena; on the other hand, every people's war establishes continuity between the various emancipatory movements; people's wars are therefore historical phenomena. For this reason, the structure of this work is also chronological.

The aim of this investigation and presentation is not least to show the "inner bond" that connects the popular wars at the end of the 18th century, in the 19th and in the 20th century, but also to make clear the immanent ruptures and undesirable developments of the phenomena of popular war, petty war, guerrilla warfare and terrorism, as they appear above all in urban terrorism.

Due to the nature of the matter, a purely phenomenological presentation would not do justice to the topic, because since people have developed theories about the people's war and the guerrilla, **these theories have in turn influenced further developments more or less decisively.**

This is particularly clear at present (1986): In my opinion, the now rich fund of experience and "guerrilla theories" plays a far greater role for rural and, above all, urban guerrillas than military theories did for the people's wars of past eras.

More concretely: Urban terrorism, which is currently (1986) once again causing a stir, is - in contrast to the Spanish People's War or the American War of Independence - inconceivable without the chequered history of the guerrilla and the theories about it - from Engels to Lenin to Mao, from Mao to Debray and Guevara to Marighela!

This alone makes the discussion of the theories of the "socialist classics" on the subject of "revolutionary violence - guerrillas - people's war - terrorism" appear meaningful. (cf. chapter 3 and chapter 7, among others).

Chapter 1

Terminology and history

The terms that have been coined by nations in the course of history for the "little war" are more diverse than the purposes for which it was and is waged.

In addition to the terms detachment war, outpost war, light war (Clausewitz), which were commonly used in the 18th and early 19th centuries, terms such as partisan war, partisan war, underground war, underground struggle, irregular war, insurrection war, later also revolutionary war, people's war, subversive war, covert war, covert struggle were in use.

Occasionally it is also referred to - pejoratively - as gang warfare or erroneously and simplistically as terrorism.

During the Spanish People's War against the Napoleonic invasion armies (1807 - 1814), the term "guerrilla" (small war) emerged, which is most commonly used today, especially in the West.

Contrary to widespread opinion (Haffner, S. 1966:5), the guerrilla is not an invention of the communists, although the small war with the beginning of decolonisation after the end of the Second World War under the leadership of communist parties (China, Malaya, Vietnam, the Philippines, etc.) has come to the attention of the wider world public.

The ancient Greeks knew and practised small-scale warfare, as did the Romans and Germanic tribes.

The small-scale war tactics of Arminius / Hermann the Cheruscan against the Romans, in particular the annihilation battle in the Teuteburg Forest in 9 AD, where three legions inflicted one of their most devastating defeats on the Romans in the famous Varus Battle...

"Small-scale wars also took place in the Middle Ages and in the early modern period, in the 16th and 17th centuries." (Hahlweg, W.: 1968:25) In my opinion, Hahlweg's book is the best academic work on the history of guerrillas.

In fact, guerrilla warfare is almost as old as mankind itself.

(Cf. Wilkins, 1963:30; Guevara, a, 1972:124; Kutger, 1963:79)

Guerrilla in the 18th century

The 18th century is characterised by the thoroughly purposeful interaction of regular line troops and small war units.

The small war detachments consisted of specially qualified and equipped soldiers who nevertheless remained part of the regular army.

Small-scale warfare had a supporting function in the context of overall warfare and occasionally proved to be of strategic importance beyond its purely tactical-operational function.

One example is the retreat of the Prussian army from Bohemia in November 1744, where small Austrian detachments inflicted heavy losses on the Prussian army and forced Frederick the Great to evacuate Prague on 20 November 1744. (Hahlweg, W., 1968:27,28)

The experience of the War of the Spanish Succession, the First and Second Silesian Wars and the Seven Years' War helped to further develop the technical and practical side of guerrilla warfare, and small-scale warfare and the military personnel involved in it were thoroughly accepted.

However, this changed at the end of the 19th century and in the 20th century, when the guerrilla as an agent of social revolutionary movements and revolutionary state creation, which were directed against the state and the military, became increasingly objectionable in traditionally conservative military circles due to its totality of method and objective.

The wars of absolutism were not total wars in which it was a matter of life and death for the civilian population, of the attempt to enslave and exterminate entire peoples, as was exemplified by the Second World War, but were limited in terms of ends and means.

The political goals were also defined by the absolutist state without the people being granted any significant influence over them. (Haffner, S.:14,15; Hahlweg, W.: 26).

As a rule, there was no general conscription, the armies consisted of professional soldiers and, in addition, of recruits hired or pressed as required, the combatants were exclusively military personnel and generally had no primary interest in the political goals pursued with their help. Incidentally, this is probably one of the reasons for the success of so many wars of liberation, from the American War of Independence to the Vietnam War: The "irregulars" fighting for their **own interests** were and are (1986) confronted by mercenaries or conscripts with no or only **secondary** personal **motivation.**

The situation was different in the colonies, however, where it was often a question of exterminating or enslaving entire peoples, and the armed conflicts therefore took on other, usually more total and brutal forms.

In addition to the limited political objectives that determined the appearance of war in the 18th century and the early 19th century and consequently limited military conflicts to the military, there was a second reason that made the involvement of the whole people, i.e. also outside the strictly regulated military apparatus, appear **dangerous** for national defence, for example. In the chapter on popular armament in his epoch-making work "On War", Clausewitz writes: "In cultivated Europe, popular war is a phenomenon of the 19th century. It has its supporters and its opponents, the latter for political reasons, because they consider it a revolutionary means, a state of anarchy declared to be lawful, which is as dangerous to the social order within as it is to the enemy..." (Clausewitz, C. von, 1963:173)

With the American War of Independence (1775-1783), the French Revolution and the associated wars of liberation against the French invading armies in the Vendée (1793-1796), in Spain (1808-1814), in Tyrol (1809), in Germany (1809) and finally in Russia (1812), the guerrilla underwent a decisive transformation and expansion of its objectives, as well as an accompanying qualitative change in its forms: While small-scale warfare had been continuously perfected and refined into a military art over the course of the 18th century as an integral part of regular "cherished" warfare, a new actor now came into play: the people.

The military historian Werner Hahlweg and Lenin were in complete agreement that the participation of the masses in warfare at the end of the 18th and beginning of the 19th century represented a caesura in the history of modern warfare, raising the small war to a completely new level.

Hahlweg writes: "While small-scale warfare in the military-technical sphere was more or less carried over unchanged from the previous epoch, its manifestation changed with regard to the impulses that arose from the political, social and economic spheres, which made it as long-lasting as it was intense in terms of its objectives. Small-scale warfare had become an essential part of the struggle for the existence of nations.

For the development of small-scale warfare, the seemingly modern era of 1775-1789-1815 represents a turning point: this is where the path to our present day begins. The small-scale wars of this epoch exhibit almost all the characteristics, combination and combination possibilities that can be found today in advanced, further differentiated forms in modern guerrilla warfare.

The repeated and close connection between small-scale war and people's war thus represents what is actually new in the development of this form of war during the period 1775-1788-1815." (Emphasis mine). (Hahlweg 1968:60)

In his article "The Case of Port Arthur", published in January 1905, LENIN writes: "Those times are irretrievably gone when wars were waged by mercenaries or representatives of a caste half-alienated from the people...Wars are now waged by the peoples..." (Lenin, a, 1952:43)

As the peoples themselves stepped onto the political stage and thus no longer left the craft of war exclusively to the military, not only did the political objective become more total, but also "warfare as a means of politics" (Clausewitz 1963:22) became irregular in several respects:

Insofar as the essence of small-scale warfare consisted in surprise, in avoiding regular battles, and conversely in covert individual combat, it was always "irregular". However, as the people entered the military arena largely unencumbered by centuries-old traditions and thought patterns, the distinction between combatant and civilian also became blurred: This was already evident in the counter-revolutionary uprising of the Vendeér peasants, who ambushed the revolutionary armies, only to return to their farms by stealth and peacefully go about their work as harmless civilians until the next attack.

So while the small war detachments of the 18th century consisted of soldiers and remained identifiable as such (even when fighting undercover), the identifiability of the fighter was now over: every man, every woman, even every child was a potentially dangerous opponent.

Now the war no longer took place on clear fronts, the front was now everywhere, the war was waged in the depths of space, not only in a geographical but also in a social sense. Not only the covert way of fighting, but even more so the involvement of the civilian population transcended war as a predominantly military form of action into a form of total confrontation between groups or nations.

So reports the journal of a German fighter corps fighting on the English side in the American War of Independence:

It is "almost impossible to surprise the enemy on any occasion, because every house near which one comes is, so to speak, a forward picket; for the farmer or his son or servant, and even his wife and daughter, shoot with a shotgun or use surreptitious means of signalling the approach of the enemy". (Hahlweg, 1968:33; Schulz, 1985:10,11)

Chapter 2

Guerrilla theory in the 19th century

The Spanish People's War against the French, which after 7 years (1814) of fierce fighting with the support of regular British troops led to victory for the Spanish, became a model case for waging a people's war as a guerrilla in the 19th century.

The Spanish guerrillas were the first to combine all the elements that are still characteristic of small-scale wars today:

Mobilisation of broad masses of people. Organising these into divisions that are mobile everywhere; fighters who are based in civilian areas and can no longer be identified as such by the enemy, "swim in the people like fish in water" (MAO).

Leaning power that supports the guerrillas; restructuring of the guerrilla units into quasi-regular army units after a corresponding period of development and growth; protracted war of attrition until the enemy is "ripe" for large-scale offensives by the regular units that have grown out of the guerrilla units and the own units have been able to gain appropriate military experience.

The (re)attainment of national sovereignty as a motive of the people's war can hardly be overestimated, as in almost all people's wars, the attainment of national sovereignty is always a demand of the movement alongside social revolutionary goals. In addition to economic and political independence, the intention is often to reappropriate one's own oppressed culture, which was often in danger of being buried, particularly in parts of the "Third World", by the market-driven imposition of the "American way of life".

This is related to the fact that very often after the victory of anti-imperialist movements, the liberated nations placed special emphasis and activities in the development of their national culture.

In the Chinese People's War against the Japanese and the Kuomintang, in Vietnam, Algeria, Iran and Nicaragua - to name just a few examples - the desire for a national identity in the broadest sense always played an important role in popular uprisings, alongside social revolutionary intentions.

The importance of guerrilla warfare as a means of national defence, which first became clear in the Spanish People's War, also inspired well-known Prussian reformers and patriots such as Freiherr von Stein, Scharnhorst, Clausewitz and Gneisenau to think about their own ideas.

Not only von Stein but also Scharnhorst were in favour of a general uprising against the French in the event of an invasion.

As military men, Gneisenau and Clausewitz were primarily interested in the practical aspects of guerrilla warfare and the general arming of the people as a means of national defence.

However, Gneisenau and Clausewitz were by no means guided by purely military considerations, but also took political and ideological issues into account in their deliberations. It is precisely this that sets these Prussian officers apart from most of their comrades to this day.

Neidhardt von Gneisenau

Gneisenau's "Plan for the Preparation of a Popular Uprising", which he submitted to the Prussian King Frederick William III, is particularly noteworthy. The contradiction between Gneisenau and some of his colleagues is striking: According to Gneisenau's idea, the Prussian **monarchy**, which was based on the lack of popular sovereignty, was to be protected or even saved with the help of the popular uprising, actually the ultima ratio of peoples striving for emancipation!

In Spain the people had risen up themselves, in Prussia the popular uprising was to be organised and controlled by the state, the authorities were to ensure by decree that the people would rise up in the event of an uprising - this would have presupposed an identity of king, army and people, which was postulated but never existed and could not exist.

However, using the example of the Soviet Russian partisan war against the German Wehrmacht, it will be shown here later that under **certain conditions** a state-initiated, organised and controlled people's war is nevertheless possible.

It is therefore not surprising that the Prussian king was sceptical of Gneisenau's "plan to prepare a popular uprising" from the outset - the shock that the French Revolution had given to all monarchies was still too fresh in his mind...

King Frederick William III's mistrust of his people, which was certainly not entirely unjustified in this respect, is also expressed in the "Decree on the Landsturm" (21 April 1813) and the 2nd Decree of 17 July of the same year, in which an attempt is made to give the popular uprising an institutional framework and to purge it of revolutionary elements as far as possible.

In the decree, the Landsturm was placed entirely under the command of the monarchist authorities; any unauthorised action, i.e. action not expressly recommended by the state, was regarded as "mutiny" and threatened with the death penalty. (Frederick William III, 1970:72)

Right in the introduction to his "Plan for the Preparation of a Popular Uprising", Gneisenau makes it clear that he **is a reformist within the framework of the monarchist system** and that the popular uprising is by no means intended for revolutionary purposes:

"If Prussia is threatened with invasion, i.e. annihilation, the royal house of regents seeks help and support in a popular uprising" (Gneisenau, N. von: Plan zur Vorbereitung eines Volksaufstandes 1970:42)

Nevertheless, his organisational ideas with regard to the implementation of the popular uprising can *almost* be considered revolutionary, especially for a Prussian military officer of higher rank:

Under "Militia organisation in general" he even calls for the election of officers and non-commissioned officers:

.... They choose their officers and non-commissioned officers, and initially officers are employed by their organisation at half pay." (Gneisenau, N. v. op. cit.: 47)

Gneisenau draws up 6 tactical principles according to which the militia should proceed and which reflect his practical experience as an officer on the British side during the American War of Independence as well as his thorough study of the Spanish People's War.

Gneisenau writes: If the enemy troops are numerically superior, "they (the militia) move into the nearest woods in order to attack the individual quarters or detachments from there. If a legion is in danger of being cancelled, it disperses, hides its weapons, caps and sashes and thus appears to be an inhabitant of the country." (Gneisenau, N. v. op. cit.:50)

Gneisenau counters the Prussian king's objection that "lack of food, no habit of privation and endurance, still less experience in war, and a few shotgun and cannon shots disperse this legion": "...all these misgivings did not deter the Spaniards from taking up arms when they saw themselves outwitted; and notwithstanding they, accustomed to a hundred years of peace and ignorant of war, committed great errors, they still exist today as a nation, and this only by insurrectionary war." (Gneisenau, N. v., op. cit.: 51)

Gneisenau's suggestion regarding the procurement of weapons is also noteworthy: "Whoever can get hold of an enemy rifle will receive 10 thalers for it and from now on will fight with this rifle, provided he prefers it to the pike." (Gneisenau, N. v. op. cit.:52)

To the king's remark that this price was far too high, he replied: "A rifle now costs 12 thalers. If you give 10 thalers for a conquered one, the state gains 2 thalers, the soldier 10 thalers, his comrades desire to acquire just as much, and the enemy is one rifle poorer. The moral gain was the main purpose here, that of money was not considered." (Gneisenau, N. v. op. cit.: 53)

Friedrich Engels, the "General of the Labour Movement", wrote in connection with Gneisenau's "Plan for the Preparation of a Popular Uprising" and the decree of Frederick William III: "This law may indeed be called an exemplary manual for Francoists - and, designed by no mediocre strategist - it is as applicable now in France as it was in its time in Germany. Fortunately for Napoleon, however, it was very imperfectly executed. The king was terrified of his own people. Allowing the people to fight for themselves - without the king's orders - was too anti-Prussian. So the Landsturm was suspended until the king would call it up, which he never did. Gneisenau raged, but in the end he had to do without the Landsturm." (Engels, a, 1952:29)

Carl von Clausewitz

Clausewitz, like Gneisenau an officer in the Prussian army and, among other things, a teacher at the War College in Berlin, where he gave lectures on small-scale war in 1810/11 and wrote his epoch-making work "On War" between 1816 and 1830, which is still required reading for reactionary military officers and revolutionary socialists alike, was similar to his colleague and friend Neithardt von Gneisenau: he was a staunch supporter of both the Prussian monarchy and total people's war.

His ambivalent understanding of politics is hardly expressed more succinctly anywhere than in the "Confessional Memorandum" he wrote in 1812, where the appendix states: "It is not the king who fights the king, not one army against another, but one people against another, and the king and the army are contained in the people." (Clausewitz, C. V. , b, :88)

In his work "On War", Clausewitz, an outstanding expert on the theory and practice of people's war in his time, drew up a catalogue of conditions that he considered to be prerequisites for the effectiveness of people's war.

"The conditions under which alone the People's War can become effective are as follows:

1. that the war was waged within the country,

2. that it would not be decided by a single catastrophe,

3. that the theatre of war takes up a considerable amount of land

4. that the character of the people supports the measure

5. that the country is very cut through and inaccessible, either by mountains or by forests and swamps or by the nature of the soil culture...
The use of the landstorm and armed crowds cannot and should not be directed against the enemy's main force, not even against considerable corps; it should not crush the core, but only gnaw at the surface, at the perimeters." (Clausewitz, C. v., C, op. cit. :173)

Not only Clausewitz's lectures at the war school in Berlin, but also the fact that in the chapter on "arming the people" he includes principles of small war in his work on "great" war and war in general, shows that he was one of the very few military men to anticipate the possibilities of people's war long before its universal significance today.

Chapter 3

Marxism and revolutionary violence

Preliminary remark:

While the national question was the starting point of the people's wars of the early 19th century and, accordingly, of their theorists, Marx/Engels' theory of revolutionary violence and the guerrilla points beyond this and anticipates aspects of the people's war that became increasingly important, especially in the second half of the 20th century: It is no longer just the struggle between nations and peoples, but also the struggle between classes that is now included in the considerations.

The mere fact that the most important and spectacular victories of guerrilla movements in the 20th century (China, Vietnam, Yugoslavia, Cuba, etc.) were won by movements based on "Marxism-Leninism" makes it seem necessary to go into great detail on the theory of revolutionary violence and the guerrilla, as or insofar as it was developed by the "socialist classics".

Marxism not only inspired the most important liberation movements of the 20th century, but also served and still serves as the ideological basis of legitimisation for the most diverse movements, parties, groups and factions.

Sinn Fein/IRA in Ireland, Herri Battasuna/ETA in the Basque Country, parts of the PLO in the Middle East (e.g. the PFLP), the FMLN in El Salvador, the People's Fedayeen and their various splinter groups in Iran, the PKK in Kurdistan, the RAF in the Federal Republic of Germany, the Red Brigades in Italy, the AD in France, the CCC in Belgium, etc. etc. - all these guerrilla movements or groups fighting today (1986) refer to Marxism-Leninism - reason enough to take a closer look at the statements of the socialist classics in this regard.

Marx and Engels' position on revolutionary violence is characterised by a double front: on the one hand, Marxist social theory rejects "conspiracy" and "putschism"; on the other hand, both Marx and Engels resolutely oppose those "class collaborators" who shy away from revolutionary violence and, by preaching peaceableness, create and strengthen illusions where only decisive action can lead to victory...

Engels' draft "Principles of Communism" (1847) already states: "But the Communists also see that the development of the proletariat is being violently suppressed in almost all civilised countries and that the opponents of the Communists are working towards a revolution with all their might. If the oppressed proletariat is finally driven into a revolution by this, we communists will then defend the cause of the proletariat just as well by deed as we do now by word." (Engels, F. , b, 1980:372)

In the "MANIFESTO OF THE COMMUNIST PARTY", Marx and Engels reaffirm their views on the necessity of revolutionary violence: "The Communists openly declare that their aims can only be achieved through the violent overthrow of all previous social orders." (Marx, K. / Engels, F. 1980/1848:493)

In his "Anti-Dühring", Engels resolutely opposes those socialists who fear violent class confrontation and more or less openly dream of "growing peacefully into socialism": "That violence is the tool with which the social movement asserts itself and breaks up ossified, dead political forms - not a word of this in Mr Dühring. Only with a sigh and a groan does he admit the possibility that violence may be necessary to overthrow the exploitative economy - unfortunately!

And this dull, sapless and powerless preacher's way of thinking claims to impose itself on the most revolutionary party known to history." (Engels, F., C, MEW 20:171)

There is complete agreement between Karl Marx and Friedrich Engels on the question of revolutionary violence: for Marx, violence is "the midwife of every old society that becomes pregnant with a new one". (Marx, K., a, MEW 23:779)

Although for Marx, as for Engels, violence is a necessary means of revolution, it is and remains a **means to an end**, always subordinate to the concrete revolutionary situation.

In this respect, Hannah Arendt rightly writes: "Whether Clausewitz calls war the "continuation of political intercourse with the interference of other means", or whether Engels defines violence as a "force accelerating the lawful economic development" - the emphasis in both cases is on political or economic continuity, on the continuity of a process that remains determined by factors that already existed before the violent action. (Ahrendt, H. Merkur 1, 1970:5)

Marx very succinctly summarised the determinacy of the revolutionary process through socio-economic development dynamics mentioned by Hannah Arendt in his famous preface "On the Critique of Political Economy": After Marx states that it is not "The consciousness of men that determines their being, but conversely their social being that determines their consciousness", (Marx, K., b, MEW 13:9), he names the driving forces for the social revolution:

"At a certain stage of their development the material productive forces of society come into contradiction with the existing relations of production or, which is only a legal term for it, with the property relations within which they had hitherto moved. From forms of development of the forces of production, these relations turn into shackles. An epoch of social revolutions then occurs" and, further below, summarising: "The bourgeois relations of production are the last antagonistic form of the social process of production, antagonistic not in the sense of individual antagonism, but of an antagonism that has grown out of the social living conditions of the individuals, but the productive forces developing in the womb of bourgeois society simultaneously create the material conditions for the resolution of this antagonism." (Marx, K., b, :9)

Marx and Engels certainly included revolutionary violence, and thus also the guerrilla, in their considerations as an important, if not the most important moment, as a means to a revolutionary end; however, neither Marx nor Engels developed a closed concept of revolutionary violence, in contrast to Castroism-Guevarism, for example, because they "analysed the possibility of the effectiveness of revolutionary violence from a superordinate point of view, without losing sight of the fundamental position towards the use of violence.

This position is aimed at

- against a "terrorist" and "adventurist" attitude as well as

- against the attitudes of "class collaborators" (Kießler, 1975:15)

The Marxist understanding of violence in the revolutionary process in particular has often been interpreted one-sidedly, i.e. incorrectly, even by parties and movements that invoke Marxism, whereby the respective interests are probably the cause of this:

Apart from the anti-communist interest in lumping Marxism, conspiracy and terrorism together, two basic positions can be identified, between which there are all kinds of transitions and hybrid forms:

While many actionist/terrorist-oriented groups absolutise Marx and Engels' affirmation of revolutionary terrorism **under certain circumstances** - here they can cite numerous statements by Engels in particular - and consciously or unconsciously disregard the fact that Marx in particular, but also Friedrich Engels, derived the social and thus also revolutionary dynamic from the development of productive forces and the relations of production, i.e. by no means generally spectacular acts of revolutionary violence, but rather attributed far greater importance in the revolutionary process to the mass nature and breadth of actions, the social democratic parties, with the growth of their reformist wings, especially since the turn of the century, have stripped Marxism of those revolutionary elements that their practical orientation, which was increasingly based on reforms within the framework of the existing capitalist system, could denounce as "class collaboration" or, conversely, that could bring social democracy into direct confrontation and conflict with state power.

For example, to give just one example of the purification of Marxist theory from undesirable aspects, the last paragraph of Engels' introduction to Marx's "The Class Struggles in

France", dated 6 March 1895, was completely deleted by the SPD party executive (according to Erich Wollenber, cf. footnote in Wollenberg, 1952:69,70).

Among other things, it says: "Does this mean that street fighting won't play a role in the future? Absolutely not..." (Engels, d, :23)

In the introduction to Marx's "The Class Struggles in France", however, it also becomes clear that Engels was very concerned, especially in view of the rapid growth of the labour movement, not to endanger it by repelling the workers with "sectarian" slogans and by giving the state the opportunity to drive the rapidly gaining influence of social democracy back into illegality and thereby weaken it through an overly "Blanquist" orientation.

The aim (in 1894) was to utilise parliamentarism for the workers' movement as far as possible without indulging in illusions about the character of capitalism and the state apparatus - but this presupposed legality. (Marek, 1966:128)

In his "Introduction..." Engels emphasises his rejection of untimely sabre-rattling: "A future street fight can therefore only be victorious if this unfavourable situation is outweighed by other factors. Does the reader now understand why the ruling powers want to bring us to the place where the shotgun fires and the sabre strikes? Why we are accused of cowardice today because we do not take to the streets without further ado, where we are certain of defeat in advance? Why are we so desperately begged to play cannon fodder for once?"

And, further down:

"The time of surprise revolutions, of revolutions carried out by small minorities at the head of unconscious masses, is over. But for the masses to understand what is to be done, long, continuous labour is required, and it is this labour that we are now engaged in, and with a success that drives our opponents to despair." (Engels, b, op. cit. :262)

Karl Marx, too, not only repeatedly named the socio-economic-political conditions for the possibly meaningful and necessary revolutionary violence, but also warned against "anticipating the revolutionary process, artificially driving it into a crisis, an impromptu revolution, without making the conditions of a revolution." (Reviews in the Neue Rheinische Zeitung, quoted here from Kießler, op. cit. :30)

The fact that Marx, like Engels, was neither a worshipper of revolutionary violence nor of parliamentary legality is also expressed in a speech Marx gave in Amsterdam on 15 September 1872, in which he states:

"The worker must one day seize political power in order to build the new organisation of labour; he must overthrow the old policy which maintains the old institutions. But we have not claimed that the ways to reach this goal are the same everywhere.

We know that the institutions, customs and traditions of different countries must be taken into account, and we do not deny that there are countries, such as America and England, where workers can achieve their goals peacefully.

If this is true, we must also recognise that in most countries of the continent the lever of our revolution must be force; it is force to which we must one day appeal in order to establish the rule of labour." (Marx, MEW 28:160, quoted here from Marek:127,128)

Summary

For Marx and Engels, violence is "the midwife of every old society that becomes pregnant with a new one."

As a "midwife", however, violence neither produces the revolution nor does it bring about the new society itself, it merely provides "midwifery", i.e. it is merely a means, albeit sometimes a very important one, alongside other means such as agitation and propaganda, demonstrations, general strikes, workers' control and so on, to ensure the successful course of the revolution and, if necessary, to shorten it.

Just as the midwife is not the essence of birth, violence is not the essence of revolution. Nevertheless, for Marx, as for Engels, it is a legitimate and sometimes indispensable tool of the revolutionary masses, although for Marx and Engels the masses can never be replaced by violence.

However, my view that Marx and Engels took an intermediate position on the question of revolutionary violence, i.e. that they were neither unconditional supporters nor opponents of violence in the revolution, but basically left this question open, only discussing it concretely from case to case, but not making it a fundamental moral and political question, but rather wanting it to be subordinated to the respective concrete historical, socio-economic-political constellations, is obviously not shared by renowned scholars such as Iring Fetscher and Günter Rohrmoser: In the chapter "The Marxist Theory of the State and the Peaceful Transition to Socialism" in their book "Ideologies and Strategies", the differentiation, not rejection, of revolutionary violence by Marx and Engels in their later writings is implicitly (re)interpreted to mean that they would have considered revolutionary violence unnecessary or even harmful in later years. (Fetscher/Rohrmoser, 181:140 ff). This impression is reinforced by the fact that an ideological bridge is built between Marx/Engels and Karl Kautsky precisely on the question of violence, which in my opinion is in no way justifiable in this form.

I consider it scientifically problematic to sweep existing fundamental differences between Marx and Engels on the one hand and Karl Kautsky on the other under the carpet, especially on the question of revolutionary violence - but this is how Fetscher and Rohrmoser proceed.

Two "classics" of Marxism, namely Lenin and Trotsky, have explicitly and very critically dealt with Kautsky's position on the question of revolutionary violence: Lenin above all in his writing "State and Revolution" (Lenin, V., b, 1970:319 ff) and Trotsky above all in "Terrorism and Communism - Anti-Kautsky! (Trotsky, L., b, 1978).

Both accuse Kautsky not only of revising Marxism on the question of violence, but even of betraying the interests of the working class.

Rosa Luxemburg also wrote in a letter to Luise Kautsky (Breslau prison, November 1917): "Are you happy about the Russians? Of course they cannot hold their own in this witches' sabbath - not because of the statistics that prove Russia's lagging economic development, as your astute husband has recounted - but because the Social Democracy of this more highly developed West consists of vile rabbit's feet who, as peaceful spectators, let the Russians bleed themselves to death..." (Quoted in Trotsky, b, 1978:XII)

Without having to agree with Lenin's, Trotsky's or Luxemburg's criticism of Kautsky on all points, it can be said that there is a gulf between the orthodox Marxist position on violence in the revolution and that of Karl Kautsky.

It is therefore impossible to avoid the impression that Fetscher and Rohrmoser's argumentation ignores the facts and deals selectively with Marxism. This impression is reinforced when the authors quote Wilhelm Liebknecht in order to implicitly document their rejection of revolutionary violence. (Fetscher/Rohrmoser, op. cit.:142)

The fact that Liebknecht, like Marx and Engels (but in contrast to Kautsky after the end of the First World War), by no means rejected revolutionary violence across the board, but was conversely the leader of the German revolution in 1918/19 (Spartacus Uprising) alongside Rosa Luxemburg and paid for his leading role in this by no means non-violent revolution with his life - not a word about this in Fetscher and Rohrmoser.

The question of why such renowned academics as Iring Fetscher and Günter Rohrmoser argue so selectively in a theoretical presentation can perhaps be answered in part by referring to the publisher and client of the work written by Fetscher/Rohrmoser: It is the Federal Ministry of the Interior...

This type of more or less tendentious literature also includes the book "Terrorismus und Guerilla" by Tophoven/Becker, which is widely used as teaching material for upper secondary schools. (1986).

(Tophoven, R. / Becker, H. 1979)

Friedrich Engels and the guerrillas

While Karl Marx dealt comparatively little with guerrillas and one finds almost only marginal remarks on this subject in his work, his friend Friedrich Engels dealt with guerrillas in great detail and analysed them from various perspectives.

Friedrich Engels is rightly regarded as the first Marxist (small-scale) war theorist, with whose well-founded judgement Marx always agreed in this respect.

Erich Wollenberg writes in his introduction to Engels Militärpolitishen Schriften: "As long as Marx lived, the two friends hardly published anything that they had not agreed on beforehand. If in the question of political economy and philosophy Marx undoubtedly appeared as the giver and Engels more "in charge" than creative, the relationship in all areas of military policy was the reverse. Here Engels was the expert whose judgement Marx was happy to defer to. Most of the military and military policy articles and essays that appeared under Marx's name were penned by the "General". (e.g. "Revolution and Counter-Revolution in Germany"), and even in Marx's writings, sections dealing with military issues are almost exclusively edited by Engels. (Wollenberg, 1952, op. cit.:7; Wallach, 1972:253; Schickel, J. 1970:116, 117; Lussu, E., n.d.: 19)

When uprisings broke out all over Germany in 1849 after the adoption of the imperial constitution in order to impose the constitution on the local nobility, Engels joined the insurgents as a "one-year volunteer" under the commander Willich, whose adjutant Engels became, and thus gained his first (and only practical) experience of revolutionary war and guerrilla warfare in four battles.

The "incomprehensibly dirty esprit of the corps of the soldier pack - meaning the professional officers who had joined the insurgents as military leaders - probably strengthened Engels in his view that "at least one of the civilians" had to be equal to them in terms of military knowledge. (Wallach, op. cit.: 252)

Willich operated with his 700-strong Freikorps in the Palatinate between the garrisons of Landau and Germersheim, primarily using guerrilla tactics: He organised vigilantes in the villages to guard the roads and provide other military support services, cut off almost all access routes to the Landau fortress with his troops and worried and provoked this garrison with night patrols and skirmishes to such an extent that the garrison was prompted to "open fire from twenty-four-pounders on a private and two men, which was as powerful as it was harmless." Engels, F., e, op. cit. : 79).

Engels' 1859 pamphlet "Po und Rhein" caused a great stir, especially in military circles, and gave rise to the assumption in these circles that the author was a general who kept to himself in the background - this makes it clear that Engels had not "cooked militaria" for nothing. (Wallach, op. cit.: 253)

Bourgeois democratic and socialist revolution

Marxism distinguishes between the **character of** a revolution, its **driving forces** and the **leading class** or **party**.

Thus, the character of the German revolution of 1848/49 could only be bourgeois-democratic, since it was primarily about the overthrow of the feudal aristocracy and the fight for bourgeois-democratic rights (freedom of assembly, freedom of contract, freedom of the press, etc.), the "dictatorship of the proletariat" was not yet on the agenda, since the objective conditions in mid-19th century Germany were not yet in place: The predominant mode of production was still agriculture, modern industry was still in its infancy, its degree of concentration and thus that of the working class was comparatively low (in contrast, for example, to Tsarist Russia before the October Revolution!), moreover, the working class was still too "unconscious" in the sense of socialist views, and a class-autonomous organisation, i.e. a revolutionary workers' party with a mass base, did not yet exist either.

(The Paris Commune also suffered from the lack of class organisation, as Marx and Engels rightly pointed out as one of the reasons for its defeat).

As large-scale industry was still relatively underdeveloped and the petty bourgeoisie was a significant social force, especially in small and medium-sized towns (competitive capitalism), the leading role in the revolution fell to this social stratum, which, according to Marx and Engels, had to prove unreliable due to its class position: Engels in particular made his disparaging position on the petty bourgeoisie clear on several occasions. His assessment of the middle classes is particularly clear in the article "The Imperial Constitutional Campaign", published under Marx's name in the "New York Tribune" on 2 October 1852, which was actually written by Engels, who was evaluating his experiences as a "one-year volunteer": "The class of the petty bourgeoisie, whose importance and influence we have already emphasised on various occasions, may be regarded as the leading class of the middle classes of 1849.

As none of Germany's major cities were among the centres of the movement this time, the petty bourgeoisie managed to take control of the movement. (....)

Wherever an armed clash leads to a serious crisis, the petty bourgeois were seized with the utmost horror at the perilous situation that had arisen for them (...) were they not forced to take up an official position in the insurrection, thereby jeopardising their fortunes in the event of defeat? And what else awaited them in the event of victory than the certainty that the victorious proletarians, who formed the main mass of the fighting army, would chase them out of office and overturn their policy?" (Engels, F. , e, op. cit.: 13,14)

Engels thus formulates a contradiction here between the "leading class or party (here it is the petty bourgeoisie) and the "driving forces" (proletarians), as was repeated in a modified form 70 years later in Russia during the February Revolution.

Engels was of the opinion that the bourgeoisie would not be willing or able to consistently carry out their own revolution, as in France, for example, but would try to withhold the gains from the workers in the event of victory.

Engels also comes to a similar conclusion in his study "The German Peasants' War": "The classes and class factions that betrayed everywhere in 1848/49 will be found to be traitors as early as 1525, albeit at a lower stage of development." (Wallach, op. cit.: 257)

In contrast to many guerrilla organisations, which usually reject a pronounced orientation towards the proletariat, even though they often use empty phrases such as "proletarian internationalism", Marx and Engels (and later Trotsky in particular) distrusted not only the actual petty bourgeoisie, but the middle class in general.

In the "Address of the Central Authority to the League" (March 1850), officially written by Marx and Engels, Engels insists on the use of "revolutionary terrorism" for the victorious realisation of the bourgeois-democratic revolution: "The workers must, above all during the conflict and immediately after the struggle, counteract as much as possible the bourgeois obfuscation and force the democrats to carry out their current terrorist phrases." (...) Far from opposing the so-called excesses, the examples of popular revenge on hated individuals or public buildings, to which only spiteful memories are attached, one must not only tolerate these examples, but take their management into one's own hands." (Engels, F. (e), op. cit.:15)

Further below, Engels emphatically refers to the bourgeois character of the revolution and emphasises the necessity of the class-autonomous organisation and arming of the proletariat: "Destruction of the influence of the bourgeois democrats on the workers, immediate independent and armed organisation of the workers and the enforcement of the most aggravating and compromising conditions possible for **the momentarily inevitable rule of bourgeois democracy."** (Engels, F., op. cit.:15)

When numerous publications on Engels rightly speak of him as the first Marxist theorist of the guerrilla (SCHICKEL, op. cit., HAHLWEG, op. cit., WALLACH, op. cit, WOLLENBERG, op. cit.), it is easy to lose sight of the historical, socio-economic-political context already mentioned: in my opinion, Engels could **not** have been primarily concerned with the socialist revolution in his military writings, but with the consistent completion of the bourgeois-democratic revolution, since neither the objective nor subjective conditions for the "dictatorship of the proletariat" were given, but conversely many relics from the feudalist era were still awaiting their revolutionary overcoming. (Rosenberg, A., 1966:56)

In almost all of Friedrich Engels' military science publications on the guerrilla, Engels deals with the guerrilla as **an agent of national liberation and the struggle against feudalist relics and for democratic rights, not as a direct means of socialist revolution!**

In this context, reference should again be made to Engels' view expressed in "The Class Struggles in France" that "the time of revolutions carried out by small minorities at the head of unconscious masses" was over and that where it was a matter of the complete transformation of social organisation, i.e. the socialist revolution, "the masses themselves must be involved, (must) themselves have already understood what it is all about, what they are standing up for with life and limb." (Engels quoted in Wallach, op. cit.:262)

This means that the more it is an actual revolution in the Marxist sense and not merely a conspiracy or overthrow, the greater the role of mass participation and, above all, the greater the role of general disintegration within the institutions of the old ruling class itself, not least the greater the role of disintegration of the regular army, which usually weakens it more significantly than guerrilla actions, however well led, without a sufficient mass base.

Engels recognised the importance of these non-military factors associated with a revolutionary situation in the neutralisation of the regular army very early on, for on 26 September 1851 he wrote in a letter to Marx "that the disorganisation of the armies and the complete dissolution of discipline was both the condition and the result of every victorious revolution".

Both the Chinese and Cuban examples vividly confirm Engels' realisation; read the relevant chapters!

If we take into account what has been said in this chapter, we can only agree with Erich Wollenberg when he states in his introduction to Engels' military-political writings that **"Engels' military writings are essentially the military programme of the proletarian party in the bourgeois revolution"**. (Wollenberg, op. cit.)

We come across this problem again in the analysis of terrorist groups in the European metropolises, which do not carry out any agitation and propaganda in the "proletarian" organisations, but invoke "Marxism Leninism"...

Engels examined the guerrilla primarily as an option for action for the national liberation of oppressed peoples, and in this context he explicitly favours people's war.

Thus he writes in "The War in Italy": "A people that wants to conquer its independence must not limit itself to the usual means of war. Mass insurrection, revolutionary war, guerrillas everywhere, that is the only means by which a small nation can cope with a large one, by which a less powerful army can be put in a position to resist a stronger and better organised one. The Spaniards proved it from 1807 to 1812, the Hungarians are still proving it today." (Quoted in Hahlweg, 1969:79)

Engels mentions several times that only a republican-minded people can successfully utilise guerrilla warfare, as the royalty shies away from it.

"Mass insurrection, the general insurrection of the people, are means that only the Republic uses - 1793 provides proof of this. These are means whose execution usually presupposes revolutionary terrorism, and where has there been a monarch who could decide to do so?" (Quoted in Hahlweg, op. cit. :79)

This is also one of the main differences between the small-scale war concept of Prussian officers such as Clausewitz, Gneisenau and, in a modified modern version, the Austrian Major von Dach with his concept of "total resistance" and the

Marxist concept of the guerrilla: for the former, small-scale war is an effective form of military defence of the nation under certain conditions.

The Marxist concept of the state differs from this traditional concept of the state, which largely abstracts from the internal social opposites ("class opposites") and implicitly understands the state as a harmonious "national community" that has to defend itself against an external aggressor, in that it also places the creation of the state at the disposal of the people.

Marxism therefore reserved the right to relate guerrillas for the first time to the striving for emancipation of peoples of colour, to understand guerrillas not merely as a "continuation of war by other means", i.e. when the regular army has failed, but to see guerrillas as an independent means of struggle of oppressed peoples, even if a regular battle has not taken place and could not take place because the weaker side does not have a regular army.

Small war tactics with Friedrich Engels

Friedrich Engels was the first Marxist theorist to deal explicitly and on a scientific basis with the special tactics of irregular warfare (guerrilla warfare and terrorism).

His writings very comprehensively outline the specific tactics required for successful guerrilla warfare; since they were written, countless small-scale wars have been fought, and when they were successful, they were very largely based on the abstract principles outlined by Engels, regardless of time and space.

In his essay "Warfare in the Mountains", published in 1857, Engels reflects on the necessary conditions for the success of guerrillas, citing four examples: The Tyrolean uprising against Napoleon's troops, the Spanish people's war also against the French, the uprising of the Carlist Basques and finally the small war of the Caucasian tribes against Tsarist Russia.

Engels comes to the conclusion, very similar to Clausewitz before him, that a supporting "leaning power" is of eminent importance for the guerrilla: while the Spanish guerrilla war against the French was only successful over such a long period of time because the guerrilla

a. could fall back on Portuguese and English support and

b. could retreat into fortresses again and again,

On the other hand, the Tyrolean uprising was only a threat to Napoleon as long as it was supported by regular Austrian troops,

Engels uses the Caucasians' small-scale war against Russia to **emphasise the importance of the offensive** over defensive tactics, which he sees as the death of the guerrilla:

"The strength of the Caucasians lay in continuous raids from their mountains into the plains, in raids on Russian positions and outposts, in rapid forays into the rear of the advanced Russian lines, in laying ambushes for Russian columns on the march...they were lighter and more mobile than the Russians and profited from this advantage." (Engels quoted in Hahlweg, op. cit. :80)

In an article published in the New York Daily Tribune on 5 July 1857. In an article published in the "New York Daily Tribune" on 5 July 1857 about Chinese resistance tactics after the Anglo-Chinese War of 1839-1842, Engels for the first time highlighted elements that today are also referred to as "subversive tactics"; in this article Engels also expresses his sympathy with the guerrillas as an agent of national liberation: "Evidently a different spirit now prevails among the Chinese than in the war of 1840-42; then the people were quiet; they left the fight against the invaders to the imperial soldiers and, after defeat, submitted with Eastern fatalism to the power of the enemy. But now, at least in the southern provinces, to which the fight has so far been limited, the masses of the people are actively, even fanatically, involved in the struggle against the foreigners. They are poisoning the bread of the British colony of Hong Kong en masse and with cold-blooded calculation (...) With concealed weapons against the Chinese on board merchant ships, and during the voyage they kill the crew and the European passengers and seize the ships (...)

They kidnap and kill every foreigner they can get hold of (...) The piracy policy of the British government led to this general uprising of all Chinese against all foreigners and turned it into a war of extermination. What is an army to do against a people that resorts to such means of warfare? Where and how much should it advance into the enemy's country, how should it assert itself there? Civilisers who throw firebombs at a defenceless city and add murder to rape may call the method cowardly, barbaric and cruel; what does that matter to the Chinese if it only brings them success (...)

If their abductions, raids and nightly massacres are barbaric in our opinion, then the civilisers should not forget that, as they themselves have proved, the Chinese cannot hold their own against European means of destruction with the usual means of warfare. (Engels quoted in Wallach, op. cit. :263)

Engels considers not only the covert way of fighting, the element of surprise, unconventional and unpredictable action in general to be promising guerrilla tactics, but also the size of the geographical area, especially in relation to the army occupying it, the people's will to resist and the resulting reserves when he analyses the second phase of the Franco-Prussian War from the point of view of guerrilla warfare:

"Once the spirit of popular resistance is aroused, even armies of 200,000 men do not make rapid progress in the occupation of enemy territory. They very soon reach the point where their detachments become weaker than the forces that can oppose them in defence; how soon this occurs depends entirely on the energy of the popular resistance... (Wallach, op. cit.:264)

This relationship between space and numbers was to play a special role in the Russian guerrilla war against the German Wehrmacht and in the Chinese war of liberation against Japan. (Cf. chapters 8 and 11)

In connection with the vastness of geographical space, to which Engels, like Carl von Clausewitz, attaches great importance for guerrilla warfare, as the invading armies lose themselves in it, i.e. either have to concentrate the occupation of the country on a few points and thus control the hinterland only inadequately or expose themselves to the danger of being wiped out individually by splitting up into smaller units, the nature of the terrain is also of elementary importance for Engels: For Engels, national uprising and partisan warfare, at least in Europe, "absolutely requires a mountainous country." (Engels, 1857, quoted in Wallach, op. cit.:264)

As much as Engels regarded the guerrilla as a legitimate and even necessary means of people's war, he (and even less Marx) was not a hothead who would have been interested in violent confrontation for its own sake.

Rather, he repeatedly warned against allowing himself to be provoked into a premature uprising by the class enemy.

Six months before the outbreak of the uprising, Marx and Engels warned the Paris Commune not to start the revolution at the wrong time:

"Any attempt to overthrow the new government when the enemy is almost knocking at the gates of Paris would be desperate folly." (Marx/Engels, 9 September 1870)

However, this did not prevent them from subsequently showing their full solidarity with the Paris Commune.

Summary

Like Clausewitz before him, Engels, on the basis of detailed analyses of various people's wars and guerrilla battles (Spanish People's War, Tyrolean uprising, uprising of the Basque separatists, small war of the Caucasians against Russia, small war in India against the English, small war of the Chinese against England, etc.) comes to certain factors that significantly determine the course and success or failure of the people's war guerrilla:

a. Permanent offensives are essential, the defence is the death of every successful guerrilla

b. The decisive factor is the independence of the people; popular war and guerrillas are all the more successful the greater the will of the people to resist.

c. The insurrection is an art, any premature insurrection is evil, the military inferiority of the guerrilla must be compensated by other factors (political, moral, social), especially in the form of the disintegration of the enemy force, otherwise the guerrilla will fail.

d. Even a large army can find itself in dire straits if it attempts to occupy a vast country whose inhabitants are hostile and determined to resist, as smaller enemy detachments will be routed as soon as they move from their bases into the hinterland.

e. In Europe at least, mountains are important for waging popular and partisan warfare, as they provide a refuge for persecuted guerrillas.

In this sense, fortresses also play an important role as guerrilla bases.

f. A foreign regular army is also of great importance as a leaning power, as the Spanish People's War and the Tyrolean Uprising in particular have shown.

g. Mobility and covert combat, generally unconventional warfare is the be-all and end-all of guerrilla warfare, open field battles should be avoided as far as possible.

h. Engels was the first Marxist small-scale war theorist to recognise and propagate the importance of the guerrilla as an agent of the anti-colonial and anti-imperialist liberation of the colonial peoples.

Not all aspects of the Marxist theory of the guerrilla could be dealt with exhaustively here, but it should have become clear that Engels on the one hand

- is very much in the tradition of conventional military science and draws on older theories, sharing many of his views with men like Clausewitz and Gneisenau,

On the other hand, it enriches the theory of the guerrilla with political and social-revolutionary aspects and points in particular to potential possibilities for revolutionary state creation, especially in colonial countries: revolutionary state creation in the sense of achieving national sovereignty and "bourgeois-democratic" relations as part of the struggle for socialism in permanence.

Chapter 4
Guerrilla in the 19th century

In the course of the 19th century, the guerrilla became increasingly important, on the one hand as an element of the war of large mass armies - the guerrilla was particularly significant in the Franco-Prussian War, in which French francterieurs were able to bind almost one-sixth (!) of the entire German armed forces (Hahlweg, W., 1968:68); on the other hand, the guerrilla also gained importance as an independent means of resistance, especially of the colonial peoples, as a means of revolt against colonialism.

Werner Hahlweg cites numerous examples of guerrillas in the 19th century:

The Greek war of liberation (1821-29), the civil war in Spain between Carlists and Christinos (1833-40), the Polish uprisings of 1830/31, 1848 and 1863/64, the revolutionary wars in Germany, Austria and Hungary (1848/49), the Danish War (1848), Garibaldi's operations in southern Italy (1860), the American War of Secession (1861-65), the German unification wars of 1864, 1866 and 1870/71, the battles in Bosnia and Herzegovina in 1878 and 1882. (Hahlweg, W. op. cit. : 61)

In the colonies, the battles in India, China, Sumatra and Algeria against the French, English and Dutch are particularly noteworthy.

It is therefore not surprising that in the course of the 19th century a whole series of military treatises on the guerrilla appeared, written almost exclusively by military men for military men.

In these writings, the theory of small-scale warfare was further elaborated and supplemented without adding anything significantly new. Werner Hahlweg names a whole series of corresponding literature. (Hahlweg, W., op. cit. :62, and footnote no. 1:261)

The most widespread instruction manual of its time was probably the "Field Instructions for Cavalry, Infantry and Artillery" drafted by Field Marshal Radetzky in 1831, which was also introduced into the Austrian army.

Radetzky's field instructions, whose introduction and sensible application, according to Hahlweg, contributed to the successes of the Austrian army in Italy against the Sardinian troops (Hahlweg, op. cit. :62), could be seen as the forerunner of modern small warfare instructions, such as those used by special units and in the individual combatant training of the Bundeswehr. (See e.g. Reibert manual)

Towards the end of the 19th century, however, small-scale warfare increasingly receded into the background again, and the instructive treatise "Der kleine Krieg und der Etappendienst" (3rd A. 1899) by the Prussian colonel Cardinal von Widdern treats guerrillas from the point of view of large-scale warfare with regular mass armies and completely subordinates guerrillas to it - a tendency that was generally prevalent around the turn of the century and especially before the First World War.

Between 1830 and 1911, the inhabitants of Algeria, Tunisia and Morocco fought with the French, and the Prussian military writer Carl von Decker wrote a two-volume work entitled "Algerien und die dortige Kriegsführung" (Algeria and the warfare there) as early as 1844, which critically states: "Finally, the country has no so-called "centre of power", no capital, with the fall of which all resistance would cease, in a word: in this country there is nothing fixed, only mobile." (Hahlweg, W. op. cit.: 75)

Carl von Decker takes a rather critical view of the war with Algeria and comes to a negative conclusion for France when he compares the objective and the necessary effort. He also asked sceptically what guarantee there was of retaining permanent possession of the country: For example, in the few towns that are held barely 20 miles from the coast? Or in the thousands of slain natives, in the burnt harvests, the miserable garbis sacrificed to the flames, the countless herds captured?" (Hahlweg, op. cit.)

In the long Algerian war, but also in the small wars of the French and English against the Chinese, the protracted battles of the Netherlands in Atjeh, Sumatra and the Sepoy uprising in India, it became clear that expansion, annexation and exploitation of foreign territories and their populations, which were part of the essence of colonialist and imperialist great power politics, inevitably led to the intensification and expansion of guerrilla warfare in the colonies.

In my opinion, what was missing for the final success of the "colonial guerrillas" was not least the **tight organisation, centralisation and discipline under a party with a common ideology**, as was particularly characteristic of the communist guerrillas and probably contributed considerably to their victory in the 20th century.

Chapter 5

Excursus: Terrorism as a universal option for action in major and minor wars

Definition and manifestations

I define terror and terrorism as all actions that are intended to cause **fear and terror** in the opponent in order to force them to act or refrain from certain actions.

Of course, according to this definition, terrorism will not only play a more or less important role in every regular war, but also in every guerrilla war.

Terrorism can be used as the only form of struggle for political goals, in which case it has strategic significance, but it is usually a tactical means within the framework of an overarching military-political strategy.

Terrorism as an abstract term in this definition is largely neutral with regard to the actors, i.e. with regard to the political objectives; it is found equally among politically right-wing, liberal and left-wing groups, albeit usually in characteristic forms.

The examples I will give below to illustrate this will make it clear that terrorism is an almost universal political option.

Examples of forms of terrorism:

1a. terrorism by political groups as a strategy of revolutionary state creation.

This includes the terrorist strategy and tactics of the Russian group "Narodnaya Volya" (70s of the 19th century), the Russian "Social Revolutionaries" (PSR) after the turn of the century, who wanted to bring about the revolutionary overthrow of the tsarist autocracy, above all by assassinating the tsars, ministers and hated representatives of the secret police.

As a strategy, the terrorism of these two groups has failed across the board.

This also includes the terrorist strategy and tactics of the RAF in Germany, which also failed; finally, this includes the very imaginative strategy of the Tupamaros in Uruguay, which also **did not** lead to the desired goal, i.e. also failed...

1b. Terrorism as a tactical tool of liberation movements.

These include the activities of the liberation movement FMLN in the small Central American country of El Salvador, as well as those of the FSLN in Nicaragua, which has been in power intermittently since 1979 and which today, in one of the poorest countries on the American continent, is accused of massive corruption...

The tactic consisted mainly of kidnapping government officials, members of foreign embassies or rich industrialists in order to ransom captured comrades-in-arms or to extort ransom money from the prisoners for arming them.

Finally, this also includes the terrorist activities of the Afghan resistance movement against the Soviet occupying forces.

These examples are not small groups, but liberation movements with a more or less large mass base, and the terrorist activities were quite helpful as an integral part of guerrilla warfare.

This form of terrorism also includes the terror and counter-terror of the equally successful Algerian liberation movement FLN and the equally relatively successful terror of the Cypriot EOAK under the leadership of the Greek colonel Grivas-Dighenis against the British, the Turks and the communists.

Finally, the resistance movements against Hitler's fascism can usually be subsumed under this heading.

The most famous example of this is probably the assassination attempt on Heydrich by exiled Czechs trained by the British S.O.E. in 1942.

Reinhard Heydrich was jointly responsible for mass massacres of Poles, Czechs, Jews and political opponents and was a leading figure in the "Final Solution to the Jewish Question".

1c. Terrorism between different power elites as a means of "coup d'etat".

History knows a whole series of examples in which power elites replaced each other or attempted to do so using terrorist tactics.

The classic military coup, which was widespread in many countries in Africa, Asia or Latin America and is still occasionally attempted today, is also a form of terrorism or falls back on it...

This is therefore terrorism between two factions of a "caste half-alienated from the people", as Lenin described the military.

But not only in distant countries, there was also such a (similar) form of terrorism in Germany: This includes the terror of the Hitler faction of the NSDAP against the group around Ernst Röhm ("Röhm Putsch"), but also the failed assassination and coup attempt by our national hero Colonel Schenk Graf Stauffenberg falls into this category.

However, this is a special case in that the group around Colonel Stauffenberg did not have a mass base, but consisted of individual idealists who had come together to save Germany - unfortunately the attempt failed, but even if they could not save Germany, they did save Germany's honour, because it became clear that Hitler himself was rejected by some of his formerly devoted officers and they risked their lives and those of their friends and relatives to end the war as quickly as possible and thus "save Germany...."

In addition to terrorism between two factions within the power elite, the use of terror by the military against a democratically more or less legitimised government is also of great importance. This includes many successful and failed coup attempts in Latin America. The military coup in Turkey under General Evren; the most notorious example is probably General Pinochet's coup against the Allende government in Chile.

It may come as a surprise to many that state terror is usually more brutal and comprehensive and that the killing threshold for "state terrorists" is obviously considerably lower than for "amateurs", i.e. terrorists within the framework of revolutionary mass movements, where revolutionary violence is often used but the killing of people is comparatively rare. (Hobsbawm, E. J. 1982:27 ff).

2 Furthermore, there is state terrorism, which a state - often after being the product of revolutionary state creation - uses against its own population in order to secure the status quo.

A general rule can be established here: The more consolidated the state's power appears to it, the more it can dispense with terrorism and the more selectively state terror can focus on its most radical opponents.

This form of state terrorism includes: The terror of the fascists before and during the Second World War in Italy, Germany and Spain against the left.

According to this definition, the million-fold genocide of the Jews by the Nazis **does not** fall under the concept of terrorism, since terrorism **does not** aim at the complete destruction of the enemy, but aims to force him to act or refrain from acting through **selective violence**; terror is therefore, to an even greater extent than "regular" war, "the continuation of politics with interference by other means".

State terrorism also includes the "Red Terror" against the "White Terror" during the Russian Civil War, the actions of the Stalinist secret police against all opposition, the terror of the South Vietnamese government with massive support from the USA against the communist guerrillas ("Vietcong"), the terror of the "Khmer Rouge" against the opposition during the Vietnam War, the sporadic terror of British government troops against the IRA in the Irish conflict, which was also predominantly terroristic, and against the EOKA under Colonel Grivas-Dighenis in Cyprus in the early 1950s, the terror of the El Salvadorean Duarte government with massive US support against the united left-wing opposition FMLN, the terror of the US-protected Marcos dictatorship in the Philippines against the opposition, the terror under "Baby Doc Duvalier" in Haiti and so on and so forth...

Reference has already been made to terrorist tactics in the context of open warfare between nations as an element of guerrilla warfare. (Cf. Chapter 1 etc.)

4. ultimately, the term terrorism also covers area bombing of the enemy's civilian population in order to "wear them down". (Cf. e.g. Brockhaus, keyword terrorism)

Examples of this form of state terrorism are the bombing war waged by the Nazis against England in the Second World War, the Allies against Germany, the USA in Vietnam, the Soviet Union in Afghanistan and later in Chechnya.

The list of uses of terrorism given here is by no means exhaustive, but it shows how **universally terrorism was and is used, especially in the 20th century.**

Almost no non-democratically constituted government renounces it completely, and where terror cannot be carried out by its own "security organs" due to political considerations, deputies are supported.

Examples: US support for the Contras on Nicaragua's borders, for the Afghan rebels against the pro-Soviet government, Unita and so on....

This is not the place to discuss the morality or immorality of terrorist acts in the abstract, because a blanket, i.e. abstract, condemnation of terrorism is, in our opinion, sometimes absurd: a people threatened with complete annihilation, enslavement or oppression, such as the Armenians in Turkey during the First World War or the Jews during the Nazi regime, and currently the Ukrainian people by the Putin dictatorship, will probably not be granted the right to self-defence, including the use of terrorist methods. No one is likely to deny the right to self-defence, including the use of terrorist methods as a last resort, to a people threatened with total annihilation, enslavement or oppression, such as the Armenians in Turkey during the First World War or the Jews during the Nazi regime, and currently the Ukrainian people by the Putin dictatorship.

These examples in particular clearly show how much the moral judgement of certain actions depends on the political, interest-bound standpoint.

(Cf. also here what was said in the introduction to this work).

While Polish, Russian and French partisan activity during the Second World War was labelled cowardly, criminal and "band terrorism" not only by SS officers, but also by Wehrmacht officers, and was met with merciless, **mass counter-terrorism** that defied all international law, the Allies welcomed these terrorist activities of the resistance movements as a "fight for freedom" and received massive support from Great Britain in particular: The "Special Operations Executive" (S.O.E.) was founded in London, an organisation to support the resistance in the countries occupied by the Nazis:

The S.O.E. trained agents in all forms of terrorism and guerrilla warfare (sabotage, covert combat, planning, preparation and execution of assassinations, scouting, espionage, etc.) and also supported the resistance movement financially and logistically (Piekalkiewicz, Frankfurt 1971:22 ff; Hübner, S.F., Internationaler Waffenspiegel 1/83:41 ff).

The SOE was later reorganised and renamed the SAS (Special Air Service) and remains **the** UK's elite unit to this day, serving as a role model for all other nations. The motto of the SAS is: "Who dares wins!" (Who dares, wins!)

Whether you condemn the S.O.E. as a terrorist school, as the Nazis undoubtedly did, or whether you see it as an organisation fighting for democracy - that too is a question of political viewpoint.

Anyone who absolutely rejects terrorism in any form would also have to morally condemn actions such as the kidnapping of the German General Heinrich Kreipe on Crete in 1944 by the British Major Leigh-Fermor and Cretan resistance fighters, the assassination attempts on Heydrich and other mass murderers - an absurd idea!

A completely different question is, of course, the political expediency of such terrorist options - but their sense or nonsense can only be decided on a case-by-case basis.

Brown, R. MC. Affee, Stuttgart 1982; Sperber, M., Merkur 1971,1:205; Arendt, H., Merkur 1970, 1:1 ff; Trotsky, L., 1981:386 ff).

Author's note in 2024: A particularly effective and particularly evil form of terrorism are attacks with vehicles or knives against "soft targets", i.e. unarmed and defenceless civilians by extremist Islamists: This poses a danger for every democratic constitutional state that can hardly be overestimated, the most recent example being the knife attack in Solingen by an Islamist who was later caught: Here, with minimal effort and a large portion of unscrupulousness, considerable damage can be caused without long preparation, with the consequence that civil liberties are restricted...

The state does not really have a suitable strategy against this at the moment, it seems....

Chapter 6

Small-scale war tactics and terrorism in the Russian revolutionary movement of the 19th century

Narodnaya Volya

The liberation of the peasants in 1861, which earned Tsar Alexander II the nickname "The Liberator", did not endear him to parts of the Russian feudal nobility; some of them saw him as a subversive in tsarist garb.

The reforms initially introduced by Tsar Alexander II, including those to the education system, either stalled halfway or were cancelled.

The hopes of the numerically small Russian intelligentsia, which was already "infected" with revolutionary Western ideas, were first awakened and then disappointed, so that the call to end the tsarist autocracy resounded ever more emphatically from this side in particular.

For the peasantry, who groaned under the burden of their poverty and debts - they had not only had to pay for their "liberation" with large transfers of land, but also long-term financial obligations in favour of the nobility - Alexander remained the liberator despite everything. The peasants blamed their economic hardship and extensive lack of political rights solely on the landed gentry, who, in their opinion, disregarded the actual will of the "liberator tsar".

This trust in the Tsar's family only disappeared with "Bloody Sunday" in 1905, when the Tsar had his bodyguard massacre a peaceful demonstration of unarmed petitioners.

In the 1970s, the state and the church were the only social organisations, but neither was a forum for legal social protest of any kind.

There were no political parties that could have been used to articulate interests, so it was left to the numerically small intelligentsia to declare war on Tsarism. (The account follows here: Trotsky, L., c, 1973, 1982; Deutscher, I., 1962, 1972)

In its search for allies, the "revolutionary subject" with whose help the Intelligencia could realise its aspirations for democratic freedoms, it turned to the peasantry in the hope of finding **the revolutionary potential** here, with whose help and as whose leader it could bring about change in a revolutionary way.

The men and women of the intelligentsia, almost all of them members of the small middle class and the small civil service aristocracy, who gave themselves the name "Semlja y Wolja - Land and Freedom" - and thus expressed their political objective, namely a democratic-agrarian-socialist social constitution, and whose views were influenced in part by Lavrov and in part by Bakunin, went to the countryside and "among the people" to enlighten them about their misery and the necessity and possibility of overcoming it through revolution.

"A whole legion of socialists," wrote a Gendamerie general who was involved in the police surveillance of this movement,.... "went about this work with an energy and a spirit of sacrifice that has no equal in the history of all the secret societies of Europe." (Deutscher, I., op. cit.:15)

The intellectuals, who "went among the people to enlighten them" with as much idealism as a lack of realism, fell on deaf ears with the peasants.

The rural population did not become revolutionary overnight as a result of the enlightenment and propaganda, but continued to believe in the tsar despite their oppressive situation and, with their enlightenment and talk of uprising, showed the impatient revolutionaries of Zemlya y Volya at least only indifference, and often even open hostility.

These "narodniki" (folk activists), who had gone among the people to impart "instruction and knowledge" to them and who in their heyday numbered a few thousand activists at best, could easily be picked up by the gendarmerie, hauled before the courts and sent into exile in Siberia, mainly due to their naive approach and isolation.

The number of activists dwindled rapidly and the Narodniki began to revise their strategy: If the revolution **by** the people was currently unrealisable due to their inertia, then the

Narodniki had to start igniting the revolutionary spark, starting the revolution **for** the people if necessary.

Having suffered the constant loss of its revolutionaries due to arrests by the Tsarist secret service "Ochrana", the already small group was restructured into a tightly organised, centralised "party" of professional revolutionaries.

This was triggered by the events of 1878: when, in January 1878, the young Vera Sassulitsch shot the St Petersburg gendarme general Trepov because he had badly mistreated a young political prisoner, was acquitted by a jury in the subsequent spectacular trial and thus triggered a broad echo of sympathy among the public, the Narodniki believed they knew how to ignite the spark that would set off the powder keg: By assassinating the tsar and other personified representatives of the tsarist system.

This view probably results not least from the social structure of Tsarist Russia: in the hierarchical Russian bureaucracy, the Tsar represented the entire institution, he **was** the system in persona.

To kill the head of the snake was to cut off its head.

The debate after Vera Sassulich's assassination not only about the **form** of the future political struggle, but also about its **content,** led in 1879 to the split of Zemlya y Volya into the group "Narodnaya Volya" (People's Freedom), which wanted to use individual terror to overthrow tsarism and largely reduced its political programme to political-institutional demands (overthrow of tsarism, national assembly, etc.).

The other grouping, "Chornyi Peredjel" (Black Redistribution), led by Plekhanov, also strove for an egalitarian redistribution of land and continued to place particular emphasis on winning over the masses, especially the peasants. (Deutscher, I. op. cit.:16; Perrie, M. 1982:82)

The Narodnaya Volya group can be described as the first Russian organisation of professional revolutionaries; many of its organisational features can be found in Lenin's SDAPR, and its initial successes were spectacular: although the "People's Freedom" group, including the 20 to 22 members of the Executive Committee, only had around 550 members - plus around 3,000 to 4,000 sympathisers, mainly from the student youth - this small group succeeded in temporarily paralysing the secret police in a country that already had a population of 20 million at the time. 550 members - plus around 3,000 to 4,000 sympathisers, mainly from the student youth - this small group succeeded in temporarily paralysing the secret police in a country of over 90 million inhabitants and turning the "liberator tsar" into a hunted game in his own environment, constantly terrified of the revolvers and bombs of the professional revolutionaries.

Tsarist government policy, starting with the declaration of war on Turkey in 1877, the Peace of San Stefano and the Congress of Berlin (1878), which was perceived as a major diplomatic defeat, clearly demonstrated the inefficiency and weakness of the system.

It was precisely at this time that trials against the opposition took place, the "Trial of the 193" against members of the Narodniki movement initiated the terror of the Narodnaya Volya.

A shift in emphasis soon became clear in this context: now it was primarily about an unequal duel between the intelligentsia and state power; social issues such as poverty, injustice and the development of capitalism receded into the background. (Borcke, v. A., 1982:69, 79)

Narodnaya Volya was more and more concerned only with the overthrow of tsarist absolutism - the social component disappeared, now it was primarily about the elimination of the tsar, the means became increasingly militant.

On the occasion of the assassination of American President Garfield in September 1881, Narodnaya Volya issued a statement of condolences:

"In a country where freedom of personality makes honourable intellectual struggle possible, where the free will of the people determines not only the law but also the personality of the government, in such a country political murder as a method of struggle is a manifestation of the same despotic spirit whose destruction we have set ourselves the task of destroying in Russia." (From Borcke, op. cit.: 74)

The ideological affinity to liberalism expressed here also had a practical component: "Liberal support, however, was vital. It provided connections, cover addresses, conspiratorial flats and, last but not least, the financial means. (....) It is significant that the loss of liberal support was a decisive factor that led to the party's decline." (Borcke, op. cit.:77)

In the decline phase of Narodnaya Volya in the 80s of the 19th century, the active fighters had dwindled to less than two dozen.

The leaders of Narodnaya Volya - Zhelyabov, Kibalchich, Sovya Perovskaya, Vera Figner - almost inevitably resorted to revolutionary terrorism; the apathy of the peasant masses made this seem to them the only solution to the problems.

Due to its necessarily conspiratorial way of fighting, Narodnaya Volya also lost its political connection to social reality and increasingly became a **purely terrorist organisation.**

Mikhailov, a leading member of Narodnaya Volya, even considered debates about political objectives and similar questions to be inappropriate at the time of the struggle, and "Jacobinism", i.e. conspiracy and the desire for a revolutionary dictatorship of an elite, increasingly determined the thinking and actions of Narodnaya Volya. (Borcke, op. cit. :76)

While Zhelyabov came to the conclusion that the goal of Narodnaya Volya was not the liberation of the peasants or the working class, but the "renewal of the whole people in general" (Borcke, op. cit.:75), Mikhailov also believed that they were in fact fighting for the "purely radical ideals of the educated classes, which are completely alien to our peasants in the masses".

While Narodnaya Volya had initially begun with terrorist actions semi-spontaneously, namely out of revenge on the occasion of the 193 trials and as a spectacular form of action to draw attention to itself - which certainly succeeded - terrorism had gained a momentum of its own in the final phase of Narodnaya Volya, which finally prompted Shelyabov to admit: "We terrorised". (Borcke, op. cit.: 75)

This was evident not only in the loss of importance of theorising and political reflection within Narodnaya Volya, but also in the idealistic glorification of its fighters: Morozov reports that new members were not asked about their political views on "socialism, anarchism, constitution, republic".

"We only asked: Are you prepared to immediately give your life, your personal freedom and everything you own for the liberation of the fatherland?" (Borcke, op. cit.:75)

Shelyabov, the most prominent member of Narodnanja Volya, and like most of them - in contrast to Goldenberg or Romanenkto, who later ended up with the quasi-fascist "Black Hundreds" - not a terrorist on principle, had already begun to problematise the increasingly purely terrorist strategy in the early 1980s. (Borcke, op. cit. :74)

In mid-1882, the chief ideologist Tikhomirov went into exile for these reasons, leaving Vera Figner as the only member of the Executive Committee, who was arrested in February 1883 as a result of Degaev's betrayal in Kharkov.

This was the turning point at which the "party" became an instrument of the police.

Although Degaev instigated the assassination of the police chief Sudeykin (December 1883) as part of his revolutionary rehabilitation, and there were repeated attempts at reconstruction with the help of assassinations - the most famous example being an assassination attempt on Alexander III, in which Lenin's older brother Alexander Ulyanov took part and was later executed as a result (Borcke, op. cit.: 72; Trotsky, L. ,c,1982:35 ff, esp. pp. 49 ff), but the assassination of Strelnikov, the prosecutor of the Odessa military tribunal, in March 1882 was the end of individual political terrorism for the time being: the reaction under Alexander III took no account whatsoever and, in contrast to the comparatively liberal Alexander II, did not rely on (partial) reforms but on repression with the help of the secret police Ochrana, which was known as the best secret service in the world at the time.

Similar to the Decembrist uprising under Alexander I, the autocracy reacted with massive repression and succeeded in "freezing Russia a little." (Borcke, op. cit.: 73). (Borcke, op. cit.: 73)

When the Party of Social Revolution (PSR) was founded in 1901, a process similar to that which characterised the development of Narodnaya Volya was repeated - under modified conditions: Although the PSR's spectacular terrorist actions initially helped to raise its profile, they also led to a similar process of "terrorisation" to that which had already characterised the political development of "Narodnaya Volya". **The problem of infiltration** of the struggle organisation by informers from the Ochrana secret service was also repeated: the Ochrana agent Evno Asev succeeded in rising to the top of the struggle organisation when the old leadership of the central party struggle group was arrested at the right moment.

During this time, Asev repeatedly formed new combat groups, which were then broken up by the secret police.

When Evno Asev was finally exposed in 1908, this had a lasting demoralising effect on the party. (Hildermeier, M. 1982:101 ff).

Without wishing to pre-empt the discussion of the urban guerrilla complex in Chapter 17 ff, it can be noted that the development of Narodnaya Volya, like that of the PSR, already points to the fundamental problems of a terrorist-oriented party or grouping, albeit under modified conditions.

Let us summarise:

The political individual terrorism of Narodnaya Volya and PSR was a substitute for the lack of revolutionary action by the masses and thus the result of the gap between the terrorists, whose social origins were the middle class, and the "dark people". (Hildermeier, M. 1982:101)

The increase in the importance of the terrorist strategy, first of the Narodnaya Volya and then also within the PSR, was accompanied by a glorification of the "heroes of revenge", i.e. the members of the combat groups, which was synonymous with an increase in irrational and individualising views within both groups.

However, the following points must be noted in the context of the terrorist strategy of Narodnaya Volya as well as the PSR:

1 Both Narodnaya Volya and the PSR considered terrorism necessary only until a democratic parliament gave the people political participation rights - for Narodnaya Volya this is documented, among other things, by the text of the declaration of condolences on the occasion of the assassination of the American President Garfield in 1881; the PSR also disbanded its fighting groups after the opening of the Tsarist manifesto, in which the latter promised the people civil rights, a constituent assembly, etc. The PSR, too, dissolved its fighting groups.

The fact that terrorism at times appeared to be the only possibility for effective social protest was due not least to the rigid social structures that illegalised and punished any attempts at political participation and any institutional organisation of interests.

2) The individual terrorism of Narodnaya Volya and the PSR arose from a state and social order in which dependency, exploitation and political oppression could still be linked to a few personified symbols - tsars, ministers, generals of the gendarmerie.

Only in this context does the revolutionaries' serious assumption that by killing the most important personifications of the system they could also eliminate the system itself make sense.

The importance of the simple desire for revenge, which is understandable given the situation, should not be underestimated either.

3) The substitutive character of both organisations results not least from Russia's "historical delay" in the political sense as well; Narodnaya Volya and later the PSR fulfilled the task of social protest as a substitute; the concrete forms of this protest in the form of terror are not least the result of the still insufficient process of political differentiation, which only began to take place somewhat after 1905 and accordingly also led to more differentiated and thus also more effective forms of social protest and political articulation.

4 While the terrorist strategy initially led to partial successes, it became increasingly obsolete with the development of mass activities in 1905 and 1917: as a genuinely

substitutionalist method, individual terror was increasingly replaced by revolutionary mass terror, namely in December 1905 and the February Revolution of 1917 as a temporary means of directly overthrowing the tsar.

Above all, individual terrorism a la Narodnaya Volya was replaced by less violent but nevertheless more effective means of struggle such as strikes and mass demonstrations, and in 1917 also increasingly by workers' control, in which large sections of the population were able to participate, making individual terror against individuals largely superfluous and leaving it justified only in the immediate struggle for power.

After the turn of the century, the decidedly terrorist strategy was increasingly replaced in Russia by political options that emphasised the collective development of consciousness not through terror, but through collective methods of social protest and resistance, while at the same time masterfully combining this non-violent mass resistance with politically controlled, selective terror; However, the actors were no longer the social revolutionaries of Narodnaya Volya or the PSR, but the Bolsheviks led by Lenin and Trotsky, who knew how to combine the tight, disciplined organisational form of Narodnaya Volya with skilful agitation and propaganda, especially among the masses of workers and soldiers, and also assigned a place to terrorism, now expanded to "partisan warfare", as a **tactical** means in the struggle for power.

Chapter 7

Guerrilla in the 20th century

Lenin

Lenin and revolutionary violence

Like Marx and Engels, Lenin's analyses are based on the premise that Marxists cannot be in favour of social peace as long as there are class antagonisms, but conversely must always stand on the ground of class struggle, which can take very different forms depending on the concrete situation.

"The Marxist stands on the ground of class struggle and not of social peace", says Lenin in his writing "The Partisan War" Lenin, V. I., c, vol. 11, 1974:209)

In "The Military Programme of the Proletarian Revolution" he also makes his fundamentally militant position on class war clear: "Socialists cannot be against every war without ceasing to be socialists" (Lenin, d, vol. 1, 1970:874)

"To deny or forget civil wars would be to fall into extreme opportunism and renounce the socialist revolution." (Lenin, d, op. cit. :875)

Just like Engels, Lenin absolutely justifies national wars of the peoples exploited and oppressed by imperialism (China, Persia, India, Latin America, etc. against the great powers):

"The denial of any possibility of national wars under imperialism is theoretically incorrect, historically obviously false, practically it resembles European chauvinism: we, who belong to the nations that oppress hundreds of millions of people in Europe, Africa and Asia, are to declare to the oppressed peoples that their war against "our" nation is "impossible!" (Lenin, op. cit.:875)

The fact that Lenin was not only a student of Engels in spirit, but had also studied Clausewitz, becomes clear in the "Military Programme" when he writes: "It would be theoretically fundamentally wrong to forget that **every war is only the continuation of politics by other means."** (Lenin, op. cit. :877)

Like Engels, Lenin also calls for the arming of the proletariat and the willingness to fight for their own liberation with weapons in hand if necessary: "An oppressed class that does not strive to gain knowledge of arms, to be trained in arms, to possess arms, such a class is only worthy of being oppressed, mistreated and treated as slaves." (Lenin, op. cit.: 877) and: "Arming the proletariat for the purpose of defeating, expropriating and disarming the bourgeoisie - that is the only possible tactic of the revolutionary class..." (Lenin, d, op. cit.:877)

The Russian Revolution of 1905 and Lenin's military theory

The parallels between Engels and Lenin's military theory by no means end with the similarities outlined above; like Engels, Lenin also dealt with guerrilla warfare, and Lenin was also able to analyse guerrilla warfare in practice: the revolution of 1905 gave him the opportunity to do so.

In order to understand Lenin's partisan theory, its historical significance, its origins and its meaning, it is useful to examine the social conditions that prompted Lenin to deal with this topic, albeit in a somewhat abbreviated form:

In the first volume of his "History of the Russian Revolution", its chronicler Leon Trotsky, next to Lenin the most important theoretician of Russian Social Democracy and leader of both the 1905 Revolution and the October Revolution, described very vividly the historical, socio-economic-political and cultural conditions that led to the outbreak of the revolution in 1905 in the chapter "The Peculiarities in the Development of Russia" (Trotsky, c, op. cit. :13):

For Trotsky, the characteristic feature of Tsarist Russia is its **historical delay**, i.e. the fact that Russian capitalism developed at a time when capitalism was already fully developed in the USA and Great Britain and was also about to become the predominant mode of production in Germany.

The result of this historical delay is what Trotsky calls "the law of uneven and combined development": On the one hand, the backward country appropriates the latest achievements of technology without likewise following in their development the intermediate stages through which the old capitalist metropolises passed; thus Trotsky shows that the degree of concentration of Russian industry is higher than in other industrial nations, and also the "fusion of industrial capital with banking capital" - both essential characteristics of the more advanced capitalism - "was again carried out more completely in Russia than probably in any other country" (Trotsky, c, op. cit. op. cit.:19)

On the other hand, alongside the few but highly developed industrial centres, agrarian production methods prevailed in the countryside: At the turn of the century, almost 90% of the labour force was still employed in the countryside.

But just as in the cities, where the middle class was comparatively weak, the class differences in the countryside also took on extreme forms: On the one hand, a small class of feudal landowners, on the other, the mass of peasants producing at subsistence level, who were often in debt and in some cases performed additional wage labour on the manorial estates.

This socio-economic situation was secured by the tsarist "autocracy" as the political head of the semi-feudal aristocracy, which controlled any democratic endeavours that arose and nipped them in the bud and suppressed them.

All the "objective" and "subjective" conditions for the bourgeois-democratic revolution were thus in place in Tsarist Russia after the turn of the century: "bourgeois-democratic" because, according to the classical Marxist view, the socialist revolution could only break out after the full development of capitalism and its immanent contradictions.

This view was first revised by Trotsky specifically for Russia with reference to the "combined and uneven development" of Russia and postulated the possibility of a permanent socialist revolution. Incidentally, Lenin did not endorse this view until shortly before the October Revolution.

In his pamphlet "Two Tactics of Social Democracy in the Democratic Revolution" (Lenin, e, vol. 1, :529 ff), written in June/July 1905, Lenin still firmly affirms the Bolsheviks' view that the revolution was "bourgeois-democratic" in character (not in terms of its driving forces!) "bourgeois-democratic": "The degree of economic development of Russia (the objective conditions) and the degree of class consciousness and organisation of the broad masses of the proletariat (the subjective condition, which is indissolubly connected with the objective) make an immediate complete liberation of the working class impossible.

Only very ignorant people can ignore the bourgeois character of the democratic upheaval that is going on; only very naive optimists can forget how little the mass of workers know so far about the aims of socialism and the means of its realisation. And yet we are all convinced that the liberation of the workers can only be the work of the workers themselves...**Whoever wishes to arrive at socialism by any other road than that of political democratism will inevitably arrive at conclusions which are absurd and reactionary in both the economic and the political sense!"** (Lenin, e, op. cit.: 540)

After Lenin had pointed out how alien the "democratic masses" still were to the socialist programme and how unorganised they still were, he gave the impatient "anarchists" advice:

"First organise hundreds of thousands of workers throughout Russia, arouse sympathy for your programme among millions! Try to do this, do not confine yourselves to sounding but hollow anarchist phrases - and you will immediately see that the realisation of this organisation, that the spread of this socialist enlightenment depends on the fullest possible realisation of the democratic transformation." (Lenin, e, op. cit.:540,541)

By 1917, however, the situation looked very different: Industrialisation had made rapid progress, and the huge losses of the war and the activities of various left-wing organisations had accelerated the development of class consciousness.

Lenin thus makes it clear that:

- it is a revolution whose character is bourgeois-democratic

- that the broadest possible democracy must be an elementary interest of the working class in order to enable "socialist enlightenment" and the organisation of the proletariat

- that the organisation of the working class and the arousal of sympathy for the socialist programme **are prerequisites** for the socialist revolution

This **cannot** be replaced by militant phrases and isolated actions.

As much as Lenin is a realist and has no illusions about the possibilities and limits of the Russian Revolution of 1905, he is a firm advocate of radical and resolute action within these framework conditions - the "objective conditions" - and expressly favours all suitable forms of armed struggle, indeed considers them to be superior to other forms of struggle such as the general strike if the appropriate conditions are present; these necessary conditions are:

1. "To be successful, the uprising must not be based on a conspiracy, not on **a party**, it must be **based** on the **advanced class.**

2. the uprising must be based on the revolutionary upsurge of the people

3. the uprising must begin at a turning point where the activation of the politicised masses of workers is at its

greatest and the fluctuations in the ranks of the enemy are also great." (Lenin, f, vol. 2:424)

But once these conditions are given, the refusal to regard insurrection as an art is a betrayal of Marxism and a betrayal of the revolution." (Lenin, f, op. cit.:425)

Lenin uses the same formulation here as Engels when he wants the uprising to be understood as art.

In "Marxism and Insurrection" Lenin also formulates a reason why he had voted against the insurrection only a few months earlier, although a section of the party base had urged him to do so:

1. "The class, which is the vanguard of the revolution, was not yet behind us. We did not yet have a majority among the workers and soldiers of the capitals. (....)

2. there was no revolutionary upsurge of the whole people at that time.

(3) At that time there were no fluctuations on a large, general political scale among our enemies and in the ranks of the undecided petty bourgeoisie. Now the fluctuations are enormous" (...) (Lenin, f, op. cit.:425)

Lenin never tired of describing the uprising as an art on the one hand and warning against approaching it amateurishly and not taking it seriously, **while on the other hand always pointing out its necessary social conditions;** as in his essay "Advice from an Outsider", where he erroneously refers to

Marx (the actual author was Engels) and cites tactical preconditions for armed struggle:

"1. Never play with the uprising....

2. a large preponderance of forces must be concentrated in the decisive place and at the decisive moment, otherwise the enemy, who is better trained and organised, will destroy the insurgents.

3 (...) The defence is the death of the armed uprising (Lenin, h, :661)

4. endeavour to surprise the enemy and wait for the moment when his troops are scattered.

5. it is necessary to achieve daily (...) successes, however small, and thereby to maintain the moral preponderance at all costs." (Lenin, h, vol. 2, :494)

We see here that certain principles of small-scale war tactics also reappear in Lenin's work:

There is the realisation that in "subversive warfare" the defensive must lead to defeat, there is the importance of the element of surprise, there is the importance of fragmenting the enemy troops in order to be able to wear them down one by one, there is the realisation that an unfavourable strategic numerical ratio of government troops and irregulars can be offset by the right tactics, that an unfavourable strategic numerical ratio of government troops and irregulars can be compensated for by the right tactics, which are capable of reversing this ratio at the tactical level - Lenin's repeated emphasis that insurrection is an art also stems from this understanding: Proper war tactics are able to make up for some unfavourable initial conditions - only the participation of the masses cannot replace even the best (partisan) tactics...

In his essay "The Lessons of the Moscow Uprising", first published in "Proletari" in August 1906, he analyses the armed December Uprising; the most important findings are summarised here:

(1) Revolutionary progress calls the counter-revolution into action, which tries to crush the revolution by all means, including terror and pogrom. (Lenin, g, op. cit.: 658)

But "the reaction can go no further than the artillery bombardment of barricades, houses and the crowds on the streets. The revolution can go further than the fight of the Moscow combat groups." (Lenin, op. cit.:659)

This means that at some point the counter-revolution will have shot its powder and that it will then be up to the broadening and deepening of the revolution whether it finally wins.

2. **"It goes without saying that there can be no question of a serious struggle as long as the revolution has not become a mass movement and has not taken hold of the troops."** (Lenin, g, op. cit.: 660)

Here, then, Lenin confirms Engels' insight that every genuine revolution necessarily leads to the demoralisation and disorganisation of the regular troops, and conversely that no revolution is possible without the demoralisation and disorganisation of the regular army, i.e. that the two are mutually dependent.

3) Lenin emphasises the necessity of taking radical and decisive action against the enemies of the revolution once the decision has been made to revolt. (Lenin, g, op. cit.:661)

At the end of his analysis of the Moscow uprising, Lenin reaffirms that the development of mass consciousness in the spirit of socialism as a prerequisite for armed struggle must be the main task of revolutionaries: "The development of the consciousness of the masses will, as always, be the basis and the main content of all our work." (Lenin, g, op. cit.:660)

Lenin's most important treatise on guerrillas, which first appeared under the title "Partisan Warfare" in "Proletari" in September 1906, was characterised not only by his study of the military science writings of Clausewitz, Engels and others, but also by his experiences of the Moscow uprising in 1905.

Lenin begins his discussion of "Partisan War" with the observation that Marxism differs from all primitive forms of socialism in that **"it does not bind the movement to any form of struggle"**. (Lenin, c, vol. 11, :202ff)

For Lenin, therefore, it was not a strategic but a tactical question - in this respect Fetscher/Rohrmoser can certainly be agreed with. (Fetscher/Rohrmoser, op. cit.: 155,156)

Lenin also calls for an "attentive response to the mass struggle that is actually taking place" (underlined by Lenin, op. cit. c, :202)

Lenin identifies two different goals that the partisan war pursued during the 1905/1906 revolution: On the one hand, the liquidation of individual counter-revolutionary individuals, above all of the "security apparatus", and on the other, the raising of funds through epropriation (Lenin, c, op. cit. :206)

Lenin identified with "revolutionary terrorism", including against hated individuals, and cited the example of the Latvian Social Democrats, who regularly published lists of informers and agents in their newspaper (30,000 copies), whose liquidation was publicly recommended.

For Lenin, the characterisation of terrorist acts, i.e. their classification as "individual terrorism", which Lenin decisively rejected, or as "revolutionary terrorism", which he expressly advocated, was not based on the objects or subjects of terror, **but on the social framework conditions.**

The decisive factor for Lenin is therefore the connection to the mass movement and the existence of a revolutionary situation.

In "Partisan War" he writes further: "Nobody will dare to describe this activity of the Latvian Social Democracy (meaning the liquidation of counter-revolutionaries) as anarchism, Blanquism or terrorism. Why? **Because here the connection between the new form of struggle and the uprising that took place in December and is maturing anew is clear.**"

(Lenin, c, op. cit.: 207)

Incidentally, the Russian revolutionary Leon Trotsky takes the same position. (Trotsky, b, 1978)

Furthermore, for Lenin, partisan warfare as a means of self-defence, especially against quasi-fascist gangs such as the "Black Hundreds", is entirely legitimate, indeed necessary. (Lenin, c, op. cit.: 207)

For Lenin, partisan warfare is an "inevitable form of struggle at a time when the mass movement is already approaching the insurrection in practice and there are more or less long pauses between the great battles of the civil war." Since for Lenin guerrilla warfare is an inevitable phenomenon in a revolutionary situation, it is logical that he considers it necessary to bring it under the control of his party in order to use it as effectively as possible to achieve his goals.

Lenin certainly saw the danger of guerrilla warfare in disorganising and demoralising the revolutionary movement, in that it was all too easy for unreliable elements to "make revolution on their own account", i.e. to enrich themselves privately through "expropriations", to take private revenge and generally to discredit the goals of the socialist movement through undifferentiated action and thus repel the masses from the revolution.

He therefore attempted to bring order to the guerrilla war by calling for the organisation of the guerrilla war by his own party and emphasising the importance of disciplined combat groups of his own, to which not only party members should belong.

Despite the importance of guerrilla warfare in a revolutionary situation, Lenin emphasised "that the party of the proletariat must never regard guerrilla warfare as the only or even the most important means of struggle; that this means must be subordinated to others, brought into harmony with the most important means of struggle and refined by the enlightening and organising influence of socialism." (Lenin, c, op. cit.: 211)

Similar to Marx and Engels, Lenin thus represents an intermediate position between decidedly violence-orientated tendencies and those who, like Kautsky, reject violence at all costs and condemn revolutionary terrorism in practice.

That for Lenin the relevance of guerrilla warfare is very situational is shown in his writings after the February Revolution of 1917, which assert the necessity of the uprising; now the situation has fundamentally changed: The "bourgeois-democratic" revolution has triumphed for the time being, and with (relatively) little bloodshed.

An important cause was the internal disintegration of the army, caused on the one hand by the catastrophic losses suffered by the Russian army during the First World War, but also by the tireless anti-Tsarist and anti-imperialist agitation and propaganda of the Social Revolutionaries and the Bolsheviks within the army.

During the period of "dual power", i.e. between February and October 1917, the significance of the partisan war faded almost completely into the background; it was no longer a question of smashing an apparatus of power, which more or less prevented any legal work by the Bolsheviks in the mass organisations by constantly arresting, exiling or liquidating revolutionaries, but of winning over the masses to the Bolshevik programme.

Here, however, it was not petty warfare but only the tireless highlighting of the mistakes, half-measures and fears of the coalition parties and the presentation of one's own party as the only legitimate representative of the interests of the masses that could make progress.

Lenin had realised this, and the slogans of the Bolsheviks were as simple as they were an expression of the needs of broad sections of the people: "Power to the soviets, land to the peasants, peace to the peoples, bread to the hungry." (Lenin, i, vol. 2, :492)

Once it was clear to Lenin that his party had won the battle for the sympathy of the broad masses of the people, he was able to end his letter to the Central Committee of the SDAPR with the confident words: "Victory is certain and nine-tenths of the time there is also the prospect that it will be bloodless. To wait would be a crime against the revolution." (Lenin, i, op. cit. :492).

The further course of history proved Lenin right in this question: The October Revolution was decidedly bloodless, and it was only the subsequent battles of a civil war character that cost countless victims... (Deutscher, I. Vol. 1, op. cit.; Reed, J. Berlin 1982; Hobsbaum, E. J. , op. cit. :30)

The Bolsheviks encountered comparatively little resistance when they "seized power" - the civil war, with its bloody terror on both sides, only began when the disempowered aristocracy struck back with active support from abroad...

Summary

For Lenin, partisan warfare is one method among others that can take on great significance in a revolutionary situation, i.e. when the appropriate conditions exist - but only then! - can attain great significance.

Partisan warfare must therefore be organised, controlled and directed by the party. Since for Lenin, too, (partisan) war is only "the continuation of politics by other means"

(Clausewitz), it is subordinate to the revolutionary movement and the party in every respect.

Lenin considered guerrilla warfare primarily in terms of the extent to which it could be a revolutionary means of eliminating undemocratic conditions that were unfavourable to the working class.

Partisan warfare in Soviet Russia - that of the Civil War 1918-1920, the struggle against the German invasion forces 1941-1945 and partisan warfare as part of the current defence strategies of the Warsaw Pact states (1985) - has its origins in the Russian Revolution of 1905 and the practice of small-scale war tactics first applied here by Russian communists in the context of the general class struggle, which strongly influenced Lenin with his ideas and practical conclusions and demands.

The partisan war thus developed from the general conditions of the 1905 revolution: the revolutionary situation and military inferiority of the insurgents, which made tactics necessary; the Russian partisan war drew its impetus from the "deep forces of the proletarian revolution". (Hahlweg, op. cit.:94)

Although the proletarian guerrilla war coincides to a large extent with the people's war, as I have already described it above, its economic-social origins, its function not as a means of national struggle but of class struggle, give it its special character.

Lenin rethought partisan warfare in terms of both its general prerequisites and its specific conditions in order to apply it in practice in the revolutionary situation in Tsarist Russia as an integral part of his overall revolutionary strategy.

Finally, it becomes clear above all that the "avant-garde guerrillas", especially substitutionalist urban guerrilla groups, **are completely wrong to invoke Lenin**: For Lenin, the guerrilla is only permissible as a revolutionary tactic **within the framework of an already revolutionary situation**; he firmly rejects tying the movement to a single form of struggle.

These views are diametrically opposed to the modern strategy of the urban guerrilla, as discussed in chapter 15.

Chapter 8

The small-scale war in the 1st World War until the beginning of the 2nd World War

Belgian Franctireur War - Russian Civil War - T. E. Lawrence Guerrilla - Major Niedermeyer's Persian War

In his famous work "Der totale Widerstand" (Dach, H. v., No. 4, 3A, Biel 1966), the Swiss Major Hans von Dach names only 4 significant small-scale war actions during the First World War, 15 between the First and Second World Wars, but as many as 35 guerrilla conflicts during the Second World War.

From the end of the Second World War until 1966, von Dach records 30 small wars. (Dach, op. cit.: 278)

If you take into account the fact that numerous other small-scale wars, some of them spectacular, have dominated world events since the end of the 1960s, it becomes clear just how important guerrillas have become, especially since the second half of the 20th century.

As important as the guerrilla is today (1986), it was insignificant for the overall political process before and during the First World War.

The figures used by Major von Dach are probably at least approximately correct, and they indicate how minor the significance of partisan warfare was, with a few exceptions, during and after the First World War.

In his history of small-scale warfare, the historian Werner Hahlweg also only refers to four more significant small-scale wars during the First World War, which will be briefly discussed below.

The Belgian French war in 1914 against the German invasion army, Russian civil war from 1918, T. E. Lawrence's small war with the Arabs against Turkey, Major Oskar Ritter von Niedermeyer's failed attempt at insurrection in Persia against the British

Apparently, the invasion by German troops in 1914 infuriated the Belgians to such an extent that, according to a German white paper, "workers, factory owners, doctors, teachers, even clergymen, even women and children" were seized at gunpoint, and the "Gazet van Antwerpen" of 7 August 1914 wrote: "The inhabitants of our city limits are in an indescribable rage. In Luxembourg, all the gamekeepers and poachers are lying in wait. It is a guerrilla war alongside that of the regular troops." (Hahlweg, op. cit.:98)

It was clearly a people's war in the tradition of the 19th century, as was also characteristic of the French Franco-Prussian War of 1870/71 against the Germans.

The fact that factory owners and workers, gamekeepers and poachers are fighting together makes a significant difference to the revolutionary partisan warfare during the civil war in Russia after the October Revolution of 1917:

Whereas in Belgium during the First World War it was still a national people's war against foreign occupiers, which allowed existing class differences to fade into the background and at least temporarily allied antagonistic social groups against the common external enemy, during the Russian Civil War of 1918-1921 the dividing line was not only between the nation and the invading troops, **but also between the classes**:

Proletariat and large sections of the impoverished peasantry, led by the Bolsheviks on the one hand, middle class, bourgeoisie and nobility, led by former tsarist officers on the other, supported by England, France and the USA.

To the extent that the Russian proletariat was concerned with the defence of newly won rights and the former ruling classes with regaining their old privileges - which was not possible without foreign support - the roles were now reversed in Russia: The most revolutionary and internationalist proletariat at the time, the Russian working class, waged not only a class war but also a national war and used slogans such as "defence of the socialist fatherland against the imperialist invaders" as a matter of course, while conversely, precisely those social groups that had previously been absolute supporters of continuing the war against Germany now openly speculated that the Germans wanted to march into Petrograd and Moscow and smother the red rule in blood.

When the peace negotiations at ⬜rest-Litovsk were temporarily broken off after 10 February 1917 and German troops then began to invade the interior of Russia, the Bolsheviks were faced with the acute problem of national defence.

This problem also arose sharply for the revolutionaries because the Bolsheviks did not have sufficient regular armed forces at this time to take on the fight against the Germans, especially as many troops were tied up fighting the domestic counter-revolution.

This concrete emergency situation in Soviet Russia after the October Revolution and the partisan theory developed by the Bolsheviks since 1905 explain why many Bolsheviks considered resorting to small-scale warfare as a means of national defence.

The "Considerations on the necessity of waging a partisan war against the German oppressors", which were handed down in a document by Rakowski, the chairman of the "Great Russian peace delegation of Kiev", must also be seen in this context. (Hahlweg, op. cit.:98)

In this essay, Rakovsky also considers the partisan war in Ukraine against the Germans to be unavoidable because renewed open acts of war against the Germans could prompt them to launch a successful campaign against Russia. This would have been a deadly threat to the young Soviet power.

Rakowski's "Considerations..." states : "Constantly worrying the enemy, destroying his detachments in individuals at every favourable opportunity, always surprising the enemy in the rear, also threatening the access and traffic routes, the partisan detachments and individual spies must bring the enemy to complete exhaustion and to renounce the occupation of further areas, since the area already occupied by him would eventually become a burden to him, and the few troops with which the Germans are currently content here would soon no longer be sufficient." (Hahlweg, op. cit.: 106)

Rakowski also emphasises the importance of simultaneous parallel actions, the partisan war was to be waged from the Baltic to the Black Sea, the individual divisions were to be coordinated accordingly and placed under a unified high command. Finally, the partisan groups were to be so numerous that "their net would completely cover the front occupied by German gangs", and they were also to prevent the removal of grain and other goods important to the Russian population through sabotage and other small-scale war tactics. (Hahlweg, op. cit.:107)

Rakovsky's "Considerations..." already anticipates all those factors that were so characteristic and successful for Soviet partisan tactics during the Second World War.

Rakovsky's consideration of the unfavourable ratio of space and numbers for the Germans, i.e. the size of the country to be occupied and the relatively small number of German occupation troops that could be provided for this purpose, is particularly noteworthy: This advantage of the Soviet power over the inherently militarily superior German troops, which Rakovsky recognised, was intended to buy the Soviet power enough time to be able to build up appropriate troops of its own.

However, the peace treaty with Germany was finally signed and there was even (temporary) co-operation between the German Wehrmacht and the Red Army.

The third and still probably most famous example of a non-communist-led guerrilla is the small-scale war waged by the Arabs against the Turkish army between 1916 and 1918 under the leadership of the British colonel T. E. Lawrence.

The warfare of Colonel Lawrence, who was an archaeologist and linguist by training and anything but a typical military man, is to be seen in the context of the regular war, namely the First World War, even though the Arab side had national motives.

In order to defeat the Turks as Germany's allies with as few losses as possible, Great Britain capitalised on the hatred of the Turks and the Arab peoples' desire for independence from Turkish rule: Colonel Lawrence, who was a friend of King Feisal I and also his advisor, acted as liaison officer between Great Britain and the Arabs and led the small-scale war against the Turks.

The fact that in the Turkish army a cannon or a machine gun counted for more than a soldier's life led to the special characteristics of the small war led by Colonel Lawrence:

The destruction of enemy soldiers played only a very minor role, Lawrence was more concerned with the destruction of Turkish war material and the communication routes, especially the railway network, because the Turkish warfare was based on both, the relatively modern equipment and the transport by means of the railways.

The war of T. E. Lawrence and the Arabs was first and foremost a "war of sabotage", in which speed, manoeuvrability and the independent operation of small battle groups were of paramount importance. The be-all and end-all was speed and covert combat: A combat group would blow up a bridge or a railway track, disappear immediately, and by the time a Turkish search party arrived at the "accident site", an explosive charge would already have detonated at another location, destroying a Turkish supply depot or ammunition depot.

Due to his impressive personality, T. E. Lawrence, who later died in an accident in England, went down in history as "Lawrence of Arabia" and is still held in high esteem by the Arabs today.

In contrast to the small-scale war of Lawrence of Arabia, which was very successful as a supplement to the regular war against Turkey, the attempt by the Bavarian Major Oskar Ritter von Niedermeyer, who was also known as the "German Lawrence 2", to unleash a war of insurgency against the British in Persia and Afghanistan during the years 1915 to 1917 ended in disaster: Despite the fact that Major Niedermeyer and his small force fought valiantly, completely on their own, the plan was adventurous from the outset, as the goal and means were completely out of proportion, nor were the Persians and Afghans apparently interested in pulling chestnuts out of the fire for one side in a dispute between two foreign imperialist powers that were equally unsympathetic to them.

Major Niedermeyer writes in his memoirs:

"Equipped with the least military power, we were to achieve the greatest possible political and military success. Here, for better or worse, we had to appear more than we were, we had to bluff...

We soon realised that we should and had to be sacrificed in our isolated position." (quoted in Hahlweg, op. cit. :105)

In the end, most of Niedermeyer's fellow fighters were captured by the British, while Niedermeyer himself managed to escape to Turkey.

The adventurous endeavour of the "German Lawrence" is an example of how small-scale war tactics, if they are not the "organic" result of social processes, i.e. if they do not emerge from the depths of the social and political space, but are used as a purely military form of action, can by no means move mountains.

The German troops under Niedermeyer had neither the confidence nor sufficient support of those who wanted to lead them to revolt: They were neither fighting on their own familiar ground, nor were they used to the hot climate. Above all, unlike Colonel Lawrence, who was indeed a **friend of the Arabs**, knew their language and culture very well and was seriously interested in the fate of the Arabs, they were **not** primarily interested in the fate of the Persians and Afghans.

Due to the lack of support among the civilian population, the small force's isolation from the regular army also became a serious disadvantage in terms of supplies.

Small-scale war tactics can only be superior if they arise from a close connection between at least significant sections of the population and the actors of the "theatre of war", if they are well anchored and accepted in the social space, if they arise from the depths of the social space!

This is an essential conclusion from the experiences of the successful small wars/guerrilla/partisan wars of history!

All too often, the strategists of regular armies overlook the fact that guerrillas can only develop their full effectiveness in the context of social processes that are not of a military nature, and that guerrillas as purely military tactics can by no means work miracles.

Summary

With the general enforcement of compulsory military service and modern mass armies, as well as the industrial development of ever more effective weapons of mass destruction, the importance of small-scale warfare declined rapidly, which naturally also had an impact on the theoretical study of it.

The small wars of the First World War were all more or less an integral part or result of the regular war and nowhere did they acquire an independent, decisive significance.

Only during the Russian Civil War following the First World War did petty warfare play a role, especially at the beginning, which in retrospect prompted one Russian revolutionary to say: "At the beginning of the Civil War, we were all partisans." (quoted in Hahlweg, op. cit.:111)

It is no coincidence that this conflict, which was initially carried out by guerrillas, is out of the ordinary and anticipates later developments in other countries: It was essentially a class conflict that was fought by military means.

Ultimately, military power was not a prerequisite, but **the result of** previous non-military, social and political processes: Even after the bourgeois coalition government under Kerensky had fallen like a ripe fruit almost without resistance, the Bolsheviks in power had hardly any other means than their powers of persuasion and their ability to organise and motivate the sections of the population who sympathised with them to fight against the foreign-backed counter-revolution, whatever the cost. (Trotsky, op. cit., Jacobs, W. D., 1963:102)

The military strength of the Red Army initially resulted from its "moral" superiority, its support among large sections of the population (peasants, workers and soldiers), against which even the financial and military support of the counter-revolution from abroad was no match.

However, there was undoubtedly a reciprocal effect: every new military victory also strengthened the morale of the Red Army, weakened the morale of the enemy and thus the counter-revolutionary resistance.

Chapter 9

The Second World War

The Soviet-Russian partisan war against the German Wehrmacht

The murderous imperialist policy of the National Socialists

Like almost every war, Nazi warfare was "the continuation of politics by other means", and this policy and the means by which it was continued or enforced were not least responsible for the development and extent of Soviet-Russian partisan warfare during the Second World War, "the largest irregular resistance movement in the history of warfare", as Lieutenant Colonel Kutger characterises the partisan movement that emerged in the rear of the German invasion forces. (Kutger, J. P., 1963:89)

The economic driving forces as a very often essential element of politics - including that of the Nazis - are well known and do not need to be analysed in detail here; it will suffice to point this out:

According to the Nazis' plans, the "people without space" was to be given the opportunity of imperialist exploitation of foreign peoples wherever possible, but especially in the East, which had been missed due to the "historical delay", with the help of the occupation policy, whereby it was less about the geographical space as such, but about its exploitation in several respects: the natural resources of the occupied countries were to be utilised as well as their agricultural potential, and the total plundering of the "non-Aryan peoples" played a special role in the National Socialist plans.

Himmler said this quite openly: "Whether the other nations live in prosperity or whether they die of hunger, that interests me only insofar as we need them as slaves for us, otherwise I am not interested." (Himmler quoted in: Cartier, R.: Der 2. Weltkrieg, 1977, Vol. 1: 322)

Whether it is the expulsion and partial extermination of the South and North American Indians, the enslavement, exploitation and oppression of black people or the Nazis' extermination of the Jews and the "Eastern peoples": The economic driving forces and motives as the cause of the extermination of peoples are just as similar as their pathetic attempts at moral legitimisation by dismissing the victims as "sub-human" or "savages".

So as little as racism is a German invention, it was reserved for us Germans to kill millions and millions of innocent victims with Prussian thoroughness in the shortest possible time, and **no political regime has ever before represented such a depraved attitude as the "Thousand-Year Reich", which fortunately did not last too long...**

In their political approach, the Nazis drew on Ludendorff's concept of total war: the general, who had failed in the First World War and was a driving force in the German fascist movement from the outset, felt superior to Clausewitz and developed a "theory of war" whose only significance lay in its disastrous historical role: **For Ludendorff, war - in contrast to Clausewitz - was not an option to be avoided if possible, but a desirable state to which politics had to subordinate itself.**

Politics was not the end, but the **war**, and **with Ludendorff politics degenerates into a means for the war as an end:** Ludendorff's policy consists above all in the liquidation of everything that harms the war; **thus the war becomes total and politics totalitarian.**

Blitzkrieg strategy

It is an irony of history that the Nazis drew their inspiration for waging the initially so successful Blitzkrieg not from a German military, but from a prophet of modern mechanised warfare who had long gone unrecognised in his own country, the British Captain Lidell Hart - incidentally a friend and biographer of T. E. Lawrence, see Chapter 8: Lidell Hart had been able to gain experience as a captain during the First World War, gave it some thought and came to the conclusion that the time of the absolute dominance of the infantry and positional warfare was over, that a future war would have to be fought by the British side primarily with air-supported tanks: For Lidell Hart, mobility and speed were the decisive criteria in a future war, while those responsible in the British War Office continued for a long time to think in terms of traditional military doctrines, i.e. continuing to give infantry first place.

While the British refrained for far too long from the massive integration of armoured weapons into their war concept, an article published in 1924 in "Army Quarterly" (IX) by Lidell Hart on the necessity of mechanisation and its strategic-tactical consequences met with keen interest among the officer corps of the German Wehrmacht. (Wallach, J. L., op. cit.: 225)

The German Blitzkrieg strategy is in its basic features the consistent, partially modified application of the ideas developed by Lidell Hart.

An essential role was played by the surprise attack, the fastest possible destruction of the enemy's weapons potential before it could be used; the German air force in particular played a decisive role in this.

Partisan warfare in Stalinist military doctrine

M. V. Frunze, who alongside Trotsky played a decisive role in building the "Red Workers' and Peasants' Army" and had been Commissar of War since Trotsky's resignation in 1925, pointed out in his 1921 essay "The Unified Military Doctrine and the Red Army" that in view of the technical superiority of the potential enemy armies, Soviet Russia's defence efforts also included preparations for waging partisan warfare. (Hahlweg, op. cit.: 112)

Frunse emphatically emphasised that the prerequisite for the effectiveness of small-scale warfare was the timely development of a plan and the creation of all the necessary organisational and logistical foundations - it is no coincidence that this is very reminiscent of Gneisenau's "Plan for the Preparation of a Popular Uprising", as both had the state-organised and controlled popular uprising against an enemy power in mind.

Frunse demanded that it should be "a task of our general staff to work out the idea of small-scale warfare in its application to our future wars against a technically superior opponent". (Hahlweg, op. cit.:112)

In fact, a military instruction book for partisan warfare was published in 1928, which was reprinted in 1933 and described partisan warfare as an important component of general warfare. (Bonwetsch, G., Göttingen 1985:92; Hahlweg, op. cit.:112)

However, by the beginning of the new 5-year plan at the latest, such an orientation increasingly faded into the background in favour of a view that no longer relied on strategic retreat and the development of comprehensive partisan activity, combined with regular warfare, but on an "offensive defence concept". (Bonwetsch, op. cit.:93)

Officially, despite the bad experiences with Finland, the fiction was now maintained that the war could be carried immediately into the territory of the aggressor and would be supported by the revolutionary action of the "international proletariat".

Contrary to widespread opinion (Piekalkiewicz, op. cit.:93), **no** significant preparations were apparently made for the partisan war, apart from the formation of so-called "extermination battalions", a reserve of less capable soldiers behind the front, whose task was actually to cleanse their own territory of scattered enemy elements and agents - and probably also their own "counter-revolutionaries" - who were later integrated into the partisan army. (Bonwetsch, op. cit.:93; Jacobs, W. D. op. cit.: 104)

The reasons for the extensive renunciation of guerrilla warfare in Soviet military doctrine before the "Great Patriotic War" are probably essentially the following:

While Rakovsky, like Frunze, had included the depth of geographical and social space as a strategic factor in warfare in terms of its significance for the "strategic retreat", analogous to the practice of "scorched earth" and guerrilla warfare already practised during Napoleon's invasion, In view of the fact that the armaments production so important for warfare was located in the European part of the Soviet Union, this option no longer seemed sensible, and the party leadership evidently believed that the growing armaments production meant that they were well equipped to resist an army like the German Wehrmacht without the guerrilla option. Another reason cited by Bonwetsch for abandoning the option of guerrilla warfare seems entirely plausible:

"However, the rigid adherence to the offensive as the only strategy will have been fuelled not least by doubts about the reliability of their own population. The mass repressions before the war testified to this irrational, deep-seated mistrust." (Bonwetsch, op. cit. :94)

In other words, the mass reprisals not only against the kulaks in the 1930s were both an expression and a cause of the indifferent or even hostile attitude of part of the Russian population towards the CPSU during the Stalin era. Nobody could have known this better than Stalin himself, and even if it is difficult today, especially for Western Europeans of our generation, to say to what extent the power of the Communist Party in Stalin's era was based on the support and cooperation of sections of the population and to what extent state power was based on the terror of the secret services, it is nevertheless clear that the front lines could by no means be drawn as clearly as during the civil war; this can already be seen in the "purges" within the Communist Party itself.

It can therefore not be denied that parts of the Soviet population, especially in Ukraine, did indeed initially celebrate the German occupiers as "liberators", as has been claimed several times, including by Guderian. (Cartier, R., op. cit. :306; Bonwetsch, op. cit. :104; Jacobs, op. cit.: 106)

When Germany invaded the Soviet Union on 22 June 1941 and destroyed over 1200 Soviet aircraft on the ground on the very first day, and many Red Army soldiers were scattered as a result of the Blitzkrieg, the party leadership returned to partisan warfare, and on 3 July 1941 Stalin made his first public appearance after the German invasion and called on the population to resist on the radio:

"Not a single wagon, not a single locomotive, not a kilo of grain and not a litre of fuel must fall into the hands of the enemy. In the occupied territories, partisan groups must organise themselves on foot and on horseback to wage a war of attrition, blow up bridges and roads, set fire to camps, houses and forests. The enemy must be hounded to his destruction!" (Cartier, op. cit. : 308)

Initially, however, this call, which was followed by numerous similar ones, was by no means enthusiastically heeded by the civilian population. Initially, the partisan groups were mainly made up of scattered Red Army soldiers, party members living underground and NKVD commissars, who were involved in political organisation and control and may have deterred many civilians due to their by no means always good reputation.

However, the **rigorous extermination policy** of the Nazis and the Wehrmacht very quickly made even the most politically naive "Soviet people" realise that it was impossible to live peacefully with the German occupation because it represented a threat to the entire Slavic people and not just the communists.

The war thus became a **struggle for the existence of** the Russian people, and the "Great Patriotic War" created a new **coalition of action** among the Russian people, ultimately strengthening Stalin's position.

The peculiarity of the Soviet partisan movement is that it was neither a spontaneous popular resistance nor a long-planned guerrilla war.

If in August 1941, just two months after the German invasion, there were **over 231 partisan groups with a total of 12,000 men** in Belarus alone, this was not an expression of spontaneous popular resistance, but was due to the fact that the combatants were initially almost exclusively scattered members of the Red Army, who naturally had to continue to obey the orders of the Soviet leadership, as well as party members and NKVD commissars, whose task was to organise partisan groups.

The Red Army favoured partisan fighting over the dubious fate of a Russian prisoner of war with the Germans, and the party members and NKVD commissars acted partly out of political conviction and partly on the orders of the party.

The partisan groups were subordinated to their own central staff, whose commander-in-chief was Lieutenant General Ponomarenko.

The Central Staff enjoyed the same status as the Supreme Command of the Red Army, although there were apparently constant quarrels between the two. (McClure, B., 1963:138)

Regional staffs worked under the central staff, which were initially inadequately coordinated with the Red Army, but later excellently.

Connections were maintained via air transport and later messages, primarily by radio.

At the lower tactical level, there was the brigade, which was divided into sections or otyadie. Especially in the beginning, the leaders of the partisan groups were primarily recruited from Red Army officers with civil war experience, who were dropped by parachute at night over their future operational area or who sneaked through the German lines. (McClure, op. cit.:138; Piekalkiewickz, a, 1972:117)

The first phase of the guerrilla war can be dated from June 1941 to September of the same year.

During this period, successes remained comparatively low, as neither the coordination of actions with the regular army functioned as desired, nor was there sufficient support among the people. Partisan activity was also closely linked to the course of the regular war throughout the course of the war: As long as the Germans were in a permanent advance towards Moscow, the Red Army, like the rest of the population, showed signs of demoralisation.

However, the situation gradually began to change in autumn 1941: Despite the disastrous experiences of the Napoleonic troops with the Russian weather conditions, Hitler ordered Army Group Centre under Colonel General Feodor von Bock to march on Moscow in October 1941, as the Wehrmacht was to be on the Volga before Christmas - a completely unrealistic objective. (Cartier, op. cit. 348, 349)

At this point, the "mud period" set in, meaning that, as in every autumn, it began to rain in October 1941.

Although the Germans were prepared for the rain, they obviously had no real idea of the effects, which an old

Ukrainian proverb describes as follows: "In autumn, a spoonful of water makes a bucketful of mud."

As every year, the rivers overflowed their banks, huge floods turned into unforeseen obstacles, and the vehicles designed for European conditions got hopelessly stuck; the horses sank up to their bellies in the mud, it was sometimes no longer possible to pitch tents, and as the Russian houses had mostly burnt down in the meantime, the soldiers had to camp in the mud.

By 20 October, the speed of cars and lorries between Gzhatsk and Mozhaisk had already dropped to three kilometres per hour (!) - there could no longer be any talk of a blitzkrieg! (Cartier, op. cit.: 350)

It now became apparent that the war was being waged by the German leadership in the "abstract", i.e. without consideration of the concrete situation: weather, terrain, morale of the troops.

The crews were starving because supplies were blocked due to the vehicles stuck in the mud, and now the partisan activity began to have its first demoralising effect. (Cartier, op. cit.:352)

In order to avoid a winter campaign, Hitler had forbidden the distribution of winter uniforms as well as the creation of rear positions to which the Germans could have retreated.

Around the turn of the year 1941/42, the tide began to turn for good, and it also marked the beginning of the second phase of the guerrilla war.

The crisis in the German advance and the failed attempt to attack Moscow, as well as the fact that the Red Army was able to hold its ground at the last moment, changed the situation.

In addition, the Russian population in the territories occupied by the Germans had now had experience of the Nazis' extermination policy and had therefore moved from an initially perhaps indifferent to an openly hostile attitude towards the Germans.

The partisan war now increasingly became a people's war, and civilians, mostly farmers, began to register as partisans with the party cells working underground.

The blitzkrieg strategy did its part to cause an epidemic spread of all types of guerrillas: The further the German tanks penetrated into Russia, the larger and longer the communication and supply routes became and the more difficult they were to control and sabotage by the Germans and the better by the Russians - a circumstance that Lieutenant General Ponomarenko and his partisan army knew how to exploit...

As early as autumn 1941, the "partisan republics" began to expand; in the area of Army Group North alone, 11 partisan groups were counted, one of which alone controlled an area 100 km in diameter. (Cartier, op. cit.:351)

In the spring of 1942, the first partisan republics were created, which were completely under the control of the Communist Party and where not even battalion-sized troops were allowed to venture. The partisan republic in the Ushachi region, for example, covered an area of 3245 square kilometres with a population of 80,000. (Hahlweg, op. cit. :126; Piekalkiewicz, op. cit. :125)

The significance of the partisan movement is difficult to fully grasp, but a few figures should give an impression:

Cautious estimates by Western historians assume that the Soviet partisans succeeded in tying up around 50 divisions of the German Wehrmacht!

To secure the railways and roads alone, 300,000 to 600,000 men had to be constantly deployed! (Bonwetsch, op. cit.:112)

The information on Germans killed by Russian partisans varies considerably: while Bonwetsch gives a figure of 30,000 to 40,000 dead, basing this on Wehrmacht data (Bonwetsch op. cit.:112), Lieutenant Colonel Kutger refers to Ponomarenko's data and gives considerably higher figures, which are also cited by other historians and military experts and, although somewhat exaggerated, seem to me to be more likely than Bonwetsch's data: More than 300,000 Germans, including 30 generals, 6336 officers and around 500 members of the Luftwaffe were killed as a result of partisan action.

In addition, 3000 trains are said to have been derailed and 3262 railway and road bridges, 1191 enemy tanks and armoured vehicles, 4027 lorries and 895 depots and warehouses destroyed. (Kutger, op. cit.:89; Piekalkiewicz, op. cit.:129)

These statements are also supported by the testimony of the German General von Manstein during his court-martial, where he recalled "that in 1944 almost a thousand raids were made on roads and railways in the rear area of Army Group Centre in the course of seven hours and that these raids took place daily in the Crimea". (quoted in Kutger, op. cit.:90)

The information on the strength of the partisan army also varies considerably.

While Bonwetsch estimates them at 80,000 (early 1942), 150,000 (mid-1942 to mid-1943) and 280,000 (summer 1944) (Bonwetsch op. cit.: 101), Piekalkiewicz considers Soviet figures of 700,000 fighters to be possible (Piekalkiewicz, op. cit.: 127)

However, the actual significance of the partisans was not primarily in the number of Germans they killed, but in their strategic complementary function, above all in their importance for delaying the war in order to give the Soviet Union time to exhaust its reserves, as well as in their supplementation of the regular warfare and not least in psychological terms.

As early as the end of 1941, the activities of the Russian partisans took on strategic importance in the battle for Moscow (Cartier, op. cit.: 299-357)

On 2 October, Hitler gave the order to attack Moscow, and within a few days the Russian army group under the command of Marshal Semyon Timoshenko lost almost 640,000 men as prisoners to the Germans and was beaten back by the German assault.

On the left wing, German armoured divisions under the command of Colonel General Erich Küppner advanced as far as Kalinin, and the right wing under the command of "Panzer General" Guderian advanced via Orel to Tula. Army Group Centre under Colonel General Günter von Kluge advanced to within a few kilometres of Moscow.

However, at this point the weather began to deteriorate rapidly, the autumn rains and mud caused supplies to falter, and the now massive partisan attacks did the rest to block the supply of ammunition and rations. As the disorganised German supply system was only able to adequately supply around three percent of the troops and the crews were already demoralised and weakened by losses, the weather and hunger, even a new attack on Moscow, when the ground was finally frozen and firm enough for a tank attack, did not achieve the desired objective.

The coldest winter for decades took the completely unprepared German army by surprise and forced it into improvised winter quarters, thus creating ideal conditions for the infiltration of Russian partisans. (McClure, B.: op. cit.:133)

Thanks to this preparatory work by the partisans, the Red Army finally succeeded in encircling the German headquarters and causing a panic-stricken retreat. The German troops suffered huge losses, and "with savage fury the guerrillas hunted down small groups of German infantrymen and cut them down in the woods, where they tried to evade the Soviet tanks". (McClure, op. cit.: 133)

The tactics

The partisans' equipment: Initially, the partisans' clothing and equipment was improvised; in addition to German looted weapons and uniform parts, weapons provided by NKVD commissars were also used. The experience report of the partisan leader A. N. Prokopienko (Piekalkiewicz, op. cit.:117 ff) describes in detail not only the tactics and form of organisation, but also the supplies and weapons made available to him.

Later, the equipment was continuously improved because the Germans increasingly found themselves on the defensive as the war progressed and the number of captured weapons increased considerably, especially in 1944.

Finally, the British and Americans also sent weapons and equipment. (McClure, op. cit.:140)

The central staff of the partisan army endeavoured to bring the leaders of the combat groups up to a minimum fighting standard through training, which was successful in the further course of the war.

The officers trained in regular partisan schools in the hinterland, especially in Tbilisi, were trained in all matters important to partisan warfare, primarily by NKVD commissars. (Piekalkiewicz, op. cit.:117 ff; McCLure, op. cit.:141)

Reconnaissance and espionage were the essential foundations of the partisan groups, on which raids, sabotage and assassinations were based; this presupposed a good relationship with the civilian population, which was guaranteed during the course of the war for the reasons mentioned above. Combat operations focussed mainly on officers' quarters and weapons depots, and the standard tactic was to move silently and attack suddenly in response to a signal. The decisive factor in such raids was not only a good scouting system, but also the prior destruction of communication structures such as telegraph lines, etc., so that help could not be summoned immediately and pursuit was delayed.

Such surprise attacks were usually carried out with generous use of ammunition and hand grenades; the most popular handgun was the submachine gun, as it was sufficiently effective and accurate at short distances, had a high firing capacity and was easy to conceal.

If prisoners were taken, then at most for interrogation, after which - according to Brooks McClure - they were shot.

The Russian partisans obviously did not adhere to the Hague Land Warfare Convention any more than the Germans did. (McClure, B., op. cit.:146)

Here, however, I have my doubts as to whether this is consistently true, at least other war reports by Russian soldiers say otherwise. (Bondarev, J., 1975: 400 ff)

Another important form of action was the ambush in unclear terrain, and the instructions in a Russian partisan manual entitled "Comrade of the Partisan" were probably often put into practice in this or a similar way: "Look! The enemy is coming! Let him come within 20 or even 10 metres, and then suddenly fire with rifles, machine guns and hand grenades. The enemy must not have time to use his firearms. Then, if necessary, go into close combat! Shoot with your sidearm! Thrust with your knife! Don't let the enemy gain the initiative for a moment! (quoted in McClure, op. cit.: 146)

The "Gensosse des Partisanen" also recommends the use of small-calibre rifles to wound the driver and co-driver and then to finish them off with the blank weapon. The advantage was that the lack of loud detonations meant that help would not have to rush in so quickly and the German vehicles could be unloaded in peace. (McCLure, op. cit.: 147)

The use of snipers also played an important role: The Russian snipers, equipped with the special version of the Russian standard infantry rifle Moisin-Nagant 91/30 with mounted telescopic sight (Boger, J.:DWJ 2/83:166), were sometimes able to deliver lethal hits at 600 m and more under favourable conditions - a very demoralising way of fighting for the enemy, as at this distance often not even the sound of the shot could be heard and the sniper lying in ambush could hardly be located.

In addition to the usual tactics of small-scale warfare, which have remained essentially the same from the beginning of the 19th century to the present day, terror also played a major role in Russian partisan warfare: Germans captured by partisans were often tortured in order to obtain information from them - a practice that was apparently adopted by the Germans. (McClure, op. cit.:147; Piekalkiewicz, op. cit.:122)

The use of terrorist methods against the Germans in the context of "psychological warfare" probably played an even more important role: the purpose of the frequently used brutalities, which were also acts of revenge against the German occupiers, was to frighten and unsettle the enemy German soldiers by spreading fear and horror, which apparently succeeded. (McClure, op. cit.:147)

As the war progressed, it became increasingly difficult for Wehrmacht officers to send individual couriers or small patrols outside the controlled areas, as they were likely to be liquidated and the soldiers developed a panicky fear of partisans in such a situation.

Rumours of the cruelty of the partisans towards German prisoners, of the harsh winters and the savage fighting methods of the Russian soldiers apparently reached far into the western front, and German soldiers are said to have committed suicide when they learned of their planned transfer to the eastern front...

German "gang warfare" against Russian partisans

It proved to be a serious mistake for the Germans in the course of the war that they had entrusted the Gestapo chief and ruthless mass murderer Heinrich Himmler with the fight against the partisans: The tactics employed by his "security forces" of responding with mass reprisals against the civilian population after losses at the hands of partisans not only ruined what may have been initial sympathies with the Germans here and there, but also aroused and increased the hatred of the civilian population with each new mass terror, motivating them to join the partisan groups. (McClure, op. cit.:149)

In addition, there were disputes between the Wehrmacht and Nazi organisations over the question of the correct tactics to use against the partisans and over territorial jurisdiction.

On 21 June 1943, Himmler ordered the creation of the Central Staff for Combating Partisans under the command of SS-Obergruppenführer Erich von dem Bach-Zelewski, and this so-called "poachers' brigade", a "police unit"(!) made up of convicts, poachers, wood thieves and other criminals under SS-Obergruppenführer Dr Oskar Dirlewanger, became sadly famous due to its cruelty, which was unusual even for the SS, and its high casualties - almost 100% every year! (Piekalkiewicz, op. cit.:130)

Only the so-called Fremdvölkische units, which were more familiar with the mentality of the partisans and their approach and way of life, were able to achieve relative success.

The largest and most successful of these anti-partisan units was that of the Polish-born Mieczyslaw Kaminski, who rose to the rank of SS brigade leader within a few months due to his cruel and successful methods of fighting partisans as a non-German.

His unit was made up of pro-German, mainly farmers, who were given back the property they had been deprived of through forced collectivisation and were also generously remunerated in other ways.

Kaminski's forces numbered 4,000 men with the best equipment provided by the Nazis, who were stationed in the area south of Briansk in Lokot and were able to keep this area largely free of partisans.

But in the spring of 1943, Kaminski and his men were also forced to retreat with the Wehrmacht - apparently he could not rely on not being betrayed when the Red Army arrived.

It was not until 1944 that a "Combat Instruction for Fighting Gangs in the East" was published, followed by the supplementary leaflet "Fighting Gangs", but even these had little effect because the partisans were now far too strong, the Germans far too weakened and had long been on the defensive, and despite all the sophisticated techniques of "fighting gangs", the elements that were the cause of the partisan activity remained: The occupation, exploitation, oppression, enslavement and annihilation of the "Eastern peoples"!

Hitler's attempt to postpone the final end of the "Thousand Year Reich" by calling for a "Volkssturm" and in the form of the pathetic "Werewolf Campaign" in the long looming defeat could not be realised because the majority of the German population had long since grown weary of the Nazis and thought of anything other than a total popular resistance against the Allies, for example analogous to the Spanish People's War of 1807 - 1814 or the Russian partisans.

For the unorganised old men and children who, according to Hitler's plans, were to form the Volkssturm, an instruction pamphlet was written, which above all processed the experiences of the Russian partisan war and where the recognition of a fact shines through, which was so decisive for the success of the Soviet partisans and the insignificance of the Volkssturm: "Without a clear political goal, the fighter, even if he is skilfully led in his missions, can only achieve temporary successes."

Summary

In terms of the tactics used, Soviet guerrilla warfare did not differ significantly from the usual forms of action that had previously characterised small-scale warfare in general, such as covert combat, irregularity, surprise attacks, sabotage, raids, assassinations, targeted use of terror, avoidance of open regular battles, etc.

Only the development or reuse of Only the development or reuse of particularly suitable weapons, above all the submachine gun and the hand grenade, which are ideal for close ranges of up to 50 metres, has increased the potential effectiveness of the guerrillas and opened up greater opportunities for them in fire raids - the results of even small combat groups in raids on soldiers' shelters could be significantly improved by using these weapons - but ultimately this also applies to regular warfare: The application of ever more modern technology has increased its effectiveness, and thus also its potential for destruction, more and more, so that the limit has long since been reached that makes "hot" war still seem opportune as a continuation of politics by other means - this Clausewitzian realisation from the time of cabinet wars presupposes a certain "harmony" of means and ends that has long since been lost in the great war.

With regard to its strategic importance, the following characteristics of the Russian guerrilla war against the German occupiers deserve to be noted here:

1) The Russian guerrillas during the Second World War were successful because they had corresponding socio-economic and political roots, i.e. they **were waged both as a national**

liberation struggle against a foreign power and as a social struggle against the National Socialist strategy of exploiting the "Eastern peoples".

Both aspects, the national and the social, formed an inseparable unity, and the communist party did not fail to call both into the consciousness of the masses.

As the CPSU had discredited the social aspect, i.e. the class struggle, among large sections of the population due to its rigid forced collectivisation, it primarily appealed to the national and cultural feelings of the population and thus achieved a political re-integration of the indifferent sections of the population that it had not expected. Terms such as "The Great Patriotic War" were coined at this time and are still part of the repertoire of communist language today (1986).

2) Another decisive factor for the effectiveness of the Russian partisan war was the increasingly perfect coordination between the partisan army under the command of a "central staff" on the one hand and the regular Red Army on the other.

The cooperation between regular troops and irregulars had already shown its effectiveness in the battle for Moscow, and the Red Army offensive that began on 20 June 1944 was initiated by the partisan demolitions (over 10,000 demolitions) carried out the previous night, which gave it its decisive significance.

3. the peculiarity of the Soviet partisan war is that it was a state-initiated and controlled struggle, which in the further course took on the character of a people's war, but nevertheless allowed spontaneous elements only under the control of the party, and remained an integrated strategic element of the regular great war from beginning to end.

In the Russian guerrilla war against the German occupying forces, many elements echo the concept of the Prussian officer Gneisenau and his "Plan for the Preparation of an Uprising". In addition, it became clear that **under certain conditions** a state-led people's war was indeed possible.

4. the Soviet guerrilla war makes it clear how ineffective so-called "gang warfare" or "counter-guerrilla" is if it remains rooted in purely military thinking and seeks to maintain the socio-economic-political conditions and relationships to which the guerrillas owe their origins.

The fact that it was precisely the mass terror and the Nazis' policy of extermination of peoples, i.e. a certain political behaviour, that turned the Soviet partisan war into a mass struggle with the character of a people's war, makes it clear that Clausewitz's maxim that war is the continuation of politics by other means applies even more to the people's war than to the great war.

5. finally, the Russian partisan war against the German troops and occupiers also shows the importance of the retreat areas in remote parts of the country and in forests and swamps that could not be controlled by the enemy, analogous to the fortresses in the Spanish People's War, the mountains in the Tyrolean uprising, the desert in the Arab-Turkish war and so on: a resistance like that of the Russian partisans against the Germans would hardly have been conceivable without the impassable forests and swamps, would certainly have taken other forms and would certainly have been less effective.

The fact that the "Slavic subhumans" threatened with mass murder often found it more promising to go into hiding in the forests and swamps and join a partisan group than the dubious fate under German occupation probably contributed decisively to the steady growth of the partisan groups.

Without the retreat areas, there would probably only have been a few, very politicised and determined people who would have offered armed resistance. The temporary terrorist strategy of the French Communist Party in the Resistance, which created a vicious circle of assassination and retaliatory strikes by the Nazis against the civilian population, tended to repel the civilian population, including the labour force. (Of course, this was no longer the case in 1944, when the Germans had to flee France).

Where the civilian population does not have the option of retreating to areas that are difficult or impossible to control, i.e. cannot be effectively protected by the liberation movement against state repression, assassinations of prominent figures in the occupying power can have devastating consequences for the resistance movement, especially if the latter does not feel obliged to fulfil any humanitarian demands. (Knipping, 1985: 135 ff; Piekalkiewicz, op. cit.: 168 - 185).

Chapter 10

Anti-fascist liberation movements in Europe during the Second World War

With the exception of Yugoslavia and Albania, whose peoples fought with particular determination for their national self-determination under the leadership of the Communists until their final liberation under their own steam - whereby British support was useful, especially in the beginning, but not decisive - no European resistance movement succeeded in driving the German soldiers out of the country without outside support and regular troops.

Most liberation movements were initially limited almost exclusively to scouting and espionage for the Allies, and even in Norway, with its largely relatively inaccessible wilderness and despite the fact that an underground army of several tens of thousands of men was secretly formed, the guerrilla war in Norway had at no time assumed a decisive war dimension.

In the Netherlands, forms of resistance such as strikes and occasional demonstrations, as well as secret boycotts, played almost the only role in the anti-fascist struggle due to the lack of a suitable reduction centre for partisans.

However, the political significance of these forms of resistance should not be underestimated.

Although more or less large underground armies were formed in almost all occupied European countries, their importance seems to have been comparatively secondary to that of the Russian, Yugoslav or Albanian armies - this even applies to the famous Resistance.

Many of the ideas associated with the legendary successes of resistance movements were probably the result of political failings and the resulting guilty conscience; this is particularly true of Germany: apart from heroic individuals who sacrificed their lives for liberation - the Scholl siblings/White Rose, the assassin Georg Elser - there was only the circle around Colonel Schenk Graf Stauffenberg, apart from church circles, who tried in an organised way to stop Hitler and his criminal gang.

But these were small groups of patriots with personal integrity who were prepared to sacrifice everything for Germany - they rightly have a high symbolic and moral status to this day, but were unable to put up enough of a fight against the established organised power of the Nazis...

Once the Nazis had come to power in Germany, they organised and purposefully ensured that all potential opponents were murdered, or at least imprisoned in camps or helplessly emigrated. Resistance could therefore only come from circles that had long been part of the establishment and were therefore initially unsuspicious, as was the case with the Stauffenberg circle.

It is striking that it was precisely in the economically more developed countries with a long cultural and liberal tradition, which regarded themselves as particularly high in terms of civilisation and culture, that resistance to fascist barbarism produced relatively few objective results, while in countries classified by these countries as relatively "uncivilised", such as Russia, Yugoslavia, Albania and China, hardly any imaginable forces could be activated to liberate them from fascism.

This cannot be explained solely by unfavourable geographical conditions - which is undoubtedly the case in Holland.

The fact that peasant societies are more predestined for guerrilla warfare than highly industrialised and mechanised nations undoubtedly played a major role in this.

Farmers who are used to hardship and daily physical strain are simply physically better land guerrillas.

Rene Allemann sees it this way: "The petty war is by its very nature (...) an outrage of the underprivileged against the favoured in general, of the country against the city in particular, which occasionally erupts through the surface of a persistent traditionalism, especially in an impoverished, "backward" peasantry." (Allemann, 1974:17)

For Sebastian Haffner, the guerrilla is bound to preconditions, which primarily include "a poor, miserable and desperate mass of people who have little or nothing to lose and for whom the difference between a permanent war and the kind of life offered by the existing peace order is relatively minor". (Haffner, 1974:28)

Another explanation can probably be found on a psychological level: According to Henri Michel, a leading historian of the anti-fascist resistance, the German victory was sudden and total everywhere (or so it seemed!): "A conference for the Czechs, a landing for the Norwegians, a battle for the Poles or the French would have been enough to collapse everything that had been believed in until then: the permanence of the fatherland, the totality of the values inherited from the past, confidence in the future. The victor seemed to possess not only power, but also credibility. Certain of himself, he claimed to bring a new order with him." (quoted in Hahlweg, op. cit.:133)

This is by no means to minimise the importance of the national anti-fascist liberation movements, but in my opinion it must be emphasised that most liberation movements ultimately remained a pawn in the strategic interests of the Allies: Great Britain in particular played a major role in the founding and activities of various resistance movements due to its experience with the colonial countries. (Piekalkiewicz, op. cit.:22 ff, 54 ff, 68 ff, 85 ff, 194 ff; Hübner, S. F., Internationaler Waffenspiegel 1/83:41; Knipping, op. cit.:127)

Ultimately, however, the boundaries were also set by these liberation movements, some of which were directed and supported from outside: this is exemplified by the assassination attempt on Heydrich by the two SOE recruits Jan Kubis and Josef Gabcik, as reported by the chemistry professor Vladislaw Vanek, who was the leader of the Czech Sokol movement and the Czech resistance under the code name "Jindra": "I learnt that an assassination attempt on Heydrich was planned at the beginning of 1942 in my capacity as leader of the Czechoslovak resistance group "Jindra".(...) I must confess that I was not very enthusiastic about this plan.

The effect of an assassination is always great, but an assassination attempt on this man in particular (...) would entail incalculable reprisals. (...) They had their orders from London, and we as a down-to-earth resistance organisation were obliged to support them to the best of our ability in carrying out the assassination." (quoted in Piekalkiewicz, op. cit.:72)

Although the Jindra group was already endangered by infiltration, it obeyed the London orders. On the one hand, the resistance was not willing or able to act independently in this form, and on the other hand, the actions planned in Great Britain were not primarily concerned with the impact on the respective liberation organisation, but with the overall political situation.

Jindra's fears were justified: As a direct result of the assassination attempt on Heydrich, 1,500 Czechs were immediately murdered by the Nazis, and 10,000 more disappeared into concentration camps. (Piekalkiewicz, op. cit.:84)

It becomes clear here that the Czechoslovak resistance movement - like most European resistance movements against the Nazis - did not succeed in drawing radical consequences from the decay of the traditional social and political structures accelerated by the Nazis: In my opinion, the subordination made clear here to the command of a completely powerless "government in exile" dependent on London also symbolises the retention of conventional thought patterns despite radically changed circumstances.

Only where the partisan resistance was organised and led by groups or personalities who acted completely free of foreign directives according to the requirements of the moment, who were flexible, imaginative, unconventional and completely unscrupulous towards the enemy and at the same time knew how to act in accordance with the mentality of their people, did the partisan war lead to success and this new elite to power: It was no coincidence that the strong personality of Tito came into conflict with Stalin, and it was no coincidence that partisan warfare was able to play such a decisive role in the SU: The Soviet leadership had been flexible enough, albeit due to serious omissions and mistakes, to dig the guerrilla concept, which had already been almost completely thrown overboard in Soviet military doctrine, "out of the mothballs of history" and apply it skilfully and in accordance with the concrete situation as a whole.

We will see something similar when we look at the Chinese situation: It took a character as convinced of himself as Mao Tse Tung to disregard the directives of the 3rd Communist International (Comintern), which in retrospect turned out to be wrong, and to wage guerrilla warfare as the specific situation demanded.

The examples could be supplemented, primarily by Greece and Italy: in one case it was the Soviet Union, in the other the Allies, to whom the resistance movement conceded so much influence that this ultimately led to the externalisation of parts of the movement and its political direction.

As a result of these considerations, I would like to put forward the thesis that although a people's war can be waged more promisingly with a strong leaning power or in coordination with still existing troops, the precondition for victory **requires** the extensive renunciation of conventional thinking and action, as well as independence from foreign directives and, finally and **above all, a very high degree of willingness to sacrifice on the part of the masses.**

Werner Hahlweg can certainly be agreed with when he writes: "The guerrillas in the Second World War, which gripped the masses to an unimagined extent, achieved great political and strategic importance in the context of the overall 1939-1945 struggle and increasingly presented themselves as a force to be reckoned with, ultimately remained the object of global political decisions at the highest level. This was all the more the case as the resistance movements and their guerrillas did not achieve final success on their own." (Hahlweg, W.: op. cit.:140; Knipping, F., op. cit.: 141,142)

The final report of the "Allied Forces Headquarters" (AFHQ) on the principles, forms and results of underground and guerrilla warfare from 1942 to 1945 concludes that large-scale subversive operations only promise success if they are backed by the war machine of a leaning power. (Quoted in Heideking, op. cit.: 1985:169)

As I have tried to show, this is indeed true for the non-communist-led liberation struggles of the Second World War, but this cannot be generalised, as we have seen in the case of the Soviet Union and will show in the next chapters using the example of China.

Chapter 11

The Chinese wars of liberation under the command of Mao Tse Tung

Preliminary remark

In addition to the essays by US officers, I have primarily drawn on Mao Tse Tung's military writings and let him speak at length - primary sources are particularly authentic and I therefore prefer them when the truthfulness of such writings is confirmed by secondary sources, which is the case here.

Although it is not always unproblematic to treat the writings of political leaders as authentic material in general, in this specific case it seems permissible to me: As Sebastian Haffner has shown (Haffner, op. cit.: 1966), Mao's military writings are not retrospectively "edited" accounts and discussions, i.e. written for political interests, but for the most part instructions, evaluations and analyses of ongoing battles as training material and instructions for commanders and party cadres.

The view that Mao's military writings should certainly be treated as authentic historical sources is also shared by

Captain Dinegar (US Army), who attests to Mao's self-critical and truthful account. (Dinegar, op. cit.: 1963)

Mao and Clausewitz

The aim of the war, which Mao emphasised several times, namely "his own self-preservation and the destruction of the enemy", led Sebastian Haffner to postulate a contrast between Mao and Clausewitz (Haffner, op. cit. 1966:14), which in my opinion does not exist in this form, but is clearly based on a misunderstanding:

In his otherwise excellent essay, Haffner clearly does not differentiate between the **nature** of war as a **particular form of social interaction** and the **aim** of war, which can **vary** greatly depending on the specific conditions.

However, the war aims at the time of Clausewitz with the then prevailing cabinet wars in Europe were of a completely different nature than the total people's war in the revolutionary China of the 20th century. If in the first case "the disproportion between the horror of the battlefields and the civilised salon atmosphere of the actual belligerents was striking", precisely because they were "cherished" wars or "cabinet wars" with very limited objectives, which were also characterised by a "disproportion between the tragic seriousness of the means and the triviality of the ends" (often only the gain or loss of one or the other province)" (Haffner, op. cit. 15), so that in this context there is also talk of the "sport of kings" or the "chess game with living pieces", the Chinese Civil War and the Chinese struggle against Japanese imperialism was a total people's war, in which the existence or non-existence of China as a sovereign nation and the social existence of hundreds of millions of Chinese was at stake.

As much as the concrete war aims differed, the essence of war for Mao was also to continue the respective concrete policy, indeed to be a special form of policy itself.

Mao states this implicitly or explicitly several times, for example in his pamphlet "On the Correction of Wrong Views in the Party" (December 1929), addressed to commanders and party cadres, where he explicitly criticises a purely military approach:

"...they regard military and political activity as mutually exclusive and do not recognise that military activity is only one of the means of fulfilling political tasks." (Mao, op. cit.:58; all of Mao's military writings mentioned below are taken from: Mao Tse-tung: Military Writings, Beijing 1969)

In his essay "On Protracted War" (1938), Mao quotes Clausewitz approvingly: "The sentence: 'War is a continuation of politics' means that war is politics, that war itself is an action of a political character." (Mao, b, : 273)

However, Mao emphasises several times - and Sebastian Haffner apparently relies on this and many similar statements by Mao - that "self-preservation and the destruction of the enemy (...) is the basis of all military principles". (Mao, c, : 183; see also Mao, d, :118 and 169)

Obviously, Haffner's misunderstanding also stems from the fact that he interprets the term "war of annihilation", which Mao frequently used, incorrectly, i.e. takes it too literally:

In his essay "On Protracted War", however, Mao clarified what he really meant by "war of annihilation": **"The aim of war is nothing other than "self-preservation and the destruction of the enemy. Destroying the enemy means disarming him or depriving him of his power of resistance, but not physically destroying him down to the last man."** (Mao, b, :277)

This makes it clear that **Clausewitz's and Mao's** understanding of the **nature** of war **certainly coincides**, although Mao's war **aims** are more comprehensive and total and this must inevitably be reflected in the **concrete form of warfare.**

Mao's much-quoted motto that "political power comes from the barrels of guns" - as Mao says in "Problems of War and Strategy" - is usually taken out of context, because in the very next sentence Mao relativises what he said: "Our principle is that the Party commands the guns, **and the guns must never be allowed to command the Party**." (Mao, e, :333,334) Emphasis mine.

The slogan of political power coming from the barrels of guns, which is quoted in almost all publications on Mao and/or the Chinese War of Liberation, unfortunately often obscures the much more complex Maoist military theory.

Despite Mao's undisputed view here that revolutionaries must be armed, Mao repeatedly criticises decidedly military-oriented positions that neglect the non-military forms of political struggle: "The theory of the omnipotence of weapons, a mechanistic view on the question of war, a view that arises from the subjectivist and one-sided approach to problems. **We hold a directly opposite view and see not only the weapons but also the people.**" (Mao, b, :261, 262)

Although Mao was the most important commander of the Chinese Red Army, lectured at the War College and wrote a series of military treatises not much inferior to those of Carl von Clausewitz, he was not primarily an army commander in the classical sense, but primarily a communist and leader of the Chinese Communist Party.

Therefore, Mao always subordinated military activity to political requirements; his entire military strategy is an organic result of his analysis of Chinese society in the first third of the 20th century.

Mao himself referred to this fact in many of his writings; his comprehensible and popular writings on questions of military strategy and tactics are always the result of socio-economic analyses of the concrete social conditions of the China of his time, and this was probably an essential element of his success...

Mao's social analysis and strategy

Especially in his essay "Strategic Problems of Revolutionary War in China" (Mao, d,:87ff) it becomes clear that Mao's military strategy and tactics as well as his entire activity as army leader are based on a Marxist analysis of Chinese society, are based on this analysis of Chinese society, are to a certain extent inevitably derived from this analysis.

For Mao, the concrete strategy and tactics of the Red Army resulted from the special characteristics of China in the 1920s and 1930s:

"China's political and economic development is uneven. They exist side by side: A weak capitalist economy and a powerful semi-feudal economy; a few modern industrial and commercial cities and a huge number of stagnant villages; several million industrial workers and several hundred million peasants and artisans suffering under the yoke of the old social order; large military powers ruling the individual provinces; two kinds of reactionary troops, namely the so-called central army under Chiang Kai-shek and the so-called motley armies subordinate to the military rulers of the individual provinces; a few railways, shipping lines and motor roads as well as a plethora of cart tracks, footpaths and trails that are difficult to pass even for pedestrians. China is a semi-colonial country. The disunity among the imperialists leads to disunity among the ruling groups in China.

There is a difference between a semi-colonial country in which several states rule and a colony in which a single state is in control.

China is a big country.(...)

China has undergone a great revolution (meaning the bourgeois revolution under the Kuomintang with its theoretician Sun Yat Sen at the head, E. R.), which prepared the ground for the birth of the Red Army..." (Mao, d, :108)

Mao's description of China's concrete situation here reveals the necessity and the goal of the revolution, but also the path that the revolution must take:

According to Mao, the revolution is necessary because a large part of the population, namely the proletariat and above all the peasantry, are exposed to double exploitation and oppression: Oppression and exploitation by the semi-feudal system, which also prevents economic development, and exploitation and oppression as a result of imperialism.

During the Sino-Japanese War, Mao makes a clear judgement: In Mao's view, the national contradiction dominates the class contradiction at home: "Of China's two great contradictions, the national contradiction between China and Japan is still the fundamental one, while the internal class contradiction still occupies a subordinate place." (Mao, f, :347)

According to the classical Marxist understanding, the prerequisites for the "dictatorship of the proletariat", i.e. the immediate establishment of socialism, were lacking in China in Mao's time because the socio-economic and political conditions were not in place: China was not yet a capitalistically developed country, the bourgeoisie and proletariat still represented a social minority, and the semi-feudal agrarian economy dominated not only economically, but also politically and culturally.

The immediate goals of the Chinese revolution were therefore those that characterise **the bourgeois-democratic revolution:**

- Agrarian revolution, i.e. the elimination of feudal and semi-feudal forms of exploitation, political liberation of the peasantry and land redistribution.

- Replacement of outdated political structures, development of a bourgeois-democratic superstructure as the basis for continuous economic and political development.

- Overcoming national fragmentation, establishing a centralised state power.

- The constitution of the Chinese nation as a truly sovereign state, which required not only a centralised state power, but also freedom from imperialist influence on China's economy and politics.

- Ultimately, the aim was also to "transform China from an agrarian country into an industrialised country, thus enabling a socialist society to develop from a society of exploitation of man by man". (Mao, g, :456)

The CCP saw its task as the fullest possible realisation of these plans, and in almost all of Mao's military writings he speaks of the "bourgeois-democratic revolution". (Cf. for example Mao, h, :5, 6. 8; Mao, i, : 47; Mao, b, : 274 etc.)

The fact that the CCP under Mao's leadership in April 1949 was not concerned with the immediate overthrow of the Chinese bourgeoisie - insofar as it was not part of the Kuomintang or had a distinctly comprador character - but conversely with the protection of the "national bourgeoisie", insofar as it was classified as non-monopoly capitalist, is also made clear in the "Proclamation of the Chinese People's Liberation Army" written by Mao on 25 April 1949, where it states under point 2:

"Protection of industrial, commercial, agricultural and livestock enterprises, etc., insofar as they are private property, shall be protected without exception against any interference." (Mao, j, :479, 480)

It was not until the last third of the 1950s that a general nationalisation of industry began.

This orientation of Mao and the CCP towards the bourgeois-democratic revolution not only corresponded to the views and directives of the Communist International (CI), Lenin, who in the case of Russia had brought his position closer to the Trotskyist position of "permanent revolution", also reckoned with the bourgeois-democratic revolution in the case of China, and it is therefore logical that the Soviet Union, still under Lenin's government, concluded a friendship treaty with the bourgeois Kuomintang, which was still relatively undifferentiated at the time, under its then leader and chief theoretician Sun Yat Sen, and supported the Kuomintang with advisors and modest arms supplies.

It is also thanks to the Soviet advisors that the organisational structure of the Kuomintang was initially very similar to the organisational principles of the Bolshevik Russian party.

Even Leon Trotsky assumed for a long time that the bourgeois-democratic revolution was the next historical stage. (On this complex, see Frank, P., 1981: 445-475; 625-633).

Shortly after the founding of the CCP in 1921 with the support of the Communist International, the Communist Party joined the bourgeois Kuomintang, which at that time, still under the leadership of Sun Yat Sen, was categorised as revolutionary and anti-imperialist.

Lenin's position on Sun Yat Sen was ambivalent, however, as he appreciated the Chinese leader of the Kuomintang as an upright revolutionary on the one hand, but classified certain elements of his views as the theory of a petty-bourgeois "socialist reactionary" and labelled him a Chinese narodniki. (Frank, P., op. cit.: 450)

When the commander-in-chief of the Kuomintang troops, General Chiang Kai-shek, took over the political leadership after the death of Sun Yat Sen, the Kuomintang's political objectives and behaviour towards the communists began to change:

The Kuomintang, which had led the national revolutionary wave from 1911 to 1924 to power, and which could also be sure of sympathy and support from abroad, increasingly came into conflict with the interests of the Chinese proletariat, especially the small farmers and agricultural labourers, whose revolutionary aspirations found a mouthpiece in the still very small Communist Party.

True to the Marxist social theory created primarily for capitalist developed countries, the CCP had initially developed its main activities in the larger cities among the proletariat, and the rapid growth of mushrooming trade unions, most of whose leaders were Communists, led to a steady increase in the Chinese Communist Party's influence and membership.

The Kuomintang under General Chiang Kai-shek, which from the outset had a strong military, even militaristic character and was primarily the party of the bourgeoisie, dissatisfied intellectuals and "enlightened" landowners, began to suppress local strikes and peasant uprisings against the exploitation and oppression that prevailed everywhere, and oppression, including by foreign powers, and at the same time harnessed the revolutionary ambitions of the politicised masses for its campaign in the north against the "warlords", i.e. semi-feudal military rulers.

The differences between the Kuomintang and the Communists increased, and in order to push back the influence of the Communists within the Kuomintang, General Chiang Kai-shek began to react with administrative measures: Communists had to resign from commanding posts within the Kuomintang army, Chiang Kai-shek demanded lists with the names of Communists in the Kuomintang, etc. - all of which foreshadowed the coming escalation between the two organisations, which reached its first climax in the Shanghai Massacre in April 1927:

After the workers in Shanghai, led by the Communists, had chased out the British administration and seized power, Chiang Kai-shek invaded the city with his troops and organised a bloodbath among the workers and Communists, killing thousands, including women and children.

This bloody deed not only marked the beginning of the terror of the Kuomintang under the leadership of General Chiang Kai-shek against the Communists, but also the break of the CCP with General Chiang Kai-shek, but not yet with the Kuomintang as a whole.

At that time, the character of the Kuomintang was quite obviously completely misjudged by the CCP as well as by the Communist International.

The CCP now followed the fatal directive of the Communist International to unite with the "left" wing of the Kuomintang against Chiang Kai-shek. However, this alliance did not last long, as the "left" wing of the Kuomintang also began to bloodily suppress the communists all too soon.

Now two tendencies began to compete with each other in the CCP: The "orthodox" tendency, supported by the Communist International, now continued its work in the proletariat under illegal and conspiratorial conditions and, at the behest of the Communist International, now controlled by Stalin, instigated several uprisings that lacked any real basis and were all suffocated in blood within a short time.

This effectively led to the virtual liquidation of the CCP in the major cities, as these were completely dominated by the Kuomintang.

The break with the Kuomintang also signalled the rise of Mao, who was a member of the provincial Central Committee at the time and thus belonged to the "second set".

Mao Tse Tung had drawn his conclusions from these events and from his analysis of Chinese society, which was still essentially an agrarian society and consequently characterised by contradictions in the agricultural sector: Since for Mao the "revolutionary subject" was basically not primarily the proletariat but, due to China's particular situation, the peasantry - to avoid accusations of heresy, however, Mao always speaks of the proletariat and the peasantry - and since the Kuomintang was overpowering, especially in the big cities, but the CCP was in danger of being completely worn down there, in Mao's view the CCP could only hold its own and grow if it worked politically where the Kuomintang was politically and militarily weak: In the countryside.

In 1928, Mao was in the Hunan-Kiangsi border area with a relatively small force that remained loyal to the Communists and had begun to build up and expand a Red Army base area there.

In his essay "Why can the Red Power exist" (Mao, h, :5), written in October 1928, Mao justifies the fact that in China, unlike imperialist countries or other colonial countries, it is possible to establish autonomous "Red" areas within a country ruled by "Whites" primarily with the political fragmentation and relative weakness of the "White" power:

"That within a country a small area or several small areas of Red Power, surrounded on all sides by the White regimes, exist for a long time, has never happened before in any country in the world (....)

For such a strange phenomenon must be accompanied by another strange phenomenon, namely wars within the white sphere of power.

One of the characteristics of semi-colonial China is that since the first year of the Republic (1912), the various cliques of the old and new military rulers, with the support of imperialism and the native comprador class and feudal lord class, have been waging incessant war against each other (...)

There are two causes for the emergence of this phenomenon, namely a localised agrarian economy (not a unified capitalist economy) and the imperialist policy of division and exploitation through the creation of spheres of influence." (Mao, h, :7)

Contrary to the classic strategy of the communists, which was also pursued in Russia, namely to unleash an uprising in the most important cities under the leadership of the party of the proletariat when a revolutionary situation arose, to smash the old state apparatus, seize political power and thereby also accelerate the political movement in the countryside and steer it in the desired direction, Mao pursued a different, almost opposite strategy from the outset, which was derived from the concrete situation as well as from the political objectives of the revolution:

As Mao understood the character of the revolution to be essentially bourgeois-democratic, the working class played a numerically subordinate role in relation to the rural population, and the current problems arose in the countryside, Mao's strategy for the revolution was to **mobilise the peasant masses.**

The motto of the "encirclement of the cities by the countryside" is the result of the conditions described here, and thus originally resulted from China's political and economic backwardness and from a policy of weakness of a party that was therefore orientated towards the peasant masses.

The CCP had to become active where it was strong but the Kuomintang was relatively weak. This also resulted in the

CCP focussing on the peasant masses: Away from the large and medium-sized cities, the railways and transport routes, the Kuomintang was no longer present with its "security forces"; there its power to a certain extent seeped away into the vastness of the undeveloped or barely developed space.

There, individual representatives of the Kuomintang - small police posts, individual officials, etc. - were easy to sweep away when the mass of the rural population was in a revolutionary mood - and it was!

Mao's political strategy was as simple as it was successful: create bases in these areas that were difficult to control, force the agrarian revolution, i.e. above all redistribute land and protect these areas from Kuomintang repression with the help of the numerically growing Red Army and local peasant detachments.

As early as 1928, the inaccessible mountainous area of the "Five Djing" in the Djinggang Mountains was a Red Power base area that was completely controlled by the CCP and the Red Army.

Mao realised early on that these bases could only exist and develop safely as long as the wars within the "White" power groups continued and prevented them from encircling and destroying the Red areas in a concentrated manner.

In "The Struggle in the Djinggang Mountains", Mao names five further conditions for the existence and further development of Red Power:

"1. active masses of the people 2. a firm Party organisation 3. a sufficiently strong Red Army 4. terrain conditions suitable for military operations 5. sufficient economic resources for supplies" (Mao, i:17)

Mao was realistic enough to know that it would only be a matter of time before the white terror would strike on a massive scale.

In Mao's view, the strategy and tactics of the Party and the Red Army should take into account the situation in the enemy's camp: In a phase of stabilisation of the enemy, forces should be concentrated, adventurous advances and fragmentation of forces should be avoided so as not to expose oneself fragmented to the already superior enemy, while in a phase of instability of the enemy, advances into new areas and the implementation of agrarian revolutionary measures should be undertaken. (Mao, i:18)

In his evaluation of the experiences made in the base areas in 1928, Mao came to conclusions that essentially remained the guiding principles of his military theory and practice during the war, which lasted more than 20 years:

"1. an independent power must be an armed power. Wherever the territory of this power may be, it will be immediately conquered by the enemy if there are no or not enough armed forces there." (Mao, i:26)

A special phenomenon throughout the War of Liberation is the fact that the at times very high losses - after about a year of fighting only about a third (!) of the original units were left (Mao, i:26) - were replaced by captured soldiers of the enemy.

From 1928 to 1949, the integration of captured soldiers and even lower-ranking officers into the Red Army was often a decisive way of compensating for losses.

As unusual as this method may seem, it is by no means new, and Mao, as a disciple of Sun Tse, is likely to have taken inspiration from him.

In Chapter II (Warfare), Sun Tse says under point 13: "Treat the captured soldiers well and take care of them. This means defeating the enemy and increasing one's own forces." (Sun Tse, 1972:52)

In 1947, when the Kuomintang was already completely demoralised and its officers even sold weapons to the Red Army (Hanrahan, 1963:232), 80 to 90 % of the captured

Kuomintang soldiers were taken into the Red Army. (Mao, k:398)

The relatively developed democratic structures within the Red Army played an important, if not decisive, role: in contrast to the Kuomintang, whose armies consisted of mercenaries or forced recruits and who were treated extremely rigorously - harassment of all kinds and beatings were the order of the day - the Red Army's recruitment was often based on its ability to persuade politically and on the deliberate use of democratic practices to undermine the morale of the enemy troops.

Sooner or later, word of the **relatively** democratic structures of the Red Army was bound to get around, and in a semi-feudal country like China in the 1920s and 1930s, where large sections of the population wandered around begging, robbing or hiring themselves out as mercenaries to the many "warlords" due to impoverishment, it was precisely these social strata - also referred to by Marx as the "lumpenproletariat" - who were not at all averse to joining an army, which had written the future improvement of their economic and social situation, democracy and liberation from the hated feudalist relics and imperialism on its banners and which, most importantly, did not put off the masses until after the seizure of power, but had already begun with the concrete reorganisation of economic and political structures on the ground, i.e. in the liberated areas as well as in the army itself.

Mao, who like many Marxists apparently had reservations about "lumpenproletarians", wrote with regard to the social composition of the Red Army: "The Red Army is made up partly of workers and peasants and partly of **vagrant proletarians**.

The presence of too many vagrant elements in the Red Army is of course not good. But these people know how to fight, and since we are in combat every day and have significant losses of dead and wounded again and again, it is not always easy for us to find supplements even among them. The only way out under these circumstances is to strengthen political education." (Mao, i:27)

From the very beginning, Mao consciously and successfully used democratisation as part of "psychological warfare", and as early as 1928 he wrote: "In China, not only the people need democracy, but also the army. **The democratic order within the army is an important weapon for undermining the feudal mercenary armies."** (Mao,i:30)

"The release of prisoners and the medical treatment of the wounded have proved to be the most effective method of our propaganda towards the enemy troops. As soon as soldiers, battalion commanders, company and platoon leaders of the enemy are taken prisoner by us, we start propaganda among them.

We divide them into two groups: One is for those who wish to stay, the other for those who wish to leave. We release the latter after providing them with travelling expenses. This destroys at a stroke the enemy's lying propaganda that "the communist bandits kill everyone indiscriminately." (Mao, i:33)

Obviously, the former enemy soldiers were completely, i.e. ideologically, integrated to such an extent that they became absolutely reliable fighters for the Red Power cause. There is no other explanation for the fact that "some of the soldiers captured in February and March of this year(....) are now already battalion commanders." (Mao, i:28)

In view of the fact that the Red Army made a large part of its recruits from enemy troops over a period of more than 20 years, the importance of the "psychological warfare" described here cannot be overestimated. However, democracy always had its limits where it collided with party discipline.

The Red Army was supplied almost exclusively by collecting ransoms from the "local despots". (Mao,i:29)

A lively trade developed between the Red Army and the local farmers and traders, and the fact that the Red Army fleeced the rich but paid the poor farmers and small traders for every nail and every grain of grain in an extremely correct manner - in contrast to the Kuomintang, which simply levied taxes, often requisitioned and responded to any resistance with terror - certainly contributed significantly to the entrenchment of the Red Army in the base areas. (See, for example, Mao, j: 482)

The armed forces of the base areas were divided into three categories:

"Red Army", "Red Guards" and "Department of Insurgents".

The "insurgent detachments" were mainly armed with lances and shotguns (Mao,i:30), and in accordance with the short range of these weapons (shotgun up to 50 metres, lance considerably less) and the low standard of training of the "insurgent detachments", their main task was to suppress the counter-revolution and protect the new local organs of power.

Initially, the "insurgent detachments" worked conspiratorially, i.e. they were civilians and limited themselves to partisan activities and propaganda work; after the conquest of the respective area by the Red Army, these detachments worked openly. (Mao,i:31)

The armament of the Red Army and the Red Guards consisted mainly of five-shot repeating rifles (Mauser K 98 system, mostly weapons taken from the Kuomintang, which had these weapons manufactured under licence in China. These Chinese Mausers are currently (1986) being offered at ridiculously low prices on the private German arms market. The locks bear the stamps of the Kuomintang...

Both units also had nine-shot repeating rifles, as Mao reports. These were presumably British Lee Enfield rifles.

In addition, machine guns were occasionally used, although these probably played a subordinate role at the beginning, as the Red Army, like most "irregular troops", suffered from a chronic shortage of ammunition.

In contrast to the Kuomintang, which was also relatively modernly equipped due to foreign support, the Red Army had neither tanks or other armoured vehicles nor fighter aircraft for air support, even heavy artillery was of course not available at the beginning, and the level of training and fighting strength was also generally significantly lower than that of the Kuomintang troops at the beginning, as the constant losses of the Red Army were also supplemented by former partisans who had little or no training.

On the whole, Mao was well aware of the weaknesses of the Red Army, and in addition to his constant demand for intensification of military training, his attention was mainly focused on constant revolutionary offensive, for "if the feudal and military rulers' camp does not continue to quarrel and war, if the revolutionary situation in the whole country does not develop further, the small areas of independent Red Power will suffer from extremely severe economic pressure, and the possibility of their prolonged existence will become doubtful." (Mao, i:37). (Mao, i:37)

Mao's fears were fully confirmed by the "encirclement and extermination campaigns" launched by the Kuomintang a few years after the publication of this document, after the Kuomintang had pushed back its semi-feudal rivals.

It may come as a surprise that Mao, for whom "political power comes from the barrels of guns", resolutely opposed a policy based solely on mobile partisan tactics.

For Mao, the establishment of base areas in which continuous political work could be carried out had absolute priority over purely military actions, which might bring temporary spectacular successes, but in his opinion could not serve to consolidate the revolution.

In his famous essay "A spark can start a steppe fire" (1930), Mao emphasises that "The policy of mobile guerrilla actions alone cannot fulfil the task of accelerating the revolutionary upsurge throughout the country." (Mao, I:72)

Mao emphasises that only the political line pursued by him and his comrades Chuh-Teh and Fang-Ji-Min, "which aims to create base areas, systematically establish political power, deepen the agrarian revolution, develop the armed forces of the people in a comprehensive process (...), advance political power in waves, etc." can ultimately lead to the victory of Red Power. (Mao, I, :73)

In view of the absolute numerical inferiority of his armed forces, Mao adopted a tactic that he used again and again with success in the war of liberation, which lasted over twenty years, and which was one of the main recipes for success in tactical terms:

"If we use correct tactics - that is, we fight only when we are sure of victory and will definitely take prisoners and loot, otherwise we will not engage in any battle at all - we can gradually expand the Red Army." (Mao, i:52)

It is clear that such a strategy requires a protracted war in which attrition and demoralisation play a major role and individual "decisive battles" play a subordinate role.

Partisan warfare

For Mao, guerrilla warfare was of strategic importance, especially as long as his own forces were conventionally inferior to the enemy. Mao also recognised the fundamental tactical requirements of guerrilla warfare:

- The enemy is not given a regular battle, because he can then exploit his military superiority; he must be worn down by "pinpricks", made to run into nothing, forced to make long and unsuccessful "pursuit marches", which tire and demoralise him, wear him down and, at the moment of weakness, unexpectedly attack him and destroy him as far as possible.

"If the enemy advances, we retreat; if he stops, we worry him; if he is exhausted, we strike; if he retreats, we pursue him." (Mao, I, :79)

As simple and old as this rule is - it also comes from Sun Tse - its consistent observance by the Red Army has almost always led to success. (Cf. also Sun Tse op. cit.:50, 68)

One of the secrets of success and also a prerequisite for such small-scale war tactics is understanding the overall situation not only in a military sense; according to Mao, the necessary method consists of "familiarising ourselves with the situation of the enemy as well as our own situation in all respects, determining the laws that determine the actions of both sides and applying them to our own actions." (Mao, d,: 97). (Mao, d,: 97)

Mao's study of SUN-Tse's writings can also be recognised here: In Sun-Tse (Chapter 3 "The Strategy of Attack" it says under points 8 and 9: "The victor is the one who exercises caution and waits for his opponent's imprudence." And: "Therefore it is said: If you know your opponent and know yourself, you may fight a hundred battles without danger." (Sun-Tse; op. cit.:56)

Mao therefore polemicises resolutely against hotheads who run against the enemy without having gained an accurate picture through prior reconnaissance:

They "inevitably run into each other's heads, precisely because they do not understand or do not want to understand that every military plan must be based on the indispensable reconnaissance as well as on the careful consideration of the situation of the enemy and their own side and the interrelationship between the two". (Mao, d, :98)

It is worth pointing out here that although Mao was very well read, i.e. he had studied the authoritative writings on the theory of war, from Sun-Tse's "Thirteen Commandments of the Art of War" to Clausewitz and Engels, and according to W. D. Jacobs (Jacobs, 1963,:263) had also studied T. E. Lawrence, he nevertheless insisted on learning and correcting false views through practice. "**Learning warfare through war itself - that is our method.**"

Mao's entire military writings are not abstractions or pure theories, but served not only to analyse concrete experiences but also as instructions for action and training material for party cadres and commanders (cf. Haffner, op. cit.:6), and they must be understood as such:

They were written for revolutionaries in the still economically underdeveloped China of the 1920s and 1930s, and abstractions and transfers to other countries, other times and other framework conditions are therefore, in my opinion, only possible to a very limited extent, if at all.

Mao would probably have been the last person to propagate his armed revolution as a general method for communist parties to seize power - possibly in the imperialist metropolises - on the contrary: he was always aware of the fact that only the special conditions in China forced the illegal and persecuted communist party to take the path of civil war.

Although the civil war in China resulted from the necessity for the communists to defend themselves against the extermination policy of the Kuomintang and thus actually served the purpose of naked self-preservation, war in China has always also been a means of advancing the revolution.

Paradoxically, however, the very fact that the Kuomintang institutionalised the civil war while the CCP, with the help of the Red Army, organised a new system of order, of which the Kuomintang now appeared to be the disruptor, contributed considerably to the Communists' gain in prestige:

The greatest handicap of a communist movement, namely to appear to the people as a wilful destroyer of "peace and order" (however imperfect this may be), was now on the side of the Kuomintang due to the policy of the base areas: in the base areas, the Kuomintang appeared as a terrorist, chaotic organisation that wilfully destroyed the new order, which was more advantageous for the poor peasants; unlike many other revolutionary movements, the CCP had obviously recognised the significance of these facts.

In countries where a policy of revolutionary consolidation through the creation of base areas does not seem possible, Mao considers a different revolutionary strategy to be necessary:

"In accordance with these characteristics, the task of the proletarian party in the capitalist states is to educate the workers through a legal struggle over a long period of time, to gather forces and thus prepare for the final overthrow of capitalism. There it is a matter of a protracted legal struggle, of using parliament as a tribune, of economic and political strikes, of organising the trade unions and training the workers.

The forms of organisation there are legal, the forms of struggle bloodless (not military). ...**As long as the bourgeoisie has not really failed, as long as the majority of the proletariat is not imbued with the determination to wage armed insurrection and civil war, as long as the peasant masses do not voluntarily begin to help the proletariat, armed insurrection and civil war should not be started."** (Mao, e,: 327, emphasis added by the author).

It can already be said at this point that the guerrilla and terrorist groups fighting in the "imperialist metropolises" and referring to Mao are, as we can see, wrong to do so.

To use Mao as an ideological legitimisation for guerrillas in a non-revolutionary situation is to distort and falsify Mao's political theory of guerrillas and revolution.

The Kuomintang's "encirclement and extermination campaigns" against the communists

By 1934, the CCP had succeeded in bringing almost the entire province of Kiangsi, with several million inhabitants, under the control of the Red Power and establishing "Soviets" in the provinces of Fukien, Hunan, Honan, Hopeh, Anhui, Szetschuan and Schensi. (Dinegar, 1963:210)

In the meantime, however, General Chiang Kai Shek had concentrated his troops against the Red Army, and in December 1930 the Kuomintang began the first "encirclement and extermination campaign", which was followed by four more and in which he deployed a total of more than 1.25 million soldiers.

These "encirclement and extermination campaigns" of Chiang Kai-shek and the counter-operations of the Red Army formed the main form of civil war in China in the 1930s. (Mao, d, :112)

In the first "encirclement and extermination campaign" (December 1930/January 1931), two brigades of the Kuomintang commander Dschang Hui-Dsan and the staff of his division were smashed, all 9,000 men destroyed and the division commander captured, which led to the panic-stricken flight of the troops. (Mao, d, :114)

During the second "encirclement and extermination campaign" (May 1931), the 200,000 "White" soldiers faced only 30,000 Red Army soldiers, who had, however, had four months to rest.

Despite its great numerical inferiority, the Red Army captured more than 20,000 rifles in this campaign and brought the enemy campaign to a complete standstill. (Cf. Mao, d, :145)

During the third "encirclement and extermination campaign", the Kuomintang troops numbered 300,000 men under the supreme command of General Chiang Kai-shek.

In contrast to the first two campaigns, whose strategy consisted of "advancing step by step and expanding the respective positions", Chiang now changed his strategy to "advance straight into the depths" with the intention of pushing the Reds towards the Gan River and destroying them there.

The Red Army evaded and tried to entice the Kuomintang troops to advance into their base area in order to destroy individual troop units there; this did not succeed, but the Red Army was nevertheless able to win all three subsequent battles by encircling individual enemy troop units and again captured more than 1,000 rifles.

In the fourth "encirclement and extermination campaign", the Red Army again succeeded in destroying two

Kuomintang divisions by tactically encircling them and again captured more than 10,000 rifles.

In his book "Strategic Problems of Revolutionary War in China" (first published in 1936), Mao precisely developed the principles that enabled the Red Army, which was vastly inferior in terms of numbers, armaments and logistics, to prevail against the Kuomintang:

In addition to the psychological aspect, i.e. the different motivation and fighting morale - here convinced to fanatical fighters for the revolution, there mercenary mentality - the following is also decisive

- The tactic of luring the enemy into one's own base area, where the Red Army enjoys the full sympathy and support of the peasant masses in all possible forms: Scouting, rations and partisan support.

The tactic of retreating to the base areas was the preparation of a tactical offensive; the enemy was thus lured into terrain that was unfavourable to him in every respect (Mao, d:139)

The counter-offensive, i.e. the start of actual combat operations, began when the enemy was in the base area, where it was exposed to attacks by both the Red Army and local partisan units.

The strategic encirclement by the Kuomintang was answered with a strategic retreat, while at the same time the counter-offensive was initiated by the Red Army beginning to infiltrate or break through gaps in the encirclement ring, thus encircling and "destroying" individual enemy divisions.

Mao considers the following prerequisites to be essential for the success of such operations:

"1. the population provides active support to the Red Army;

2. the terrain is favourable for our operations;

3. all the main forces in the Red Army have been concentrated;

4. the opponent's weak points have been identified;

5. the opponent has been exhausted and demoralised;

6. the opponent has been misled into making mistakes;

The first condition, namely the support of the people, is the most important of all for the Red Army." (Mao, d:130; author's emphasis).

For Mao, the be-all and end-all of successful (small-scale) warfare is to seize the initiative through the counter-offensive and to condemn the opponent to passivity as far as possible, turning him into an **object incapable of action** that must then be destroyed as completely as possible.

"To achieve this goal, the following conditions are necessary: the concentration of forces, the war of movement, the war of quick decision and the war of annihilation." (Mao, d:152)

At first glance, it may seem surprising that Mao, who from 1928 to the end of the 1940s repeatedly emphasised the necessary protracted nature of the Chinese People's War, even called for protractedness as a condition of victory: To grow, the Red Army needs time, and to wear down the enemy, to drive up the costs for him and slowly demoralise him also requires a longer period of time - so it may be surprising that Mao calls for war with a quick decision here.

This apparent paradox is resolved, however, when one considers that these were not quick decisive battles in the strategic sense, for example according to the German "Blitzkrieg pattern", but quick decisive battles in operational and tactical terms.

Mao also justified the need for quick decisive battles as follows:

1. the Red Army has no sources of support in terms of weaponry and, above all, ammunition supplies, so it cannot engage in long battles for this reason alone.

2. after concentrating its main forces in the tactical counter-offensive phase, the Red Army, unlike the enemy, has only one strong unit at its disposal, which must quickly destroy the enemy division it has encircled so that it can immediately turn its attention to the next enemy unit.

3. if the Red Army fails to reach a quick decision in a single battle, the enemy's other units not too far away can come to the aid of the one encircled by the Red Army, and the tactical superiority of the Red Army will then turn into absolute, i.e. also tactical, inferiority (Mao, d,:166)

The fifth "encirclement and extermination campaign" and the "long march"

The Kuomintang's fifth "encirclement and extermination campaign" against the Red Army began in October 1933 with the deployment of 900,000 soldiers under the command of General Chiang Kai-shek in the Fukien-Kiangsi region.

The "regular" Red Army numbered around 180,000 fighters, plus around 200,000 partisans who were poorly equipped - they only possessed around 100,000 rifles - and were ill-suited for regular warfare due to inadequate training. (Dinegar, op. cit.:211)

The Kuomintang troops were generally well equipped, they had armoured vehicles and air support, while the Red Army did not even have heavy artillery. (Dinegar, op. cit.:211)

In this campaign, General Chiang Kai-Shek apparently changed his strategy based on the advice of the German General von Seeckt:

He now proceeded to crush the enemy. With the help of fortified blockhouses and a veritable fire-wall, an iron ring was closed around the Red Army, whose leadership realised the new Kuomintang strategy too late and made the mistake of retreating to the base area using the tried and tested method instead of breaking out immediately.

Captain Dinegar (US Marine Infantry) writes:

"The area was literally burnt and, if necessary, depopulated. The Kuomintang admits that at least one million peasants were killed in this campaign alone in order to make Mao's economic and psychological blockade effective. This new policy was also successful.

Not only did it restrict Mao's mobility, but it also terrorised the peasants to such an extent that, despite all their sympathies, they no longer supplied the Reds or cooperated with them. This was bad enough in itself; in addition, this policy forced the Reds to exploit the peasants in exactly the same way as the Kuomintang did - which destroyed much of the peasants' faith in the Reds' good intentions." (Dinegar, op. cit.:211)

In August, the Red Army had lost more than 80,000 men, and according to the then commander of the 1st Army Corps, Chu En-Lei, the Red Army lost more than 60,000 men in a single one of these prolonged sieges. (Dinegar, op. cit.:212)

Exactly what Mao later rightly characterised as dangerous in his evaluation of these events had occurred: the Red Army had been deprived of the initiative because it had almost completely lost its ability to move; it was now engaged in a **defensive war of position** against an opponent who could sooner or later completely wear down the Red Army in this form of war due to its numerical, logistical, training-related and weapons-related superiority.

The worst thing was that the Red Army was now unable to retreat, and even mobile tactics had been made impossible; moreover, supplying the Red Army began to become a serious problem, as the Kuomintang's terrorist tactics towards the peasant masses meant that they could no longer dare to support the Red Army in any way.

In order to regain mobility and the initiative, the Red Army first had to break through the tightly meshed, fortified siege ring of the Kuomintang; it first had to **break out**, whatever the cost.

At the end of August 1934, Mao and Chu-teh and other commanders of the Red Army met to discuss the situation and it was decided to break out and retreat.

This "strategic retreat" was intended to save the Red Army from complete annihilation by the Kuomintang and enable it to seize the initiative again later.

The entire supply arsenal was broken up; some of the supplies were buried or destroyed, and a large part was also taken along, which later proved to be a big mistake, as the extensive material severely restricted the Red Army's ability to move and therefore had to be thrown away en route.

The 8th Route (March) Army under Mao's leadership marched from Jütschün to Jutu, where it united with other units to form an army of 90,000 to 100,000 men. (Dinegar, op. cit.:214)

As they only marched at night and overcast skies and moonless nights prevented the Kuomintang from conducting aerial reconnaissance, the Kuomintang leadership did not realise what was going on.

The positions vacated by the Red Army were temporarily replaced by local partisan troops in order to deceive the enemy.

Two "diversionary columns" were formed to ensure that the deception manoeuvre, i.e. the start of the strategic retreat, would succeed unnoticed by the Kuomintang.

The partisan column under Fang Chi Minh exerted pressure on the enemy in north-eastern Kiangsi; it was completely routed by the Kuomintang after completing its task.

The second group of guerrillas under Han-Jing established themselves in the mountains south of the border of Fukien and Chekiang; this group later managed to fight their way independently to Zhensi, where they arrived after a few years. (Dinegar, op. cit.:215)

In the Kuomintang's fifth "encirclement and extermination campaign", Mao and Chu-Teh used small guerrilla units to shield the large main army by deceiving and distracting the enemy.
The "Long March" began on 16 October 1934, and in the six weeks that followed, four Kuomintang defensive lines were breached, each fortified with concrete machine gun nests and blockhouses.

A total of nine battles were fought in the first 38 days, costing the Red Army 25,000 men. Mao's 8th Route Army marched straight north-west towards Szetschuan to clash with Hsu Hsiang-Tschien's troops.

However, Chiang Kai-shek saw through this goal because this time the Red Army abandoned its method of deceiving the enemy; the Kuomintang was therefore able to throw 110 regiments in the Red Army's path and set up sophisticated roadblocks.

Only the fact that the Red Army high command must have been demoralised and headless at this point can explain why Mao and Chu-Teh did not use their tried and tested tactic of dispersion - concentration - dispersion at the beginning of the Long March. (Cf. also Dinegar, op. cit.:216)

On 20 June 1935, after a veritable odyssey, they reached the north-west of Szetschuan. There they met up with the 50,000-strong 4th Front Army under the command of Hsu Hsiang-Tschien and Tschang Kuo-Tao.

Almost half of the troops, around 50,000 men, had been killed or wounded en route.

Throughout the "Long March", the Red Army carried out political work as far as it was able: where possible, the peasants were armed, the local landowners expropriated, property deeds destroyed and the land redistributed. (Dinegar, op. cit.: 221)

The "Long March", the largest withdrawal and evasion movement of a guerrilla army in history - the Red Army covered a distance of over 10,000 kilometres on foot! - brought its soldiers and commanders many valuable experiences later on; but the losses were also considerable: not only did the old base areas have to be abandoned and the civilian population living there left defenceless to the revenge of the Kuomintang, but the Red Army also suffered huge losses.

Of the 130,000 men who had begun the long march, only around 30,000 reached their destination, i.e. the province of Schensi. (Haffner, op. cit.:11)

Dinegar gives slightly different figures, but a similar ratio: 100,000 : 20,000 (Dinegar, op. cit.: 224)

Unlike other historical and political figures, Mao was perfectly capable of **self-critically** reflecting on his own actions and openly admitting the mistakes he had made.

He later criticised the events that led to the "Long March": "We did not plan organically; we had not thought the campaign through properly. The enemy's high command had laid out its strategy far-sightedly: we only thought about what was in front of us. (....) We panicked and fought foolishly." (Dinegar op. cit.:214)

On the other hand, Mao was never prepared to regard the consequences of the fifth "encirclement and extermination campaign" as a complete defeat; thus, on the occasion of an evaluation of the events in "Strategic Problems of the Revolutionary War in China", he wrote: "What is a defeat of the Red Army? Only if a counter-operation has failed completely can it be called a defeat from a strategic point of view, but even then only a partial and temporary defeat. For a total defeat in the civil war would mean that the Red Army was completely destroyed, which was never the case." (Mao, d, :114)

The Sino-Japanese War

Japanese imperialism took advantage of the fact that civil war was raging in southern China to continuously tear off pieces of northern China from 1931 onwards, without any significant resistance from the Kuomintang: Chiang Kai-shek wanted to deal with the enemy within first.

The fact that Mao not only correctly assessed the importance of the national question for a semi-colonial country like China, but also approached the tasks ahead of him in a very cold-blooded manner, is shown above all by the fact that he declared war on Japan with his remaining army of around 40,000 men and forced the mortal enemy of the Red Army, the Kuomintang under the leadership of General Chiang Kai-shek, to enter into an alliance with the Communists after the Sianfu Incident, to form a "united front".

Mao was even prepared to formally subordinate himself to the Kuomintang, but was not foolish enough to agree to the disbanding of his own troops in the Kuomintang army.

This alliance not only gave the Red Army some breathing space, but also gained the sympathy of parts of those circles that had previously viewed the Communists with suspicion.

By adding the national revolutionary / anti-imperialist aspect to social revolutionary warfare, Mao also opened up the party's influence to sections of the population that had previously been hostile or at best indifferent to the CCP's social revolutionary ambitions.

The Sino-Japanese War officially broke out in June 1937, and as far as Japan and the Kuomintang were concerned, it was a conventional war.

In a conventionally waged war, the one who has the more developed economy, the greater economic resources, the better, more modern equipment and the better trained soldiers is usually superior - in everything Japan was superior to the Kuomintang; in the course of the war, three quarters of Chinese territory was occupied by the Japanese and the Kuomintang was pushed back to the far south - leaving the terrain free for the partisan struggle of the Red Army and the Chinese peasant masses against Japanese imperialism.

The guerrilla war against Japan (1st phase)

In the case of Japan, too, Mao's strategy resulted from analysing the concrete conditions in his own and his opponent's camp, both in subjective and objective terms.

In his essay "Strategic Problems of the Partisan War against Japanese Aggression", written in May 1938, Mao therefore begins with the question of why the guerrilla war is of strategic importance in this national war, although in his own opinion regular warfare plays the main role and the guerrilla war plays an auxiliary role in the "war of resistance against Japanese aggression". (Mao, c, : 179)

For Mao, the necessity of guerrilla warfare arose from the fact that Japan was a small but strong country (see above!) attacking a large but weak country.

An essential basis of his strategy here is also the motto adopted by Sun-Tse of creating the opponent's weakness and exploiting it as far as possible.

In the VII Commandment of the Art of War, Sun-Tse states:

"13 In the morning one has fresh courage, during the day it wanes, and in the evening one thinks of returning to camp. Therefore, the one who skilfully wages war evades the enemy as long as he is in high spirits, and delivers his blow when he is sluggish or thinking of returning to camp. This is the control of courage.

14 If the opponent is in order, wait for disorder. If he is calm, wait for confusion. This is the guidance of the heart.

(15) If the enemy is near, wait until he is far away; if he is powerful, wait until he is exhausted." (Sun-Tse, op. cit.: 68)

The superiority of the Japanese army, i.e. their better equipment and higher standard of training of the Japanese soldiers, could only be effective where the Japanese army was given the opportunity to use it, i.e. to face it in a regular battle.

The Kuomintang did so, and because it was less well trained and also on the defensive, it was defeated and pushed back into southern China.

In his 1938 essay "On the Protracted War", Mao developed his strategy against Japan, which to a certain extent "inevitably" resulted from his (realistic) analysis of his own concrete situation and that of the enemy, and in which he precisely defined the course of the war of resistance against Japan, its stages and its respective concrete forms.

This particular writing is remarkable for several reasons:

On the one hand, because of their whole aim, in the propagation of a **protracted** war.

The fact that this writing is at the same time a theoretical derivation of a concrete political-military strategy, an instruction for commanders and a post-factum **prognosis** of the course of the war **clearly sets it apart from the usual military writings.**

According to Mao, the Sino-Japanese war must go through three stages:

"The first stage will be the stage of the enemy's strategic attack and our strategic defence, the second stage the strategic consolidation of the enemy and our preparation for the counter-offensive, the third the stage of our strategic counter-offensive and the enemy's strategic retreat." (Mao, b, :253)

The strategic attack of the opponent

Due to its imperialist nature and military superiority, Japan invades China, so Japan has the initiative and, due to the weakness of the Chinese forces - Kuomintang and Red Army - is able to penetrate far into the interior and occupy all important points - cities, railways, roads, production facilities, etc.

Since the enemy, i.e. Japan, was superior in this phase, it could not be attacked openly; large parts of Chinese territory had to be sacrificed to it for the time being, because for Mao, quite analogously to the principle of "self-preservation and the destruction of the enemy's forces", which he often emphasised, self-preservation and the growth of his troops were more important than the temporary assertion or gaining of territory.

Asserting or gaining territory can be **the result** of one's own strength, which, however, must first be won.

It is unmistakable that Mao learnt from the mistakes made during the fifth "encirclement and extermination campaign" by the Kuomintang: Precisely because the Red Army had tried for too long to hold on to its base area, even though it lacked the forces to do so, it had had to bear the consequences that were disastrous for it...

Although, in Mao's view, the Red Army was strategically in a defensive position during the first phase of the Sino-Japanese War, or, as Mao also put it, operating "on the inner lines", it could and had to seize the initiative at the operational-tactical level, i.e. to constantly attack the enemy through mobile guerrilla warfare and to smash individual enemy units as completely as possible.

The tactics employed were essentially the same as those used successfully against the Kuomintang's first four "encirclement and extermination" campaigns.

These experiences are clearly reflected in Mao's book "Strategic Problems of Partisan Warfare against Japanese Aggression":

"It is possible and necessary to carry out offensive actions in operational and tactical terms within the framework of the strategic defence, to fight battles or battles with a quick decision within the framework of a strategically protracted war and to carry out operational or tactical actions on the outer lines within the framework of strategic operations on the inner lines. **This is the strategic course that must be followed throughout the war of resistance. It applies to both regular warfare and guerrilla warfare.**" (Mao, c, :184)

It was precisely this strategic course that was responsible for the success, i.e. the successive expansion of the base areas before and during the four "encirclement and extermination campaigns" and saved the Communists from annihilation by the Kuomintang; a deviation from this course, i.e. the untimely surrender of base areas, was the Red Army's undoing during the fifth "encirclement and extermination campaign".

It is therefore no wonder that Mao, enriched by this dearly bought experience, henceforth propagated the ability of a militarily inferior army to "**walk away**" when the situation demanded it as an elementary condition for ultimate victory.

Thus he writes in "Strategic Problems of the Partisan War against Japanese Aggression":

"The ability to walk away is the most prominent feature of partisan units. Going away is the main method of getting out of a passive situation and regaining the initiative." (Mao,c,:189)

For the concrete implementation of "offensive actions within the framework of the defence, of combat actions with a quick decision within the framework of a protracted war and of actions on the outer battle lines within the framework of actions on the inner lines", Mao once again lists the necessary procedures and conditions:

"1. the basic guideline of guerrilla warfare, however, must be the attack, which is much more offensive than that of regular warfare. Moreover, this attack must take the form of a surprise action." (Mao, c, :185)

2. in disturbing the enemy, in binding him and in disruptive actions, as well as in working among the masses - in all these guerrilla activities the principle of dispersal of forces applies.

3. however, if the task is to destroy an enemy unit or smash an enemy attack, the reverse principle applies: "Concentrate a large force to defeat a small enemy force." (Mao,c:186)

In the same paper Mao writes above:

"... I am not against two or more directions of operations; but at one and the same time there must be only one main direction. The Chinese Red Army, which had appeared on the scene of the civil war as a weak and small force, has since inflicted repeated defeats on its strong opponent, and these military successes, which astonished the world, were based to a large extent on the concentrated deployment of its forces. ...When we say: "one against ten, ten against a hundred", this formula refers to strategy, to the war as a whole and to the overall balance of power between the enemy and us; (...) But this is not meant in relation to operational or tactical actions, here we must never behave in this way.

Be it in the counter-offensive, be it in the attack - we always have to concentrate strong forces in order to strike a blow against part of the enemy forces." And further: "**Our strategy is: one against ten, our tactics: ten against one.**" (Mao,d,:153f) (emphasis mine).

Mao's teacher Sun-Tse can also be recognised here, who says in the VIth commandment under **rule no. 7**: "So if I show the opponent behaviour without insisting on it, I preserve my integrity and fragment the opponent. Through this protection I will be a united force. But if the opponent has divided himself, he will form ten parts. Then I will attack his unit with tenfold power: There will be many of us, but few of the enemy. If someone knows how to strike with the masses against a minority, he has to fight only a few, and it is easy to defeat them." (Sun-Tse, op. cit.:63)

The Red Army actually followed these principles throughout the war of liberation against Japan, always endeavouring to establish at least a threefold, but preferably a four-, five- or sixfold tactical superiority over the enemy.

4. protractedness was another condition of the Red Army's eventual success: The Red Army was weak at the beginning, so it needed time to grow, also to be able to develop the necessary political work in the base areas. The protracted nature of the war also played a major role in Mao's strategy

with regard to the international situation, as the onset of the Second World War was bound to weaken the Japanese troops due to the resulting fragmentation.

However, Mao's calculation that the protracted nature of the war would lead to internal disintegration in the enemy's camp, culminating in a popular uprising of the progressive, anti-imperialist and democratic forces in Japan, only worked to a modest extent: In most cases, the effectiveness of ideological indoctrination combined with total control and ruthless terror of dictatorial or semi-fascist state apparatuses is underestimated: As true as it is that state terror usually only accelerates rather than weakens a revolutionary oppositional tide, i.e. a democratic or communist movement on the offensive - history knows a number of examples of this - this does not seem to apply to a situation where the left and democratic forces find themselves on the **defensive** without the possibility, like the Chinese Red Army, of being able to mount a "strategic retreat":

Neither in Hitler's Germany nor in Franco's Spain was a really significant resistance able to form once the left had suffered a defeat; even Mussolini's fall was probably only made possible by the emerging differences within the right-wing power bloc and by the fact that Italian fascism was less total and less profound than German fascism in particular.

However, Mao did not wait for external influences - the international situation, disputes within Japanese imperialism, etc. - but rather used them as argumentative support for his conviction that the Red Army could eventually win if it only took enough time.

Mao recognised Japan's elementary weaknesses at an early stage, as they also had a similar negative impact on the German Wehrmacht:

"Japanese imperialism, however, has two fundamental weaknesses: First, it lacks armed forces, and second, it wages war on foreign soil." (Mao, c:187)

The consequence of the fact that the area occupied by Japan was far too large in relation to the Japanese troop strength was that only the central points could be occupied, while the hinterland was largely outside the control of the Japanese armed forces.

The situation was similar to that of the Kuomintang, except that in contrast to the war between the Communists and the Kuomintang, there were hardly any Chinese who would have voluntarily supported the Japanese.

The hinterland, which could not be controlled by the Japanese or only with disproportionate effort, was immediately seized by the Communists as a field of operations, and at the same time the CCP began with anti-Japanese propaganda, the formation of local militias and partisan units and of base areas according to a tried and tested model.

It is no coincidence that parallels to the Russian guerrilla war against the German Wehrmacht come to mind here: Here, as there, the occupying forces had far too much territory to control, which the guerrillas knew how to exploit...

This time the situation was much more favourable for the Communists: **By tapping into the national sentiments of the Chinese, by propagating the anti-imperialist struggle against Japanese aggression and thus combining national and social revolutionary struggle, by presenting itself as the most determined force against brutal Japanese imperialism, the CCP steadily gained prestige and popularity,** and in the slowly but surely expanding "Liberated Areas" and partisan base areas it was able to recruit more and more new fighters and thus more than make up for its losses.

Thus the 8th Route Army under Mao's command and the new 4th Army grew from 40,000 men in 1937 to more than a million men by the time the Japanese surrendered in 1945 - a remarkable result!

Partisan warfare and war of movement

The characteristic feature of the war of movement in the last phase of the Chinese War of Liberation is the fact that it was essentially based on the same operational and tactical principles as the guerrilla war; for Mao, the guerrilla war was the preliminary stage of the "regular" war of movement.

Contrary to widespread opinion, the actual partisan war, i.e. above all the irregularity and clandestinity, by no means played the decisive role that is often claimed today - at least not in "objective" terms. (Cf. Hanrahan, op. cit.: 233)

This becomes clear if you look at some figures: In 1947, for example, when the civil war between the CCP and the Kuomintang was again in full swing, the numerical strength of the Kuomintang troops was about 3,700,000 men. (according to Mao, k: 395)

Such armies, which were also excellently equipped - according to Hanrahan (op. cit.:231), around 20 Kuomintang divisions had been fully or partially equipped by the

Americans - could not be destroyed within a few years by small-scale warfare alone; this required large-scale battles and the massive deployment of regular troops.

Such large Kuomintang troops could have encircled and destroyed the communist-controlled base areas one by one, analogous to the fifth "encirclement and extermination campaign", or could have forced the Red Army into a "strategic retreat" if the latter had insisted on the exclusive use of guerrilla warfare.

Mao's special ability consisted precisely in applying the strategy and tactics best suited to the situation at the appropriate time and place, and in the last phase, the strategic counter-offensive of the Red Army against the Kuomintang, this was the war of movement with regular troop units. (Cf. Hanrahan, op. cit.:233)

However: firstly, the regular Red Army soldiers continued to receive support from local partisan groups - which continued to play an elementary role in Mao's warfare, especially in terms of reconnaissance and distracting and deceiving the enemy - and secondly, partisan units were also formed from regular units time and again as required.

After all, guerrilla warfare was also a necessary stage in order to reach the higher form of regular warfare.

In my opinion, the success of the Red Army was not primarily based on the fact that it was a guerrilla army - the Red Army won its largest battles of annihilation as a largely regular force - but on the existence of objective prerequisites and the subjective abilities of the party cadres and commanders to make the right decisions at the right moment by realistically analysing the specific situation - here they were certainly helped by many years of often painful experience.

All this was made possible not least by Mao's ability to combine the traditional with the new - for example Karl Marx and Sun-Tse - to act unconventionally and unpredictably in military terms, to apply his experience self-critically, to further develop what was useful and to free himself from the ballast of military traditions.

The Chinese wars of liberation against the Japanese also show that in history it is often not only the "objective" conditions that determine the historical process, but that these merely set the broad framework within which **individuals** are decisive; that at certain turning points, **personalities** are needed to help the historical possibilities achieve a breakthrough. History has nothing in common with pedantic schematism, but is a living process that is always determined by very lively human subjects - albeit, of course, always within a contemporary historical framework.

Summary

The CCP's People's War against the Kuomintang and then against the Japanese, which lasted over twenty years and probably involved a similar number of people in the political events and **cost a similar number of lives as the entire First World War (according to Sebastian Haffner, op. cit.: 9), is the first historical example of a communist-led total guerrilla against imperialist exploitation and oppression and against the internal "class enemy".**

It should be noted that this was **not primarily** a revolutionary war to establish the "dictatorship of the proletariat" and the immediate goal of building socialism, but rather, according to the CCP's own self-image at the time, the **objective** was "**bourgeois-democratic**", albeit under the leadership of the Chinese Communist Party, which gave the Chinese Revolution its characteristic character.

The CCP's strategy resulted from a generally realistic analysis of Chinese society in the 20th century - notwithstanding some mythological side effects.

In my opinion, this close connection between social analysis and its practical application in political and military terms, in addition to the existence of "objective"

conditions, must be regarded as essential for the success of the CCP and the Red Army under Mao Tse-Tung's leadership.

The following characteristics characterise the entire Chinese liberation war - the civil war as well as the anti-Japanese liberation war:

1. the principle of political work (agitation and propaganda) and of anchoring in the masses, which Mao always placed at the top; in none of his writings does Mao fail to emphasise again and again the necessity of mass mobilisation and of winning over the masses to the goals of the Communist Party, i.e. the anti-imperialist revolution.

For Mao, this was both a goal and a political prerequisite for the success of the Chinese revolution, and Mao's concept of the base areas in which the party carried out concrete political work, as well as Mao's frequently emphasised rejection of "roving bands of rebels", was not least the result of the realisation that the Chinese revolution was primarily a political and not just a military task.

2. the establishment of a Red counter-power in the form of base areas, which were not only of decisive importance as a logistical and military base for the Red Army, but also played an elementary role as a foundation for the consolidation of the revolution, as well as for its undulating spread.

3) The existence of the Communist Party was a decisive factor in a process whose goal was also seen in the establishment of a centralised state power to overcome national fragmentation and weakness.

The function of the party in the revolutionary process was also of fundamental importance in terms of its significance as an organising, centralising, controlling and disciplining body, but also as a source of impetus.

4. Strategically, the party and the Red Army pursued a policy in which "self-preservation and the destruction of the enemy" took top priority over territorial gains; Mao's view that strength also results in the possibility of local expansion, but that (temporary) territorial gains do not in themselves signify strength and justify the loss of larger troop contingents, was the guiding principle of Maoist strategy: Seizing or regaining the initiative as a prerequisite for the army's striking power presupposed the ability and willingness of the Red troops to "go away", i.e. to allow the enemy into their own base area temporarily if necessary, even at the cost of economic and other advantages, as a condition for wearing them down in an area unfavourable to them, demoralising them and being able to destroy them all the more easily with the support of the rural population.

The "war of annihilation" always propagated by Mao resulted from the realisation that the Kuomintang, like the Japanese, were enemies who would not rest until the communists, their main opponents, had been completely wiped out.

"Cats make friends with cats, nowhere in the world do cats make friends with mice." (Mao).

5. The tactic almost always used of luring the enemy into one's own base area, irritating him here through the partisan groups supporting the regular units, provoking him with pinpricks to pointless because unsuccessful pursuit marches, keeping him on constant alert through mock attacks, thereby finally tiring and demoralising the enemy, This tactic presupposed extensive sympathy, support and anchoring of the army and party among the rural population, which the communists were able to secure again and again through revolutionary measures, primarily through the expropriation of large estates and the redistribution of land to the poor peasantry.

Furthermore, this tactic required extreme mobility, and it was the long-standing partisan practice that enabled the extraordinary mobility of the Red Army even in the final phase of the liberation struggle, when the Red troops had become a mass army, and helped to concentrate and disperse these now numerically very large troop units as required.

6 As in all guerrilla wars, the permanent offensive, the constant endeavour to retain or seize the initiative, was a condition of success in the Chinese War.

7. contrary to widespread opinion, it was not the guerrilla as an isolated method, as a kind of "secret recipe", which finally led the Red Army to victory after very protracted fighting, but the flexible application of different military strategies and tactics depending on the requirements of the situation, whereby, in my opinion the guerrilla played a role more in terms of its political implications, its significance as a politico-military form of self-preservation and the gradual growth of the long completely inferior Red Army than in terms of its potential for destruction: Mao himself not only occasionally made downright disparaging remarks about the guerrilla, but also explicitly described it as a form of war by militarily inferior forces.

Mao's prediction that in the final phase of the struggle, namely the "strategic offensive" of the Red Army, the guerrilla would by no means disappear, but would nevertheless have to take a back seat as the main form of combat in favour of the regular war of movement, was also fully confirmed.

8. Although the Red Army must be described as a "regular" force, especially in the last phase of the war against the Kuomintang, it had some characteristic features that distinguished it from other "regulars": First and foremost is the fact that, in accordance with Mao's demands, the same tactical principles applied to the regular army as to the partisan groups; also, the close interlocking between partisan groups and regular armed forces makes it seem reasonable to put "regular" in inverted commas; this is also because members of the partisan detachments were transferred to the regular army if necessary. This is also because members of the partisan units were transferred to the regular army or, conversely, partisan groups were temporarily formed from individual regular Red Army units as required, i.e. for individual projects, but also for a longer period of time, especially to build up new local partisan units.

9 The Red Army's recipe for success in tactical terms was based to a considerable extent on the "artificial" creation of a balance of power that enabled the Red Army to emerge victorious from most battles and with considerably lower losses than the opposing side: **Strategically one to ten, tactically ten to one, that was one of the essential military principles of the Red Army.**

The creation of tactical superiority in the face of existing strategic inferiority through skilful manoeuvring was of course not an invention of Mao's; it characterises more or less every successful guerrilla.

10 Just for the sake of completeness, it should be pointed out that suitable terrain was a fundamental prerequisite for the Chinese guerrilla war - Mao has repeatedly pointed this out.

Mao only mentioned an important fact in passing because it was self-evident to him and did not pose a problem, but it is important in the later context: Mao derived the Chinese War of Liberation from the concrete conditions in China in the 1920s, 1930s and 1940s, and these **concrete conditions**, which Mao repeatedly re-analysed, also produced the concrete people who fought the Chinese People's War, **one of the bloodiest and most costly wars of the 20th century.** The fighters of the Red Army and the local partisan detachments were not proletarians in the majority, but people who literally **had "nothing to lose but their chains".**

The impoverished and indebted farmers, agricultural labourers, day labourers, vagabonds, workers, robbers and former Kuomintang soldiers - they all had nothing to lose but their chains, they actually had "a world to gain", as the Communist Manifesto puts it.

Only revolutionaries of the calibre of Mao Tse-Tung or people who had been used to great hardship and physical strain all their lives could wage such a total, brutal, protracted and bloody people's war as the one against the Kuomintang and the Japanese without sooner or later questioning the meaning and purpose of the whole enterprise.

Sober figures and verbal descriptions are probably only imperfectly able to depict the misery that must have prevailed in China at the time, which finally prompted the Chinese peasants to gather in droves under the banner of the CCP and the Red Army and to "make a clean sweep of the oppressor", the internal and external enemy.

Chapter 12 Guerrillas in Latin America

Political-economic conditions of the guerrilla

Karl Marx already attributed a decisive role to the colonial exploitation of the "Third World" for the emergence and expansion of European capitalism:

"The discovery of the gold and silver lands in America, the extermination, enslavement and burial of the indigenous population in the mines, the incipient conquest and plundering of the East Indies, the transformation of Africa into an enclosure for the trade hunt for black skins mark the dawn of the capitalist era of production. These idyllic processes are the main moments of the original accumulation." (Marx, a, 1979:779)

More recent, Marxist and non-Marxist orientated studies have confirmed the importance of the plundering of the "Third World" for the original capitalist accumulation, i.e. the accumulation of capital for the founding of companies.

The (Marxist-oriented) economist Ernest Mandel calculated the value of the wealth transferred from the countries of the "Third World" to the European metropolises through direct robbery, slave trade and "regular" trade, and he arrived at an amount of over 1 billion gold pounds in the period from 1500 to 1750, which is "more than the value of the entire investment capital in all European industrial companies around the year 1800". (Mandel, 1972:77)

Unfortunately, the millions of atrocities and mass murders committed against the people of Latin America have a very real economic basis: Latin America has served and continues to serve as a reservoir of raw materials, a market for the industrialised countries, a source of cheap labour, an investment field for "exuberant" capital, and so on: It is undeniable that Latin American countries, along with other regions in the world, not only played a major role in the original accumulation of capital in Europe and the expansion of European and later US capital, but are still a source of "extra profits" of all kinds today.

Wherever such extreme conditions of exploitation prevailed, there was resistance, and the repeated claims of "apathy" on the part of the Indians contradict the historical facts.

There have been repeated local rebellions in Latin America with significant participation of the Indians, and not only since the end of the Second World War: the most famous example is probably the largest Indian uprising in Peru, led in 1780/81 by the Inca and scion of an ancient Inca dynasty, Tupaq Amaru, which, after initial successes, finally ended with the capture and public quartering of Tupaq Amaru in Cuzco, the former Inca capital. (Cf. on this and the following Galeano, 1983,:56 ff ; Allemann, 1974,:318)

Colonialism and later imperialism provoked the corresponding reaction in Latin America in the form of nationalism, and the wars of liberation of the Latin American countries, led mostly by the offspring of wealthy Creole landowners such as Simon Bolivar, were waged more or less exclusively with the aim of national liberation from the "mother countries", initially primarily from Spain.

Most of these liberation struggles were fought conventionally, because the liberators such as Simon Bolivar, who were themselves part of the ruling class, were **not** primarily concerned with transforming the economic structures in favour of the poor farmers and agricultural workers, i.e. above all the Indian population.

One of the few exceptions in the series of anti-colonial liberators is apparently General Artigas from Uruguay, who alternately fought against the Spanish, Argentinians and Portuguese for a sovereign Uruguay and was almost the only one who also focussed on social restructuring of the economic foundations, above all agrarian reform - the land to those who cultivate it! - had in mind. (Allemann, op. cit.:318)

But the Mexican priest Morelos also issued the slogan: "All rich people, all aristocrats and all leading functionaries are to be treated as enemies."

But eventually he and his rebels were also defeated and shot. (Galeano, op. cit.:58)

Once Latin America was formally independent, structures emerged that to some extent still characterise almost all countries on the Latin American continent to a greater or lesser extent:

- Extreme dependence on the world market, characterised by export production. The asynchronicity of development on an international scale has led to an international division of labour on several levels.

The rich industrialised countries of Europe and North America purchase raw materials, agricultural products, semi-finished goods and other goods at low prices from the poor countries of Latin America. In order to maximise profits, wages in Latin America have been kept low through a series of sometimes even terrorist measures.

No matter how often military dictatorships may have changed and donned a liberal cloak, the principle of state power has always remained the same to this day: The protection of the haves against the have-nots, the suppression of the majority of the population by an armed minority that has the power of the state on its side....

A fatal vicious circle has led to the "development of underdevelopment": In order to achieve the highest possible profits, the mechanisms shown by Karl Marx in "Capital" are applied: on the one hand, there is considerable over-exploitation of labour power, as the price of the commodity of labour power is kept so low with the help of dictatorial measures that it is significantly lower than that for technical innovations.

This over-exploitation is made possible by rigid, authoritarian and dictatorial government methods, which in turn prevent necessary innovations and the emergence of a broad domestic market:

Trade unions are violently suppressed and can only be effective to a limited extent anyway, because there is not only a large "industrial reserve army" but also a large "relative overpopulation", which, because it is completely excluded from wage labour and not organised, can very easily be used as "strikebreakers" due to its extreme impoverishment.

However, it is often precisely these sections of the population that provide the most determined fighters in a revolutionary situation and represent a permanent revolutionary potential.

Due to these political structures and the resulting inadequate possibility of achieving higher wages and thus growing purchasing power to create a broad internal market and a corresponding middle class, the economy remains export-orientated and thus not only extremely dependent on the world market and therefore susceptible to crises, but to a certain extent a necessary "car-centred development" is also made impossible, which would be in contrast to a purely export-orientated monoculture.

On the other hand, the introduction of more modern production methods to compensate for the fall in the prices of raw materials and agricultural produce on the world market has increased unemployment and impoverishment among large sections of the population, especially in rural areas, has destroyed and continues to destroy subsistence farming and is driving micro-farmers and seasonal workers into the urban slums, where they usually search in vain for regular work.

Moreover, there are limits to modernisation where the ruling oligarchies cannot be interested in the comprehensive **education** of the masses: It is no coincidence that most revolts and revolutions in Latin America begin at the universities!

In my opinion, an essential part of the programme of all successful liberation movements in Latin America was therefore rightly aimed at the education sector, above all in the form of broad literacy campaigns, in order to create the intellectual prerequisites for broad popular participation in economic and political decision-making processes.

The problems facing almost the whole of Latin America are ultimately the result of two interrelated structures:

imperialism, i.e. the various forms of exploitation and political influence exerted on the poor by the rich countries, and the structures within society, which have now often gained relative autonomy: As long as the economy and politics of Latin American countries are determined by the interests of a numerically relatively small but unscrupulous ruling class that plunders its own population and enriches itself as a result, there is little hope that the "development of underdevelopment" can be halted.

To summarise, it can be said: The economic and political problems of Latin America appear to be difficult to solve under the given conditions, i.e. the imperialist grip and the extreme class differentiation within society and the associated political structures.

These are the political and economic **conditions** from which almost all Latin American liberation movements had to start; they had to wage a "war on two fronts", so to speak: Against imperialism, i.e. the exploitation and domination by foreign corporations and states, and against the internal enemy of democracy and self-determination of the whole people, the **ruling upper class** in their own country, which often represents a bulwark against any form of social modernisation.

So if they want to solve these problems, liberation movements or democratic movements must be as anti-imperialist/nationalist as they are social revolutionary - if they are not, they will not be able to achieve real liberation and renewal.

It follows from the problems outlined here that the problems of the Latin American countries are **not** solved with the seizure of power by a democratic movement, if they are actually successful, but are only just **beginning:** This only creates the conditions for a longer process of emancipation with an uncertain outcome!

Chapter 13 Latin America and the Left

The founding of communist and socialist parties in Latin American countries in the 1920s and 1930s was not only the result of the gradual emergence of a comparatively insignificant industrial proletariat and the associated conflicts of interest in Latin America, but must also be seen in the context of the victorious Russian October Revolution, the founding of the "**Communist International**" **(CI)** and its initially great prestige in the "Third World".

Since the (Stalinist) Communist International/Comintern was seen as the "world party of the proletariat" and was able to impose the policies to be pursued by its national sections, acting as a kind of central command authority at times, the alignment of the various Communist parties with the respective "general line" is by no means surprising.

Stalinisation, which in Soviet Russia led to the elimination of the entire opposition, the left and right wings of the SDAPR, continued in the Communist International and eventually also affected the communist parties of Latin America, albeit with some delay.

In Latin America, too, the exclusion of "Trotskyists" and the ever tighter alignment with the directives of the Communist International took place, for which, however, the geopolitical interests of the Soviet Union alone, the "bulwark of socialism", increasingly became the political guideline, while the goal of world revolution increasingly receded into the background in accordance with the Stalinist doctrine of "socialism in one country".

Instead of **conducting independent analyses of the actual situation in their own countries based on the concrete social situation,** the Communist parties in Latin America increasingly became, consciously or unconsciously, the extended arm of the foreign policy interests of the Soviet Union and adopted its schematic theory of the "bourgeois-democratic revolution", which was on the agenda in the countries of Latin America.

The orientation towards the "popular front" propagated by the Communist International in the mid-1930s and adopted by the Latin American communist parties, i.e. a class alliance between the proletariat and the peasantry as well as the "progressive part of the national bourgeoisie" against fascism and feudalism, was already controversial there and ultimately led to the loss of hegemony on the left, where there was actually something like a relatively progressive part of the bourgeoisie (Spain, France).

In Latin America, where, with a few exceptions, there has never been a genuine national bourgeoisie analogous to the European and North American centres, and where the bourgeoisie has played a rather parasitic role as a "comprador bourgeoisie", acting as an intermediary and willing tool of exploitation by foreign countries, an alliance between the proletariat and this thoroughly parasitic and corrupt clique of power, which is completely reactionary even by capitalist standards, is not really politically expedient.

This "**popular front policy**" of the Soviet Union and the Stalinist Communist International must be seen in the context of the increasing threat to the Soviet Union from fascist Germany in the 1930s and 1940s and the endeavours of the Stalinist Soviet government to conclude a pact against the Hitler-Mussolini-Franco coalition, including with the governments previously classified as imperialist.

The policy of the Communist International was thus intended to promote the interests of Stalinist Soviet power on an international scale.

The fact that the popular front orientation was **not** the product of a **revolutionary strategy**, but owed **its** existence to the national and **geopolitical interests of the Soviet Union**, is also made clear by the fact that the aim was not, as would have corresponded to an immanent logic, a popular front of workers, peasants and the declassed, but a "popular front" with those forces that were alienated from the common people and played a very dubious role in this respect.

However, for the Communist International, the alliance of the broadest possible anti-Hitler coalition had absolute priority over revolutionary processes with uncertain outcomes: this is not only evident in the case of Spain, where the democratic republican revolution was sacrificed to this coalition; this policy was also considered binding for Latin America.

For example, Carlos Lamarca, a leader of the Chilean CP in the 1930s, **criticised** the **Trotskyists** in 1938 **because they did not want to renounce the class struggle despite the coalition with Anglo-American imperialism against Hitler that the Soviet Union was seeking:**

"The Trotskyists are using the people's legitimate feeling of hatred against imperialism to concentrate the attack on English and Yankee imperialism, which have the largest volume of investment in Chile. This is a moment of aid to the penetration and domination of the fascist governments.... (Ross, RH 6:32)

The consequences of this fatal policy are particularly evident in the example of Cuba, where the Communist Party (PSP) even participated in the government of the completely corrupt and dictatorial US puppet Batista from 1943 onwards.

In return, the Cuban Communist Party was legalised and given modest leeway in its propaganda work among the proletariat, which at the time was purely trade union-based.

This **strange coalition of interests between an extremely reactionary, imperialist-controlled puppet government and a communist party**, initially caused by geopolitics, **also gave rise to social "entanglements of perspectives".**

Similar problems, as described here using the Cuban example, existed - albeit in a mitigated form - not only in Cuba, but everywhere where the Communist or Socialist parties adapted their political standpoint or relativised it beyond recognition due to real or supposed tactical requirements.

Chapter 14 Cuba

A brief chronology of Cuban history

1511 Incorporation of Cuba into the Spanish colonial system. Development of a colonial society politically and economically dependent on Spain, Spanish trading centre and supply base.

Until the 18th century, extensive export-orientated livestock farming in latifundia (export of hides), alongside small-scale tobacco farming.

19th century Boom in the sugar industry. Establishment of monocultural sugar production in plantations, based on the exploitation of slave labour.

1868 First uprising against Spain. On 10 October 1868, the republicans proclaim independence and establish a republican government in Bayamo.

This is followed by a ten-year guerrilla war against the Spaniards with arms support from the USA, in which around 50,000 Cubans and around 208,000 Spaniards lose their lives.

1878 "Peace of Zanjon", which leads to the representation of Cuba in the Spanish Cortes and the gradual abolition of slavery.

This is followed by an economic crisis due to the abolition of preferential tariffs on sugar from Cuba in the USA, which leads to a renewed uprising under M. Gomez, A. Macco and J. Marti.

The uprising is bloodily suppressed by a Spanish army of 200,000 men under the command of Captain General Weyler.

In 1897, under the liberal Madrid cabinet of P. M. Sugasta, Weyler was recalled and Cuba was granted further autonomy.

1898 In the Paris Peace Treaty of 10 December 1898, Cuba falls to the USA after it defeats the Spanish fleet. The USA establishes a military administration.

The "Platt Amendment" followed in 1901, an agreement anchored in the Cuban constitution that granted the USA the right to intervene in Cuba in the event of internal unrest.

20 May 1902 Handover of the government to the first President T. E. Palma by US General L. Wood.

1906 Liberal outrage against Palma. The USA intervenes with the help of marines. Palma is replaced first by US Secretary of War W. Taft, then by Colonel Ch. Magoon.

1909 J. M. Gomez takes over the government after the withdrawal of US troops.

1913 Military intervention by the USA due to renewed unrest, the government is taken over by the conservative M. G. Menocal. The government is dependent on the USA.

1917 Revolution under J. M. Gomez against his conservative successor M. G. Menocal (1913-1921), the USA again intervenes militarily.

Sugar cultivation brings growing profits until the economic depression at the end of the 1920s. One day after the USA declares war on Germany.

1925-1933 President Machado y Morales. Hostility towards foreign capital grows, and this and Machado's dictatorial regime leads to revolution.

1933 Overthrow of Machado. The new commander-in-chief of the army, the former non-commissioned officer and now General F. Batista y Zaldivar, who in 1934 pushed through the elevation of C. Mendieta as president in 1934.

19.5.1934 A treaty between Cuba and the USA leads to the repeal of the "Platt Amendment".

1940 Batista is elected president. Social and economic reforms are implemented.

1944 Batista loses the presidential election to R. Grau San Martin.

1948 C. Prio Socarras wins the presidential elections.

1952 Batista seizes power again with the help of the military.

11.11.1954 (Manipulated) elections confirm Batista in office again, the opposition forms but is bloodily suppressed.

The storming of the Moncada barracks by Fidel Castro and his comrades fails.

1956 Start of the guerrilla war under the leadership of Fidel Castro ("26 July Movement").

1.1.1959 After three years of guerrilla warfare and a general strike, Fidel Castro's troops march into La Habana, dictator Batista has fled.

The Cuban democratic movement

Karl Marx's famous observation that one can no more "judge an epoch of revolution by its consciousness" than one can "judge what an individual is by what he thinks of himself" (Marx,b, 1975:9) has also been confirmed by the example of the Cuban revolution:

Hardly any other revolution has been so mythologised and fetishised in such a short time as the Cuban one, and it should be said here that the revolution led by **Fidel Castro**'s "26 July Movement" was by no means - as is generally claimed - a **socialist** revolution, if one uses the term "socialist" in the Marxist sense.

Socialism according to the Marxist definition presupposes the planned, conscious action of the actors towards the goal of socialism; it means the consciously planned replacement of the "anarchy of the market" with a democratically controlled planned economy.

According to Marxist theory, the agent of this revolutionary process is the class of wage-earning employees ("proletariat"), which represents the vast majority of the population in developed capitalist society and is predestined to assume control and management of production as a "revolutionary subject" due to its function in the social production process.

A socialist revolution **without** a proletariat as a **hegemonic class** or even an "unconscious" socialist revolution is therefore ruled out per defenitionem.

If the "Cuban leadership itself only recognised in 1961 that it had made a socialist revolution" (according to Hubermann/Sweezy, 1979,:11), then this means nothing other than that it could not have been a **socialist** revolution in the Marxist sense. However, this in no way excludes a further development towards a "socialist society" in accordance with Marxist theory.

Neither in terms of its social, i.e. class-based (class-specific) composition, nor in terms of its political objectives was the "26 July Movement" originally socialist; rather, it was a **class alliance of intellectuals, workers, peasants, the declassed and - at times - even an alliance with parts of the ruling class;** for example, President Socarraz, who was overthrown by Batista, himself a tool of imperialism and completely corrupt, is said to have initially supported Castro financially in order to procure weapons. (Cf. Allemann, 1974:61 ff)

The 26 July Movement **was not** socialist in its aims either:

It was **not** about the "dictatorship of the proletariat" according to the Marxist model, but about

- the removal of the bloody Batista regime

- the restoration or further development of democracy

- the establishment of national sovereignty

- a moderate land reform.

At first glance, therefore, this was a revolution with goals that could theoretically have been formulated by purely **bourgeois or petty-bourgeois** movements.

The peculiarity of the Cuban revolution, however, was precisely that the goals of the "26 July Movement", which could theoretically have been the programme of a bourgeois movement, set in motion a decidedly anti-capitalist dynamic due to the specific conditions of the country controlled by imperialism.

There are certainly many reasons for this, but two points in particular must be emphasised:

Firstly, there is the undeniable fact of the absolute **economic and political control of Cuba by the USA.**

Monoculture and trade in sugar, the result of the interests of the colonial powers and later imperialism, was in itself a considerable **dependency** on the USA, because the USA **bought almost all the sugar** and in return supplied Cuba exclusively with imported goods.

Cuba's extreme dependence before the revolution becomes clear when one considers that before the revolution, North American companies **controlled "more than 13% of the nation's real estate"** through their sugar-linked ownership alone.

However, the ratios only really become visible when one considers that only **about 50% of the land can be used for agriculture.** (Nohlen, 1984:350 ff)

The degree of concentration in agriculture was very high, as "4000 owners owned 57% of the land". **In fact, the sugar cane plantations were "largely owned by foreign companies."** (from Mires, 1978:92)

Ownership of the sugar centres 1939 1953

Cuban 56% 114

US-American 66 % 41 %

Other 51% 6 %

(From: Mires, op. cit.:56)

Allemann quotes the following figures: in 1939, Cuban companies accounted for only 22% of sugar cane cultivation and the sugar industry based on it; in 1958, the figure was 62% (Allemann, op. cit.:64)

Allemann wrongly deduces Cuba's increasing alleged independence from US imperialism from this, but fails to mention two things:

On the one hand, the "Cuban sugar owners (....) acted as local representatives of North American capital anyway (Mires, op. cit.:56), and on the other, the fact that **there was merely a change in the form of US involvement in Cuba, namely a relative shift from sugar to the industrial sector.**

These economic processes can be summarised as follows:

"1. transfer of financial capital and technology from the agricultural sector to industry

2. dependent industrial development with increasing participation of the local bourgeoisie

3. the financial apparatus of the state was placed at the service of this economic policy.

4. intensification of the monopolistic and foreign-determined character of the Cuban economy." (From: Mires, op. cit.:57)

It is an undeniable fact that the USA has always used its full political and, if necessary, military influence to secure this system of exploitation:

Symptomatic of this is not only the so-called "Platt Amendment", which officially granted the USA the right to intervene in Cuban domestic politics, but also the very direct military interventions by US troops in Cuba.

In terms of its fundamental goals and principles, US imperialism in pre-revolutionary Cuba did not differ significantly from its actions in other countries of the so-called Third World.

For the Zurich economist Tim Guldimann, US policy is also the result of economic, i.e. imperialist exploitation interests, which the USA shares with Western European countries and Japan.

The USA has "assumed the role of the guardian of order in the interests of all other industrialised countries. (...) the "Pax Americana" guarantees "law and order" for European and Japanese capital in Latin America. Imperialism is directed at all aspects of a dependent society: politics, the economy, science, education, the military, culture, etc. Its aims are to deepen dependency, prevent opposition and culturally and ideologically indoctrinate the elites (military, students) in particular. If this policy fails, the centre resorts to its last resort, military intervention (Guatemala, Cuba, Dominican Republic). The US army has intervened ninety times in Latin America in the last 200 years." (Guldimann, 1975:146)

The significance of US imperialist control of Cuba before the revolution is also illustrated by the following figures:

In 1958, 13 US sugar companies produced 40% of the sugar; US capital controlled 36% of the land, 90% of the mining industry and the entire energy supply. **Profit transfers** to the USA, in addition to the extreme luxury consumption of the Cuban oligarchy, prevented **independent development**. (From Nohlen, op. cit.:351)

The dependence of pre-revolutionary Cuba on US imperialism also determined the character of the Cuban revolution, which, although not genuinely socialist, **was not** a pure "bourgeois-democratic revolution" either: The fact that the most important areas of material life were almost completely, and others to a considerable extent, removed from national Cuban control, and that not only the economic but also the political problems could only be solved if Cuba gained its national sovereignty, that is, also its full political self-determination - which in turn presupposed economic self-determination,- presented the Cuban revolution with two fundamental alternatives: Either to leave US capital untouched, thereby retaining the goodwill of the US administration, but also continuing a relationship of dependency that had not only led to extreme economic deformations, but had also prevented real democratisation; or to recognise that genuine democratisation and self-determination for the Cuban people was only possible via the path of open confrontation with US interests.

As we know, the members of the "26 July Movement" under Castro's leadership took the second path, naturally also **in the face of resistance** from within the ranks of the "26 July Movement".

The confrontation with US imperialism gave the Cuban revolution a **strong nationalist-anti-imperialist component,** the far-reaching socio-economic and political consequences of which Fidel Castro - unlike his brother Raul Castro or Ernesto "Che" Guevara - **may not have realised**, especially in the beginning.

After the victory of the "26 July Movement", the concrete question arose as to what to do with the nationalised land and industry; here, too, there were two alternatives: The takeover of these economic sectors by the state, which after all represented a class alliance between the proletariat, peasantry, agricultural workers, intellectuals and the "marginalised" and was represented by 26 July.

However, it is noticeable that the Cuban state was largely characterised by a lack of institutionalised forms until the 1970s.

The second alternative would have been to hand over industry to the "national bourgeoisie".

But there was no genuine national bourgeoisie with the necessary expertise, willingness to take risks, initiative, creativity and, last but not least, the "spirit of capitalism".

There was only a clique of people who, completely corrupt and unscrupulous, had enriched themselves from the misery of the Cuban population, who had turned the capital Havana into a self-service shop and brothel and had already taken the precaution of leaving the country.

The only option left to the Cuban revolutionaries - if they did not want to betray their own revolution - was to take over the management of the economy themselves.

However, this was no longer a capitalist "free market economy", but an economy that was - initially only partially - controlled and managed by the state.

Nevertheless, it was **not** socialist because the economy was not in the hands of the "associated direct producers", i.e. the proletariat, but was under the control of a group that was **not** identical to the proletariat, namely the "26 July

Movement", which Latin America expert Fernando Mires characterises as a "class pluralist movement". (Mires, op. cit.: 113 ff)

The Cuban resistance against the Batista dictatorship

When Batista seized power for the second time in 1952, this coup was directed against the completely corrupt government under Prio Socarraz and therefore met with no significant resistance at first, but not with applause either, as Batista's political "idiosyncrasies" already had a poor reputation.

By violating the political rules of the game, i.e. by replacing elections, even if they were rigged, with openly **violent action**, the law of the jungle, Batista **himself** initiated a process that **led to his overthrow by the "26 July Movement"**, which in turn had brought its own rules into play, namely the armed guerrillas.

Fidel Castro's political path by no means began with the guerrillas; the guerrillas were merely a stage in his journey from a young lawyer who, outraged by the injustices of the Batista regime, "appeared before the Supreme Court of La

Habana as the lone Don Quixote of civil justice with a bundle of legal documents to demand that Batista be punished for violating the constitution". (Fernando Mires).

Castro's public political activity during the Batista dictatorship thus began with the fact that he "legally presented the democratic illegality of the dictatorship", namely in the form of an indictment, excerpts of which are reproduced here:

"Logic tells me: if there are courts, Batista must be punished; conversely, if he is not punished, if he remains head of state, president, prime minister, senator, civil and military leader, master of the executive and legislative branches, master of the lives and property of citizens, do these courts no longer exist, has he eliminated them? Is this the terrible truth? If it is, let the judges say so, take off their togas and resign. It would be bad to conceal this truth and resign ourselves to a tragic, absurd, illogical reality without norms, without meaning, without glory, honour and justice." (quoted from Mires, op. cit. :51)

Some may see this gesture by Castro as mere **bourgeois idealism**, but the fact is that this accusation was just as important a part of the political conflicts in Cuba, just as much a part of the revolutionary process as Castro's - militarily failed - attack on the Moncada barracks on 26 July

1953, which the "official" communists of the PSP condemned as putschist and adventurous.

Although the attack on the Moncada barracks did not lead to the popular uprising hoped for by Castro and his comrades, this action was also **suitable for consolidating his prestige in the democratic Cuban movement and his credibility as a revolutionary democrat - or democratic revolutionary - in Cuba.**

It was Castro's "naive" political activity that gave him such political prestige that Batista could not afford to summarily massacre or "disappear" the young lawyer after the failed storming of the Moncada barracks - like so many other members of the opposition - but instead forced Batista to simply expel him.

And abroad, as is generally known today, Fidel Castro immediately began to **prepare the guerrillas.**

From today's perspective, the "**class pluralist composition**" (Mires) of the 26 July Movement was certainly a **basic condition for its success**, and this was due not least to Castro's ability to unite very different classes and strata.

Of course, this coincided with the increasing social confrontation between a small pro-Batista minority and a large anti-Batista majority.

Castro and Batista complemented each other in a peculiar way: Batista provided the objective conditions - unintentionally, of course - while Castro knew how to implement them subjectively, i.e. organisationally, for the revolution. Fernando Mires describes it like this: "Batista, like Machado in his day, brought about the union between those who wanted to change the present, those who dreamed of the future and those who were homesick for the past." (Mires, op. cit.:50)

In fact, the beginning of the Cuban revolution can be dated much earlier than the beginning of the armed struggle: the anti-imperialist Cuban revolution actually began in the struggle against the Spanish and can be dated back to 1868. It undoubtedly reached a climax with the seizure of power by the 26 July Movement under the leadership of Fidel Castro - in my opinion, it is still not complete today, as Fidel Castro, and after him his brother Roul, was unfortunately corrupted by power and has himself become an obstacle to the liberation of Cuba ...

Rather, it is precisely the events following the seizure of power by the 26 July Movement, i.e. the economic, social, political and cultural restructuring, that have by no means been completed to this day.

Note: **I wrote this in 1986, but it is still true:** the economy, politics and social life are still waiting for overdue reforms, especially **political participation and the realisation of democracy** are still on the agenda!

When Granma landed in Cuba, the 26 July Movement already had a **broad political base** in the population, had **built up** a **wide network of loose political relationships and no longer needed to explain to the population why it now saw the only way out in armed struggle and had now begun it.**

In the specific Cuban case, the problem for the revolutionaries was not to prove to the poor peasants the legitimacy of the armed struggle, but the **effectiveness of** this "revolutionary method of intervention".

Castro no longer needed to explain to the population **why** he had taken up arms, because every politically interested Cuban had followed Fidel Castro's political struggle against Batista and knew what the "26 July Movement" wanted - as far as the movement itself could form a concrete picture of it.

But just as the Cuban revolution was not a proletarian revolution, it was not a peasant war like the Chinese or Vietnamese war of liberation.

As true as it is that the "26th of July" received great support from the poor peasants and agricultural labourers and that many campesinos also joined the fight, it should not be overlooked that the recruitment of intellectuals from the cities, including workers and freelancers, played a very large role alongside the peasant combatants and apparently even made up the majority of the fighters compared to the peasants.

In addition, the political movement in the cities, primarily in Havana, always played a far greater role than in China or Vietnam, for example. (Cf. Allemann, op. cit.:72; Mires op. cit. :94 ff)

With Mires, one could speak of a **"Democratic People's Revolution with a national/anti-imperialist character"**; in its course, it was a rural cadre guerrilla that emerged from an urban class pluralist movement and was linked to the diverse - economic, political, military - resistance in the cities.

Strategy and tactics of the Cuban guerrillas

In his essay "What is a Guerrilla", first published in "Revolucion", the organ of the "26th July" in February 1959, Ernesto "Che" Guevara stated the most important principles on which he believed the Cuban guerrillas were based; this essay is particularly important because it is to be regarded as a particularly **authentic document** due to its **date of publication**. It states: "...Guerrilla warfare is not, as is believed, a tiny war, the war of a small group against a strong army; rather, guerrilla warfare is the struggle of the whole people against the prevailing oppression. The guerrilla is the armed vanguard of the people; all the inhabitants of an area or a country form its army. This is the basis of the guerrilla's strength, his victory, sooner or later, against any power that tries to oppress him; in other words, the basis of the guerrilla is the people.

It is inconceivable that small armed groups, however mobile they may be and however well they may know the area, could survive the organised pursuit of a well-equipped army without this strong help."

(Guevara, a, 1959, 1972,: 16 ff, emphasis mine)

Here, "Che" Guevara himself documented the basis of the guerrilla struggle up to the seizure of power on 26 July: The guerrilla is merely the armed arm, the **armed avant-garde of an already revolutionary-minded people, it is by no means the small social minority attacking a far superior army - at least not in the political sense - it is, politically speaking, part of a revolutionary-minded majority of the people.**

From a purely military point of view, however, it is initially exactly what Che Guevara deliberately denies here: "The war of a small group against a large army" - the group was so small at the beginning that after the Granma landed in Cuba and was almost completely crushed by the government troops, there were not even two dozen fighters at the start of its actions.

In **Guevara's later writings**, however, the socio-economic-political context of the Cuban guerrillas recedes more and more into the background, as he emphasises the purely military aspects in his later writings and thus, in my opinion, reduces the originally complex Guevarist theory of revolution by essential content.

As we shall see, there were also political reasons for this.

In his first writings on the guerrilla, however, Che Guevara constantly emphasised the need to have the majority of the people behind him. However, this implies a lengthy political process of radicalising the masses and **inevitably relativises the guerrilla as a revolutionary method.**

In "The Guerrilla War" Che Guevara says: "It is important to realise that the guerrilla war is a struggle of the masses, a struggle of the people; that the guerrilla is the armed nucleus, the fighting vanguard of the people, its strength is based on the masses." (Guevara, op. cit.:25)

In their criticism of Debray, the two Cuban revolutionaries Simon Torres and Julio Aronde emphasise that the "military line was subordinated to the political line" in the political strategy of "26 July".

According to Torres/Aronde, the guerrillas can also be explained by the political situation in the country, which they summarise as follows:

"1. the lack of special ideological efforts on the part of the imperialists, the bourgeoisie and the church.

2. lack of an organised struggle for their own land, which would have meant the existence of clearly defined political programmes.

3. direct confrontation between the army and the peasants, in which the soldiers protected the large landowners (rule with a machete and through land expulsion, i.e. through violence against the peasant masses).

Only under these conditions was political action not indispensable: it could be carried out with the rifle and broke the subjugation of the peasant to the rule of the bourgeois, which appeared brutally personified in the "Guardia Rural" (rural police).

The political struggle had already taken the form of direct clashes between the army and the rural population. In such circumstances, the rifle itself compensates for the lack of political activity and is in fact the only means of changing the balance of power in this sector of society." (From: Torres/Aronde, 1979,: 40)

Here it becomes very clear: the conflicts were there, under the given circumstances the guerrilla was the only possible form of conflict resolution in the Cuban situation, which was revolutionary in every respect.

What is striking is the frequent emphasis on the role of the peasantry, which has often been subsequently (mis)interpreted to mean that the Cuban guerrilla war was a peasant war a la China - which it certainly was not.

The emphasis on the role of the rural population naturally has very real references, but in my opinion it also results from the endeavour to influence the traditional - Moscow-oriented - Communists: It must be borne in mind that the activities of most Communist parties centred on the urban population, while in most cases the Communists in the countryside hardly became active to any significant extent.

The best-known exception to this rule is the popular uprising led by the communist Farabundi Marti in El Salvador in the early 1930s, which was, however, bloodily suppressed and cost over 50,000 lives.

Guevara also addresses precisely this omission when he says in "Guerrilla War": "The 3rd doctrine (...) deserves the attention of those who are guided by dogmatic conceptions, who want to concentrate the struggle of the masses in the cities, completely **forgetting** the **enormous role of the peasants in the life of all the underdeveloped countries of America"**. (Guevara, b, :24)

Due to the fact that the resistance fighters in the cities can be too easily destroyed by the repressive forces, the guerrillero must fight where he can hide, he must therefore carry out his activities in "agricultural and sparsely populated areas". (Guevara, b, :26)

The key is to support the local population, primarily the farmers:

- they supply the guerrillas with food

- They provide him with the information he needs for his surprise attacks.

Not only the fact that Ernesto "Che" Guevara begins his writing on the guerrillero and the guerrilla with its origins in the people and its connection with the revolutionary will of the people, but also the fact that he **does not emphasise the military aspects** here **at all**, but refers to the **political** starting point of the guerrilla, namely the people, shows that for Che Guevara at this time the guerrilla is nothing more and nothing less than a revolutionary method of a revolutionary-minded people at a certain point in time in a certain country; **The guerrilla as a quasi-universal revolutionary method for the entire Latin American continent is not (yet) mentioned here.**

Guevara's text "The Guerrilla War" (1960) also begins with the socio-political origins of the guerrilla, whereby Che - like Engels and Mao before him (cf. Chapter 3 and Chapter 11) - emphasises **the importance of legality** and, above all, the importance of the **violation of democratic legality** by the state as an important prerequisite for the guerrilla:

"In fact, peace is violated precisely by the forces of oppression that unlawfully hold on to power. Under these conditions, the discontent of the people grows, they move on to ever more determined forms of struggle; their revolutionary vigour increases, finally culminating in active resistance, which at a certain point leads to the outbreak of open struggle and **which is ultimately provoked by the rulers themselves"**. (Guevara, b, : 24)

The importance of democratic legality or even democratic sham legality in Guevara's view is shown by his scepticism towards guerrillas where the legality of the ruling power has not yet been completely shaken and is not yet unanimously questioned by the masses: **"Where a government has come to power in a more or less democratic way, with or without electoral fraud (!), and where at least the appearance of constitutional legality is preserved, no guerrilla movement arises because the possibilities of legal struggle have not yet been eliminated."** (Guevara, b, :24)

For Guevara, it was not enough - **although this changed later!** - to go to the countryside and start with the guerrillas, rather the support of the guerrillas had to be won from the population by the guerrillero acting politically, i.e. driving forward the revolution in the countryside.

By acting as an agrarian revolutionary, the revolutionary realises the interests of the peasant masses, who are indeed revolutionary in Cuba in the 1950s, and thus consolidates his social base, securing the support of the local population, which Ernesto Che Guevara describes as a "condition sin qua non". (Guevara,b,: 25)

Guevara writes further: "But since in the agricultural areas the struggle of the people is for their rights, above all for a change in the existing conditions of land use, the guerrillero appears above all as a fighter for land reform. He supports the desire of the broad mass of peasants to become the unrestricted masters of their means of production, their land, their livestock and everything that they have striven for over many years and that represents the basis of their livelihood." (Guevara, b,: 25)

Many of the guerrilla principles already mentioned by Mao can be found in Ernesto "Che" Guevara:

1. for Guevara, the guerrilla is merely a special form of war; the war cannot be won with the guerrilla alone, sooner or later the guerrilla turns into a regular war. (Guevara,b, : 27,28,29)

2 Similar to Mao, Che Guevara also calls for engaging in hostilities only where success is guaranteed from the outset. (Guevara,b: 28)

3. war is a war of annihilation, which means that it is not enough to merely put the enemy to flight, one must inflict devastating blows on his divisions. (Guevara,b: 28,29)

This is simply because "the supply of weapons to the guerrillas must essentially be at the expense of arming the enemy." (Guevara, b:30)

Nevertheless, prisoners are given medical treatment and released as far as possible - in stark contrast to the practice of the government troops, who almost always killed captured guerrillas immediately.

Guevara makes an exception for notorious brutal elements and torturers who were given short shrift. (Guevara, b:40)

4. "For a correct strategy of guerrilla warfare, it is essential to analyse the enemy's activities comprehensively." (Guevara,b: 30) Here, too, we can easily recognise Mao and Sun-Tse.

5 Similar to Mao, Ernesto Che Guevara's guerrillas go through several phases, and like Mao's, Guevara's **first phase is defensive in nature**, where "the main task of the guerrilla is to avoid annihilation by the enemy at all costs". (Guevara,b: 31)

This is done by retreating into impassable terrain that is known to the guerrilla but unknown to the enemy, where ambushes can be laid for the enemy. **In tactical terms,** the retreat therefore includes **the offensive**, the success of which depends on the

6. **surprise of the opponent** results.

7. the guerrillas take up positions inaccessible to the enemy - which are secured by mines and ambushes - and begin to wear down the enemy through initially small-scale operations.

The destruction of enemy connections and the liquidation of liaison officers play a particularly important role here.

8 Guevara is well aware of the need to support the urban resistance movement and to work with it in a coordinated way, but he is far from propagating the guerrilla as a universal recipe when he writes:

"Later, we can work together with the organised masses in the workers' areas, and the result of this cooperation must be the **general strike**. The strike is an extremely important factor in the civil war." (Guevara,b: 32)

This distinguishes the early Guevarist guerrilla concept from that of Mao.

The principles of the Cuban guerrillas can therefore be summarised as follows:

The guerrillas move into a redoubt, where they initially carry out only modest actions due to their small forces. (Raids on small police stations and barracks, laying ambushes for the troops pursuing the guerrillas).

The guerrillas make contact with the local rural population, carry out propaganda and implement agrarian reform in their base areas as far as possible.

The guerrillas demonstrate their growing power through increasingly bold attacks on the army; the population begins to see the guerrillas as an increasingly serious power factor that promises to better represent their interests and increasingly supports the guerrillas.

The guerrilla grows continuously, "marching columns" are formed, which form a new "focus" in another part of the country, and the same process starts all over again, only now under more favourable conditions, as the guerrilla is now known. (Guevara compared this process to a beehive).

Finally, there are guerrilla bases throughout the country, and coordination with the urban resistance movement has been continuously improved, which in turn is carrying out ever bolder actions - sabotage, strikes, assassinations - against hated representatives of the old order, etc.

Finally, the government army is so **demoralised** and the guerrilla army has become so powerful that the final blow can be struck against the hated regime.

The tactics of the Cuban guerrillas

As in the Chinese civil war of the Kuomintang against the communists, the main approach of the initially naturally vastly superior opponent was to attempt "encirclement and extermination campaigns", and accordingly for Guevara, as for Mao, the first phase of the guerrilla war is essentially characterised by the guerrillas' efforts to escape this encirclement; The first phase for the guerrilla therefore consists of the **strategic defence**, which must be accompanied by **tactical offensives** as well as the growth and continuous qualitative improvement of the guerrilla forces. The essential prerequisite for this is mobility. (Guevara, b,: 34)

However, mobility is not only important with regard to retreat, but also with regard to "counter-encirclement": the enemy is surrounded and alternately taken under fire from different directions, in each case where he has not concentrated his forces. (Guevara,b:34)

Guevara repeatedly points out the need to use ammunition sparingly, because it is not only for tactical reasons - more difficult to locate the guerrillas - but also for obvious logistical reasons that targeted single shots are preferred. (Guevara,b:35)

In this context, Che Guevara explicitly opposes "sabotage as terror", by which he apparently means bomb attacks against enemy objects in places frequented by uninvolved civilians, because this can lead to the death of completely innocent people and does more harm than good to the guerrillas and the revolutionary movement. (Guevara,b: 36,37)

For Che Guevara, terror is only legitimate if it is specifically directed against an individual, generally particularly hated representative of the regime, "who is notorious for his cruelty or special merits in carrying out reprisals and other things". (Guevara, b:37)

Guevara names the weakest points of the enemy, against which the actions are to be directed primarily at the beginning, as the means of transport such as roads and railways; ambushes and mines are to be laid there.

There is no need to go into further detail here, **because it is quite obvious that the Cuban guerrillas are by no means something fundamentally new** - as has been claimed from time to time - **but in tactical terms the skilful and flexible application of an old and tried and tested method of small-scale warfare.**

To summarise, it can be said: It was not the method per se that characterised the Cuban guerrillas - in this respect they were to a certain extent "conventional" - but their connection with concrete economic, social and political struggles, as well as their determined and - at the time - integer leadership - Guevara, Castro, Cienfuegos and others - that made them a milestone in the history of the Latin American revolution.

Chapter 15

Cuba and the Latin American revolution

As noted above, the Cuban Revolution was neither a proletarian revolution in the classical sense, i.e. by no means a revolution under proletarian hegemony comparable to the Russian October Revolution or in accordance with orthodox Marxist theory, which is primarily a theory of socialist revolution in fully capitalist developed countries; nor, as noted above, was it a classical peasant revolution along the lines of the Chinese or Vietnamese revolutions (cf: Mires, op. cit.:91 ff; Allemann, op. cit.: 70/72; Torres/Aronde, op. cit.: 40)

Rather, the Cuban revolution was characterised by the fact that almost all relevant classes and strata were more or less involved: Revolutionary-democratic intelligentsia - Fidel Castro himself is the best-known representative of this stratum - working class, marginalised and underemployed people in the countryside and in the city, the peasantry and temporarily even parts of the old oligarchy, insofar as it had come into conflict with the Batista dictatorship.

One can therefore **speak** with some justification of a **democratic anti-imperialist people's revolution.**

If the armed struggle of the "26 July Movement" often appears today as an independent method of socialist revolution in the "Third World", this is, in my opinion, **the result of a misunderstanding** that is the product of several interrelated factors, the most important aspects of which will be pointed out below.

Due to the fact that Cuba's economic structures were essentially characterised by economic interdependence, above all with the USA, and at the same time Cuba, like most Latin American countries, did not have a "national bourgeoisie" that would have been able and willing to organise the development of independent national production corresponding to the needs of the Cuban majority of the population - this "lack of will" and this "inability" of the Cuban national bourgeoisie is of course not subjective, but, as has been shown, a specific feature of the Cuban economy, This "lack of will" and this "inability" of the Cuban national bourgeoisie is, of course, not subjective, but, as shown, specific to the bourgeoisies of most "Third World" countries and the result of imperialism; these peculiarities of the bourgeoisies are in fact a component and condition of "dependent development".

Due to these facts, the Cuban revolutionaries were to a certain extent forced to take the necessary restructuring and the completely new reorganisation of Cuban production relations into their own hands.

Of course, this compulsion does not rule out the possibility that this was exactly what Ernesto Che Guevara or Raul Castro, for example, would have wanted from the outset.

Above all, it was imperialism itself that put the need for agrarian reform, the nationalisation of land, the communications network and energy supply, and finally also industry, on the agenda.

However, one should not fall into an "accountant's mentality", **an economic determinism** that sees these political processes exclusively as the result of "objective laws" and views the **acting subjects merely as the will-less executors of an "objective historical process"**. It would have been perfectly conceivable - and at least more convenient - for the movement to have bowed to the manifold economic, political and military pressures exerted by the USA, merely changing the political leadership and leaving it at a few superficial reforms. (Cf. A. G. Frank: 1979:20)

It can be regarded as proven that those parts of the old oligarchy who had something against Batista, but nothing against the system that brought about the Batista dictatorship, believed exactly this when they, like the ex-head of government Socarraz, initially provided arms aid to the "26 July Movement".

Fidel Castro's development after the revolution from a radical democrat to a Marxist, albeit a Marxist who was as pragmatic as he was unorthodox, was decisive for Cuba's further development up to the present day.

If one applies the term "socialist" in its Marxist meaning - and only then does it make sense - it is clear that Castro's proclamation of Cuba as "socialist" and even "communist" in 1961 could only be a **declaration of intent**, but not the result of previous economic, social and political processes.

This political declaration of intent, which was also pushed through against internal resistance from parts of the "26 July Movement", is therefore far from being without significance for the further national development of Cuba, but has of course had a decisive influence on the entire development of this island to this day.

Nevertheless, this sudden commitment to socialism and the "socialist camp" - while retaining specific Cuban characteristics - is not simply the result of "socialist voluntarism", but also the result of international politics, more specifically: The increasing turn towards the Soviet Union, with all its positive and predominantly negative consequences, is linked to the destabilisation, encirclement and blockade policy of the USA.

After it became clear relatively late to the relevant political circles in the USA that the "26 July Movement" would by no means leave it at the elimination of the old oligarchy, but would tackle the nationalisation of the foreign, i.e. primarily the US enclave economy, the US administration began with a policy of blockade and confrontation, which reached its temporary climax with the invasion of the "Bay of Pigs" by US mercenaries in 1961.

The economic blockade imposed by the US government, in which other countries also participated, was comprehensive and drove the Cuban leadership into the arms of the Soviet Union - which were by no means too open at first.

By openly declaring its allegiance to the "socialist camp", Cuba forced the Soviet Union, which until then had tacitly recognised Latin America as a US sphere of influence, to support Cuba in accordance with its difficult conditions. (Cf. Mires, op. cit.:108)

However, the blockade policy and military threat from the USA had far-reaching consequences: At least initially, the Cuban leadership could not and did not want to rely solely on the distant Soviet Union for two main reasons: Firstly, this inevitably meant the danger of foreign domination or at least Soviet influence on internal Cuban social development - not an attractive prospect for a movement like the "26th of July", which was not only democratic but also nationalist.

With regard to a massive US-American intervention, there was no real guarantee that the Soviet Union would not drop Cuba like a hot potato, because such a situation could have led directly to the Third World War.

Particularly in the mid-1960s, the Cuban leadership therefore endeavoured to support the revolutionary movement on the Latin American continent: The "Let's create two, three, many Vietnams" propagated by Ernesto Che Guevara were, when put into practice, not only suitable for splintering US imperialism into a multi-front war and thus decisively weakening it, not to mention relieving the Viet Cong; the liberation of further Latin American countries from the imperialist grip intended by means of guerrilla warfare would have opened up new prospects for the Cuban revolution, especially in the long term, not least in economic terms: The Cuban government also knew that the "revolution is not an island" (Mires), i.e. the construction of socialism in an isolated country, especially on a totally encircled island with mono-production and a population of just 7 million at the time, would have been unrealistic - only the connection of Cuba with a liberated Latin American continent would have opened up the possibility of turning a declaration of intent into reality in the long term.

In this context, the writing of the young French doctor of philosophy, Regis Debray's "Revolution in the Revolution?" should also be seen, which represents a further generalisation - and in my opinion also **a reduction** - of Che Guevara's guerrilla conception, although Che's initial premises, namely that the **guerrilla is a method of struggle but not a revolutionary universal recipe,** disappear in favour of an almost militaristic conception in which the armed focus is everything and the people tend to degenerate into extras. (A good description of the connections can be found in BERNER, 1969:29 ff)

In January 1966, the Tricontinental met in Havana, and it was here that the regional Latin American guerrilla organisation OLAS was founded on Castro's initiative, whose "main function was to coordinate and support the revolutionary movements of the subcontinent and, where it seemed necessary, to give them new impetus. In addition, he (meaning Fidel Castro, E.R.) intended to create a reliable instrument for his own regional policy in the form of the Guerrilla International, with the help of which he hoped above all to overcome the resistance of most traditional communist parties in Latin America to the Cuban claim to leadership". (Berner, op. cit.:70)

This should be seen in the context of the fact that "the CPSU increasingly emphatically supported the position of those Latin American communist parties that rejected armed struggle for themselves or only wanted to accept it as one of many possible forms of struggle". (Berner, op. cit.:71)

Ultimately, it was a collision between Cuban national interests, which lay in the local spread of the revolution - which had to set the traditional, partly encrusted political structures in motion - **and the geopolitical interests of the Soviet Union, which at that time could not afford or did not want a second or even a third Cuba.** (Cf. Hubermann/Sweezy op. cit. and Mires, F., op. cit.)

This is also confirmed in a Pravda article that "the supreme internationalist duty of the socialist countries is the building of socialism within their own borders and that therefore "other sections of the liberation struggle" in the "Third World" should not expect active, direct help from the Soviet

Union." (Published in Pravda, Moscow 27 October 1965, quoted in Berner, op. cit.)

The founding resolution of OLAS in January 1966 was passed "against the votes of all communist party delegates (with the exception of the Cuban delegates)." (Berner, op. cit. 1971)

The first publication, wide distribution and use of Debray's pamphlet "Revolution in the Revolution?" as educational material in Cuba speaks in favour of Berner's thesis that this pamphlet was a work launched, or at least approved, by Fidel Castro.

Obviously, Guevara's return from Congo-Brazzaville, the preparation and realisation of the guerrilla movement in Bolivia under the command of Ernesto Che Guevara is not merely an expression of "petty-bourgeois adventurism", but must be seen in the temporal and political context of the founding of OLAS and the political-strategic goals of the Cuban leadership on a Latin American scale.

The call for a general guerrilla uprising left behind by Ernesto Che Guevara in Havana: "Let's create two, three, many Vietnams" must therefore also be seen in the context of Soviet foreign policy and the policies of the other Latin American Communist parties: "To all appearances, this is a plan, supported by the OLAS International, to thwart the Soviet goodwill policy towards the Latin American governments hostile to Castro, which was initiated at the end of 1965, to unite the revolutionary left of the continent under Castro's leadership into a united front and to present the communist parties with the alternative of either joining this front or being overrun by developments - as happened in Cuba in his time. (Berner, op. cit.:72)

It is not possible to discuss all the factors that led to Cuba's increasing rapprochement with the Soviet Union in this context, **but it is clear that there were considerable differences between Fidel Castro's strategic-political concepts of the 1960s and the policies of Moscow and the Moscow-oriented Latin American Communist Parties, which were expressed not least at the theoretical and ideological level.**

The over-emphasised focus on the guerrillas, not only in Ernesto Che Guevara's later writings, but even more so in the writings of the French theorist Regis Debray - who in turn can be seen at least to some extent as Castro's mouthpiece - therefore also corresponded to the Cuban leadership's need, to work out the differences between the Cuban revolutionary model and all other doctrines already known in Latin America and to derive concrete demands from this, "the fulfilment of which **demanded a radical break with their traditional principles of action and organisation,** especially from the **traditional communist**

parties. (....) In this way, an attempt had to be made to loosen the various international ties of the revolutionary forces to non-American leading bodies in order to enable their **ideological reorientation** towards an American centre of leadership. To this end, it was necessary to bring the Cuban claim to leadership and the fighting goals of all OLAS member organisations to a common ideological denominator. But these are precisely the political intentions that Debray professes in "Revolution within the Revolution?" (...) professes." (Berner, op. cit.:72)

In fact, with the help of these military and propaganda measures, the Cuban leadership succeeded in **reorienting parts of the left towards the guerrillas** in most countries on the Latin American continent - **with varying, but predominantly negative results.**

Chapter 16

The failure of the land guerrilla in Latin America

In connection with the spectacular victory of the Cuban guerrillas, guerrilla fronts emerged in almost all Latin American countries in the course of the 1960s, which were orientated towards the guerrilla theory developed by

Guevara and Debray and attempted to trigger and advance the socialist revolution with the help of the guerrillas.

Despite their sometimes spectacular initial successes, these movements all suffered defeats and were more or less completely crushed. (Cf. Thomas Borges, Taz-Journal:43; Allemann, op. cit.:115 ff)

Without wanting to discuss the causes of this in detail, a few hypotheses for the failure of the guerrillas should be put forward:

Although the purely economic contradictions in Venezuela, Bolivia, Guatemala and Peru - to name just a few examples - were by no means less than in pre-revolutionary Cuba, the numerous failed attempts at insurrection by the revolutionary left in these countries show that economic underdevelopment and foreign domination by imperialism, extreme class differentiation and political instability are by no means **always synonymous** with a **revolutionary situation:** Revolutions are made by people, so they are not simply the result of "objective conditions".

Experience has shown that the essential conditions for social revolutions are not only the existence of serious economic crises, but also the associated **signs of social disintegration** and, above all, considerable **instability of the "ruling class"**, i.e. its factional fragmentation, the disorganisation of its political apparatus, the disintegration of the ideological "superstructure" in general and, last but not least, with regard to its minimum goals, a homogeneous opposition with central leadership bodies that can offer correspondingly attractive political alternatives and, if possible, also has a popular personality with integrative abilities.

However, while in Cuba the majority of the population formed a relatively cohesive unit, at least in the question of the exercise of political power, i.e. specifically in relation to the Batista dictatorship, through a common political perspective in ideological terms and, in the form of the "26 July Movement", also in loose organisational terms, the guerrillas were thus the "organic" result of a process of political unification, this was lacking in the majority of guerrilla fronts on the Latin American continent.

The guerrillas in Venezuela, for example, were directed against a populist government (**Action Democratica - AD**) that had considerable popular support and was by no means isolated and demoralised.

The same applies to the **populist APRA** in Peru, which the leader of the AD, Romulo Betancourt, modelled himself on. (See Allemann, op. cit.: p. 122 (h) The guerrillas were not directed against an "illegal", generally hated dictatorial regime, which the people could only confront by force of arms, but became a **means of provocation**, so to speak, intended to seduce the ruling class into **exposing** its brutal and aggressive character hidden behind the peaceful mask.

In fact, this consideration seems to have played a decisive role for all guerrilla fronts orientated more or less towards the Cuban revolution - **with fatal consequences!**

The guerrillas did not appear to large sections of the population as a necessary instrument for the conquest of freedom and democracy - as was the case in Cuba at the time - but as a kind of troublemaker that restricted the at least partially existing possibilities of political articulation and participation, and the general freedom of movement of the population in general, because the **state repression measures,** which of course did not fail to materialise, **made life even more uncomfortable for the civilian population in particular.**

With the help of a more or less skilful application of brutal state and later also state-directed and / or supported "private" repression in combination with limited reforms or even sham reforms, most governments finally succeeded, after a shorter or longer phase of defeats, in increasingly isolating the guerrillas; often they were isolated anyway due to their social composition. **The guerrillas were thus**

alienated from their social base, then forced onto the pure defensive and could thus be crushed.

The miserable failure of the Peruvian guerrillas is a classic example of how guerrillas fighting against a populist government were isolated and crushed by a skilful combination of massive repression and partial reforms.

However, this has not been able to prevent the "resurgence" of the guerrillas in the form of "Sendero Luminoso" (Shining Path, Maoist), which is neither theoretically nor practically identical to the Guevarist guerrillas of the 1960s and has so far (1986) remained localised to the province of Ayacucho.

The failure of the Bolivian guerrillas under Che Guevara's leadership is also the necessary result of a strategy that was pursued almost completely detached from the concrete political movements in Bolivia, which to a certain extent represented the consistent application of Debray's "revolution within the revolution?". (See also Allemann, op. cit.: 214 ff)

In 1979, the Nicaraguan liberation movement FSLN succeeded in overthrowing the US-protected dictator Anastasio Somoza and seizing power, with the FSLN's actions showing many parallels to those of the "26 July Movement" in Cuba at the time.

However, the later successes and the conquest of power by the Sandinista Liberation Front FSLN in Nicaragua, whose foundation in the early 1960s was actually linked to the victorious Cuban revolution, was by no means based on the application of the "focus strategy" propagated by Guevara at the time, but conversely - according to Thomas Borge, a leading FSLN member - on a political-military strategy based on the **political** mobilisation of peasants and workers in particular.

The previously pursued Castristian-Guevarist military-orientated strategy had previously led to the almost complete destruction of the FSLN.

Only the focus on the concrete problems of the farmers, workers and poor rural population created the conditions for the military success of the FSLN in Nicaragua. (Cf. Thomas Borges, op. cit.: 43)

In summary, it can be said that the Nicaraguan liberation struggle had less in common with the form of an "avant-garde guerrilla" without a revolutionary mass organisation propagated primarily by Debray (as the mouthpiece of the late Guevarist-Castrist views), but much in common with the political situation in pre-revolutionary Cuba and the course of the liberation struggle there: Both countries look back on a long revolutionary past/tradition, both have been victims of imperialism in an extreme way, in both a US-protected dictator had ursuped power, etc. and so on.

It has thus become clear that the reduction of the guerrillas to their military-technical components and options, to the options for action of a very small political minority, without any real reference to the concrete state of political development in the population, i.e. to the political consciousness of large sections of the population, ultimately determines the success or failure of any revolutionary movement.

Conclusion: This one-sided orientation towards Che Guevara's late revolutionary model, which failed miserably in Bolivia, and which characterises almost the entire development in Latin America in the 1960s and 1970s, has led the radical left in Latin America into a political dead end.

The guerrillas of the sixties and seventies in Latin America, who followed the late Guevarist model - from which most today (1986) seem to have moved away again - show the difference between guerrilla as a purely military tactic as opposed to popular war and tend to bring it back into the neighbourhood of the war of a bygone era, when small-scale war was the special form of war waged by professional military men - albeit now with completely different objectives.

In this way, the guerrilla army had, in at least one aspect, come closer to the character of the regular armies, namely being a "caste half alienated from the people" (Lenin).

The failure of this form of guerrilla was therefore pre-programmed.

Chapter 17

The urban guerrilla concept

Latin America

a. Brazil

The Brazilian social structure is also characterised by the economic, political and social processes already described above; without discussing these conditions again, the key aspects will be briefly summarised once more:

Brazilian history is characterised by a long series of local and supra-regional uprisings against the colonial powers, which were fought almost exclusively under the leadership of the "liberal intelligentsia", which was mainly inspired by the

French Encyclopaedists and the French Revolution.
(Compare this and the following: M. M. Alves, 1971, :10 ff; C. Detrez, 1971,:34 ff; Allemann op. cit., : 25 ff; Nohlen op. cit.,: 97 - 102; Füchtner, 1982,: 189 ff)

For a long time, despite its formal independence, Brazil was not a nation in the classical sense, but rather a peculiar conglomerate of "quasi-autonomous regional oligarchies", and it was only under the dictatorship of Getulio Vargas that the Brazilian nation actually began to be constituted.

Vargas' successor, Juscelino Kubitschek (1956-1961), moved the government capital "Brasilia" to the centre of the country, not least for this reason, i.e. to integrate the long-neglected hinterland into the national cycle. This new government metropolis, which was virtually created out of nothing, was a very costly undertaking and certainly contributed significantly to the lasting disruption of Brazil's national finances.

When Joao Goulart was elected president in 1961, this marked the beginning of an era (1961-1964) that ultimately led to the open dictatorship of the military in Brazil.

Following Peron's example, Goulart created his own "domestic power" with the support of significant sections of the trade union movement, which found its political and organisational expression in the **PTB** and represented a quasi-progressive variety of "Getulism", i.e. a continuation of Varga's policies with liberal aspects.

However, this policy soon turned out to be an aimless oscillation between opportunistic adaptation to the oligarchy and equally opportunistic adaptation to the left in the form of pseudo-revolutionary vocabulary, as is often characteristic of Latin American populism.

This ambivalent policy, precisely because Goulart apparently lacked the Machiavellian skills of Getulio Vargas, set in motion a process of radicalisation on both the left and the right: Among the left, especially the **Brazilian Communist Party (PCB)**, Goulart raised hopes of sweeping reform, above all "by playing only half-seriously with a decisive agrarian reform", which was just as much needed in Brazil as in the other countries of Latin America and which "he was nevertheless neither able nor willing to fulfil". (Allemann, op. cit.: 280)

On the other hand, Goulart's occasional flirtation with the left and his talk, albeit not entirely serious, of radical reforms **frightened the oligarchy and above all the military, on whom Goulart ultimately relied.**

This ambivalent policy obviously gave the impression on both the left and the right that Brazil was drifting towards a social revolution: The right, frightened by Goulart's connections to the working class, which in part constituted his social base, and by his connections right into the ranks of the communists, saw the spectre of a "cold takeover by the communists", while the left saw the dawn of mass radicalisation due to Goulart's policies.

In fact, a number of different left-wing organisations emerged at this time, ranging from the **peasant leagues** in north-eastern Brazil, organised by the lawyer **Francisco Juliao**, to **Lionel Brizola's "secret army",** which was said to be over 100,000 strong, but which dissolved into almost nothing after the military seized power.

Lionel Brizola was a brother-in-law of Goulart and governor in the far south of Brazil and allegedly endeavoured to seize power along Cuban lines. (Allemann, op. cit.:287)

Finally, the **PCB** and the young radicalised left-wing Catholics of the "**Accao Popular**" (**AP**) played an important role, both competing for the leadership of the radical students.

The PCB communists in particular, who had been forced back underground in 1949 after three years of legality, exerted a certain influence on the Goulart system through the **trade union centre CGT**, which they controlled.

It was precisely these cross-connections that gave the reaction the impression that Goulart was making himself a pawn of the communists.

This view is certainly the result of a fundamental misunderstanding, because the PCB was by no means a revolutionary factor within the Brazilian left in the sense of class struggle, but rather a "braking factor" - similar to its sister party in Cuba during the Batista dictatorship.

One reason for this is the orientation of the Latin American Communist parties towards an alliance with the national bourgeoisie, as discussed above, but also the personal experiences of the General Secretary of the PCB, the **former officer Luis Carlos Prestes**: in the 1930s, Prestes and other "left-wing" officers carried out a (failed) coup attempt and then covered a distance of around 2,400 kilometres in a "long march" with barely 1,000 men. 2400 kilometres, during which the "**Coluna Prestes**" **fought** more than **53 battles** with the government army **and more than 600 guerrillas were killed.**

However, Prestes' intention to rouse the masses and encourage them to resist the dictatorship of Artur Bernade failed completely.

Prestes, who became a national hero as a result of this undoubtedly heroic attempt to introduce reforms recognised as necessary with the help of the guerrillas, then joined the PCB and later played a decisive role in determining its policy as its General Secretary.

Prese's political conception can by no means be categorised as "revolutionary-Marxist"; it was essentially limited to the goal of a "national-democratic revolution", whereby he relied on an alliance with the "progressive national bourgeoisie"; he categorically rejected armed struggle as a revolutionary strategy, if only because of his own bad experiences, but instead stood for a purely pacifist "long march through the institutions". (Detrez op. cit.:34 Allemann op. cit.: 287)

When the first OLAS conference was held in Cuba in August 1967, the PCB leadership decided **not to** send a delegate, thereby documenting its pacifist strategy and its rejection of the Castrist-Guevarist revolutionary strategy.

This leads to the break-up of one of its most important functionaries, Carlos Marighela, with his party, the PCB.

Carlos Marighela, a member of the Executive Committee of the PCB since 1952 and provincial chairman in the province of Sao Paulo, very experienced in open and conspiratorial work and a popular political leader, had travelled to Havana without the permission and approval of his party and had attended the OLAS conference as a guest.

Although the PCB's refusal to show solidarity with the Cuban revolution and its other political goals on the international stage triggered Marighela's break with his party, the PCB, a fundamental divergence with the PCB's political strategy and largely reformist practice that had already existed beforehand was undoubtedly the decisive factor in Marighela's move.

Marighela's main divergences with the PCB, of which he had been a member for over 30 years, are expressed in a letter to the Executive Committee of the PCB, in which he not only announces his resignation from the Executive Committee, but also gives an interesting assessment of the political mistakes of his party, which is why some important passages are reproduced here:

In addition to their **inactivity** and **local limitations**, Marighela criticises "**the lack of contact with the farmers**" (Marighela, a, 1971: 86)

After criticising the party's lack of political and ideological preparation for the 1964 coup d'état, he also identifies the reasons for this in his view: "In fact, it is a historical fatalism to declare that the bourgeoisie is the leading force of the Brazilian revolution and that the proletariat must subordinate its tactics to it. This denies the proletariat any initiative and deprives it of the possibility of reacting to events itself." (Marighela, op. cit.: 88)

Above all, Marighela criticises the party's alliance policy, which is part of the "**frente amplio**", an alliance including right-wing military leaders and parts of the oligarchy against President Costa e Silva.

Marighella's criticism is not based on a rejection of all alliance politics, but he criticises the participation in this alliance primarily because leading fascists are involved and accuses the Executive Committee of the PCB of feeding illusions:

"The Executive Committee is silent about these facts and feeds illusions in the name of a supposedly "broad alliance policy" and in the name of a necessary action against sectarianism and left-wing radicalism. It (...) abandons its independent class standpoint in order to be towed by the bourgeoisie." (Marighela, a, op. cit.: 89)

For Marighela, this dependence on the bourgeoisie, criticised by Marighela, is also linked to a purely electoral orientation; the Executive Committee "wants to gently overturn the dictatorship, to reconcile Greeks with Trots! Instead of developing a revolutionary strategy and tactics, the Executive Committee preaches an impossible peaceful path and an illusory democratic renewal. (...) They continue to preach pacifism for lack of revolutionary vigour and revolutionary consciousness, which can only arise in struggle. For Brazil there is only one way out: armed struggle." (Marighela, a, op. cit.: 89)

Marighela thus justifies his propagation of armed struggle above all with the PCB's pointless orientation towards the "progressive national bourgeoisie", which leads to a dead end and cannot eliminate the problems that led and lead to dictatorship: "It is pointless to fight for power to remain in the hands of the bourgeoisie so that a bourgeois government comes to power. This was the intention at the time when the model of a national and democratic government was defended, and this is the intention today when the hypothesis of a "more or less progressive government" is put forward. (...) In fact, this means nothing other than the rejection of revolutionary action, parliamentary pacifism, capitulationism. The fascist, authoritarian constitution established by the dictatorship, which cancels the monopoly of the state, defends a reactionary agrarian structure, puts the country at the mercy of the USA, degrades the legislature and the judiciary to mere instruments of the executive and makes any formation of a democratic government through free elections impossible. Such a democratic government can only emerge through the abolition of this constitution, the overthrow of the dictatorship and the construction of a new economic system." (Marighela, a, op. cit.: 90)

It is therefore entirely logical for Marighela to propagate armed struggle, and his strategy of urban guerrilla warfare is by no means simply the product of an impatient revolutionary who is out of touch with reality, but is almost inevitable

- from his own experiences with the reformist theory and practice of his party, the PCB

- from the concrete conditions in Brazil, whose industrial centres make a purely rural guerrilla illusory

- from the repressive conditions of the dictatorship, which make "any formation of a democratic government through free elections" impossible.

While Marighela's revolutionary strategy was initially (1967) still based on the "focus theory" a la Guevara/Debray, various circumstances and considerations eventually led him to propagate a combination of rural and urban guerrillas; in the initial phase, the urban guerrillas played a decisive role in that they were to prepare the logistical and financial organisation of the rural guerrillas as far as possible with the help of bank robberies and other "expropriations". (See also Gabeira, 1982: 120; Allemann, op. cit.; Detrez, op. cit.)

The significance of the plan for a Brazilian land guerrilla against the dictatorship at the beginning can also be seen in Gabeira's biography, who is very (self-)critical of it in retrospect: "**In a way, these considerations reflected our distorted ideology. Grassroots work within the working class of Sao Paulo, among the metalworkers, seemed secondary to us compared to the enormous goal of raising a land guerrilla**. (Gabeira, op. cit.:)

This dual concept of rural and urban guerrillas also had the advantage for Marighela of fragmenting the armed forces.

A "climate of rebellion" is to be created in the urban metropolises, "while the guerrillas develop in the rural areas." (Quoted in Allemann, op. cit.: 294)

In October 1969, however, Marighela expressed scepticism about Debray's focus theory. In an interview on the "revolutionary war" Detrez/Marighela (October 1969), Marighela answers Detrez's question: "Are you against Debray's ideas?" "Some of his ideas were useful to me. As far as the Focus theory is concerned, I am probably of a different opinion." etc. (in: Smash the islands of prosperity in the Third World! 1971: 90)

The decisive factor for Marighela was that the solution to these tasks could not be achieved through a newly created party, but rather required a "secret, small, tightly knit, flexible, agile organisation of the vanguard", because "large and cumbersome organisations are the death of revolutionaries" (quoted from Allemann op. cit.:294) Similar to Debray and Guevara, military and political leadership must also be one for Marighela.

The fact that of Marighela's revolutionary strategy, namely a combination of rural guerrillas and urban guerrillas, only the urban guerrillas of the **ALN**

(Marighela) and **the MR-8** ultimately made a name for themselves is due to the failure of the Brazilian rural guerrillas: "Neither the Focus', which Brizola tried to ignite from Uruguay in Rio Grande do Sul in 1965, nor a similar enterprise launched in the Sierra da Copoeira of Minas Geraes - i.e. in central Brazil - had achieved even notable initial success, both having been quickly and effectively suppressed." (Allemann, op. cit.: 296)

For this reason, Marighela considered it necessary to prepare the rural guerrillas sufficiently through the urban guerrillas, but without giving in to the illusion that the **urban guerrillas alone** could overthrow the dictatorship. Marighela was well aware that **urban guerrillas meant "starting the fight under conditions of strategic encirclement"**.

For Marighela, the urban guerrilla is a tactical means of preventing the destruction of a future rural guerrilla and allowing it a long phase of undisturbed reconstruction. (See also Detrez, op. cit.: 36; Allemann, op. cit.: 297)

Organisational problems of the urban guerrilla

In view of the relatively high degree of urbanisation in Brazil by Latin American standards, Marighela's attempt to organically combine rural and urban guerrillas, whereby the urban guerrillas should first create the conditions for the formation of rural guerrilla fronts, does not appear to be an unrealistic concept from the outset.

But if Marighella's revolutionary strategy is focused on the cities, this in no way implies a favouring of the proletariat as **the** revolutionary subject.

Marighela, who as a successful socialist practitioner can certainly not be denied relevant experience, shares with Castro and Guevara, albeit in a very weakened form, the scepticism towards a purely proletarian orientation, as was characteristic of the ideologies of most Communist parties.

For Marighela, the "revolutionary subject" includes not only "workers, campesinos, whom the city has attracted as labour", but also students and clergy. (Marighela, b, 1969/1983: 47)

Marighela's "Handbook of the Urban Guerrillero", also known as the "Mini Handbook of the Urban Guerrillero", was published by Edition de Seuil in 1969, the year of his assassination. When it was banned at the instigation of the French secret service, 23 French publishers republished it. A single printing of the German version first published in June

1970 in "Sozialistische Politik" no. 6/7 was confiscated. In April 1971, Rowohlt Verlag printed the text in the rororo aktuell volume 1453 cited here several times under the title "Zerschlagt die Wohlstandsinseln der 3. Welt", but left it at this one edition.

(The edition on which this book is based is the 6th edition published in January 1983 by "Von der Revolution zur Revolution", Berlin).

When Marighela writes at the end of his handbook: "The intellectuals represent the central pillar of resistance against the arbitrariness, social injustice and inhuman incongruity of the guerrilla dictatorship" (Marighela, op. cit.:48), this reflects the fact **that the cadres of both the ALN and the MR-8 were largely made up of intellectuals**, primarily radicalised students, but also doctors, lawyers and professors. Marighela even had contact with priests. Mario Alves estimates that the participation of intellectuals in the urban guerrillas was close to 60%. (Alves, 1971: 9)

In accordance with the tasks of the urban guerrilla, which consisted primarily in "distracting, wearing down and demoralising the military dictatorship and the forces of repression," and also in "raiding the goods and properties of the North Americans, other foreign companies and those of the Brazilian big bourgeoisie and destroying or looting them"

(Marighela, b, op. cit.: 6), the tactics also had to be adapted to these goals.

In many respects it is similar to that of the narodniki in pre-revolutionary Russia (cf. Chapter 6, p. 55 ff), and the main problem of the urban guerrilla is that it has to operate under conditions of "strategic encirclement": The seas of houses and street canyons are the inaccessible mountains and valleys, analogous to Cuba, in a sense, the Sierra Maestra of the urban guerrilla, where the guerrilla finds shelter; provided, however, that the urban guerrilla knows how to "live among the people", he must therefore endeavour "not to appear as a stranger or to differ from the normal life of an average citizen." (Marighela, b, : 8)

However, while the Sierra Maestra in Cuba, for example, was a guerrilla redoubt that could not be controlled by the government, "liberated areas" in the classic sense are unthinkable in the city; these can only be replaced very imperfectly by the urban underground.

According to Marighela, the guerrillero should, if possible, go about his usual work, as long as he is not yet known as a guerrilla and is wanted by the authorities.

The organisational principles result from the necessarily conspiratorial nature of the struggle: from the fact that "the worst enemy of the urban guerrilla and the greatest danger to which he is exposed is (....)the **infiltration of the organisation by spies or other people who give the police information about us"** (Marighela, b, : 41), the system of a tightly organised cadre guerrilla, including "an apparatus of counter-intelligence and counter-information, is inevitable". (Marighela, b, : 22).

In addition to permanent mistrust and corresponding "counter-intelligence", Marighela propagates the "execution" not only of secret service torture specialists, but also of informers.

These two aspects, namely the strictly conspiratorial character of the organisation and the necessary terror against "agents of all kinds", arise from the conditions of the strategic encirclement of the urban guerrilla, **but in my opinion** they **are among the main causes of the failure of the urban guerrilla - and by no means only in Latin America!**

Marighella's assumption that the urban guerrillas could count on the sympathy of the masses and that they would therefore also approve of acts of terrorism such as "executions" and bomb attacks etc. is, in my opinion, a fatal error: experience has shown that there is a certain sensitivity and rejection of acts of terrorism in broad sections of the population, and only very few people approve of "individual terror" across the board - even if they are disliked members of the establishment.

At best, this can change in an already revolutionary situation, but this did not exist in Brazil!

To us, the rather cautious attitude expressed in Che Guevara's essay "The Guerrilla War", first published in 1960, in which Che Guevara **condones terror against individuals only against generally hated, particularly exposed opponents**, seems more realistic. (Compare Guevara: 196 ff).

The example of the **Tupamaros in Uruguay**, who for a long time completely renounced assassinations and apparently enjoyed great popularity for this very reason, but nevertheless carried out spectacular and effective actions and**, significantly, only suffered a severe loss of popularity after they liquidated the US agent Dan Mitrione**, makes it clear that the sense of individual terror as a politically effective measure - apart from exceptions - must at least be doubted; "executions" of "agents" express the whole problem of conspiratorial working methods: without them, the conspiracy will undoubtedly be cracked sooner or later; on the other hand, they almost always lead to a loss of popularity.

The inevitably conspiratorial character of the **urban guerrilla thus results in a decisive disadvantage**: the extreme repression of the state apparatus makes grassroots work among the masses, which Marighela also regards as necessary, more difficult: Either the urban guerrilla renounces all other forms of struggle out of caution and restricts itself to small-scale war tactics, in which case it will not only find it extremely difficult to significantly expand its social base, but there is also the danger that it will lose its political character, especially as the population will then be unilaterally exposed to state counter-propaganda. This can, skilfully used, have a decisive effect on the actions of the urban guerrillas and tend to make them appear as a purely criminal organisation in the eyes of the majority of the population - in this case, the political destruction of the urban guerrillas would only be a matter of time.

If, on the other hand, the urban guerrillas begin to open up their **top-secret organisation somewhat**, for example by participating in the organisation and "protection" of strikes or the like, **the urban guerrillas can easily be infiltrated and their cadres captured. What this means under the conditions of a military dictatorship that is not really bound by any laws is clear.**

THE TACTICS OF THE URBAN GUERRILLA

In accordance with their objectives, namely to expose the Brazilian dictatorship, to expose its repressive and anti-popular character through actions, to ridicule the government, to fragment and demoralise the security forces and finally to lead the urban masses to general resistance, the forms of action of the urban guerrillas consisted of "raids, with the aim of expropriating funds, freeing prisoners, capturing explosives, machine guns and other weapons and ammunition". (Marighela, b, : 26) As well as bank robberies, the "most popular type of robbery, which served to finance the guerrillas and guerrillas".

Marighela sees the problem that the urban guerrilla can easily be discredited as a criminal organisation, and as a countermeasure he recommends

1. the guerrilla "must not use unnecessary violence and must not touch the goods and property of the people."

2. the raid must be combined with education, i.e. with propaganda about the political aims of the urban guerrillas. (Marighela, b,: 28)

3. "invasions", which can lead to the confiscation of documents that prove government policy and the corrupt machinations of politicians.

4. occupations in order to "get hold of certain facilities and places to carry out a propaganda campaign. (op. cit.: 29) Occupations of radio stations are likely to have had the greatest effect.

5. ambushes, which were mainly used for surprise attacks on police forces to seize weapons.

6. street fights to involve the masses in the struggle.

Finally, Marighela also mentions "strikes and labour disruptions" as one of the "most feared weapons of the exploited and oppressed." (op. cit.: 31)

However, this is where the concept of urban guerrillas comes into contradiction with itself, because a serious mass strike cannot be commanded, especially not by a guerrilla organisation that is ultimately - because it works in conspiracy - relatively isolated.

The situation may be different in a pre-revolutionary or revolutionary situation, but in this case the guerrillas would only have a secondary function of distracting and binding security forces...

In addition, with larger armed forces **there is generally no element of surprise, which** means that the forces of state repression are more successful at infiltrating and can relatively easily get hold of the guerrillas; the only relative protection against this, i.e. against unchecked state repression, can only be provided by completely open political activity, which, however, requires a great deal of support from the population.

Moreover, the arrest of leading representatives is a deliberately accepted risk of any revolutionary mass movement; it opens up propaganda opportunities and can contribute to further discrediting the state organs and also offer starting points for mass mobilisations. (The most famous example of this is the broad amnesty campaign during the Spanish revolution in the 1930s).

The situation is quite different in the case of guerrillas: here, every arrest can spell disaster, as the violent extortion of information is a lever used by the state to break up the conspiracy.

If Marighela also cites the liberation of arrested revolutionaries as a task of the guerrilla, experience shows that this is usually only successful - with reasonable effort - in the initial phase of the guerrilla. Later on, it is relatively easy for the state to quickly adapt to this aspect of the guerrilla; the argument of the possible liberation of political prisoners has often served and continues to serve the state to legitimise special conditions of detention for guerrillas:

high-security wings, military camps, solitary confinement, etc.

He is expressly in favour of terrorism, by which Marighela means only the planting of bombs and setting fires.

But here, too, experience from around the world casts doubt on the political sense of this approach, as experience has shown that the blanket approval of bomb attacks leads to indiscriminate terror against unsuitable targets and, above all, all too often does a disservice to urban guerrillas - with the exception of exceptional cases - by endangering innocent bystanders, which can never be ruled out.

When Marighela claims among the "original advantages of the urban guerrilla", in addition to the surprise of the enemy and better knowledge of the area of operation, "greater mobility and speed than the police and the other forces of repression" as well as an "information apparatus that is better than that of the enemy" (Marighela, b : 18), **doubts must be raised about this:** Apparently Marighela, like so many revolutionaries before and after him, underestimates the possibilities of the state to adapt to the guerrillas, including the organisation or reorganisation of an effective secret service and the more or less skilful combination of repression, surveillance and bribery.

It goes without saying that Marighela, in his manual for urban guerrillas, mentions all those elements of small-scale warfare that we have already encountered several times in dealing with the subject...

In his handbook, Marighela also emphasises the importance of marksmanship, saying that shooting is the "basis of guerrilla existence", whereby he sees the **sniper**, who knows how to hit safely at short and long range, as the "final stage of perfect marksmanship". (Marighela, b, : 14)

The Tupamaros in Uruguay

For the sake of clarity and readability, this brief excursus on the Tupamaros only provides a general reference to the fonts used:

M. N. L. (Tupamaros): We, the Tupamaros Berlin 1974, which is the German translation of the French edition of the Tupamaros documents published by Maspero under the title "Nous, les Tupamaros". In this document, all the actions of the M.N.L. that seemed important to them are described in detail by themselves.

Allemann, Fritz R.: Macht und Ohnmacht der Guerillas Munich 1974, in particular pp. 311-354, 421-439 Allemann was a journalist and lived in Latin America for several years;

his book is well researched and provides a good overview of the subject.

Vorwerck, E.: Tupamaros in: Wehrkunde, 20th vol. 1971, issue 8: 403 ff

Hahlweg, Werner: Stadtguerilla, a, 1973: 580 ff

Conley, Michael: Protests, subversion and urban guerrillas in: Contributions to Conflict Research Vol. 3, 1974, 71 ff

Müller-Borchert, H.-J.: Guerilla im Industriestaat, 1973, 96 ff

The **Tupamaros** take their name from the tradition of indigenous uprisings against foreign rule; the name *Tupamaros* is a tribute **to Tupac Amaru, the leader of the great indigenous uprisings in Peru in the 18th century.**

In contrast to the **ALN and the MR-8** in Brazil, which were founded under conditions of extreme state repression, the Tupamaros initially fought against a system in which social and economic inequality prevailed, although relatively democratic structures would have made a legal political struggle of ideas possible. **For a long time, Uruguay was regarded as the "Switzerland of Latin America".**

The political goal of the Tupamaros was therefore to "expose" the government, albeit partially corrupt, as "anti-popular", repressive, etc., similar to what Guevara demanded in his later pamphlet "Venceremos" (we will win), and the Tupamaros actually achieved this goal; their imaginative, for a long time completely bloodless, but nevertheless or precisely because of this, popular actions, which were primarily aimed at ridiculing the oligarchy and the state and demonstrating their defencelessness against the "revolutionary avant-garde", to provoke the oligarchy and the state to lash out blindly and thus accelerate a process of radicalisation of the left, **eventually led to the point where the press was no longer allowed to mention the name *Tupamaros*, but only reported on "those whose names we must not mention" or the "nameless" - everyone in the country knew which organisation was meant...**

The Tupamaros knew how to plan and carry out their actions like no other urban guerrilla before and after them, so that the meaning was immediately clear to everyone and could usually be approved of; the characteristic feature was the **"Robin Hood method"**: in one case, for example, the villa of a government official who was notorious for being corrupt and criminal was raided in a generalised manner, including the removal of a safe weighing over 1200 kg and the leaking of the documents inside to the press. The publication of these documents, which proved the criminal involvement of government officials, triggered a government scandal.

In another case, a lorry full of food was hijacked and driven to a poor neighbourhood, where the food was distributed free of charge among the "marginales", accompanied by appropriate propaganda against the establishment.

The Tupamaros were also masters at kidnapping prominent personalities, and despite intensive searches by police forces, despite combing entire neighbourhoods house by house, the security forces were unable to locate the Tupamaros' "people's prisons" for a long time.

The Tupamaros not only succeeded in gaining great sympathy among the population, some of whom were very poor, but also in infiltrating government agencies and allegedly even army units - however, their actions did not lead to the general uprising they had hoped for.

There are probably three main reasons for the (temporary) success of the Tupamaros:

1. their predominantly intellectual social background and composition. The joking assertion that membership of the Tupamaros required a doctorate reflects the fact that the Tupamaros belonged to a considerable proportion of the intelligentsia, with specialists in all fields such as doctors, engineers, physicists, etc.

2) The second reason for the relatively spectacular (initial) successes probably lies in a strictly conspiratorially sealed-off organisational structure.

3) The third reason for the Tupamaros' success can probably also be attributed to the fact that they were founded at a time when the political system still felt bound by democratic laws and did not react effectively and repressively from the outset - the starting conditions were still very favourable.

But in the end, the Tupamaros made mistakes that contributed to their destruction: after the kidnapping of Dan Mitrione, an American interrogation specialist, the Tupamaros made such high demands as conditions for Mitrione's release that the government refused to comply.

Mitrione was subsequently liquidated, and this led to a considerable loss of popularity for the Tupamaros.

In addition, the Tupamaros were eventually infiltrated because they were probably too hasty in recruiting new cadres due to an overly optimistic assessment of the political situation; this ultimately enabled the state to set up "people's prisons", and the Tupamaros as an organisation were soon smashed.

Chapter 18 Guerrillas in Latin America - Balance sheet

That the bourgeoisie has "cosmopolitanised the production and consumption of all countries" through the "exploitation of the world market", so that "the old local and national self-sufficiency and seclusion (....) is replaced by an all-round intercourse, an all-round dependence of nations on each other", Karl Marx already stated this over 150 years ago (Marx, Manifesto: 466), but today more than ever this statement proves its almost universal validity and topicality: this statement finds its expression above all in the age of imperialism and in globalisation, but also in the fact that the **"intellectual products of the individual nations become common property"**.

These "intellectual products" undoubtedly also include the attempts of revolutionaries of all nations to analyse the particular social conditions and to derive instructions for revolutionary action to overcome the reality they perceive as bad from this and from the practical experience of political struggles: Latin American revolutionaries also drew some of their ideas from the "Manifesto of the Communist Party" quoted above, from the writings of Lenin, Mao, but also from those of Marighela, Guevara or Mariategui.

But just as imperialism presents itself in different forms from continent to continent, from nation to nation, revolutionary theory and practice is also a product of these concrete conditions under which the national liberation struggles and the struggles between the classes take place.

The overly enthusiastic reception of revolutionary strategies and their transfer to more or less different social conditions and developments have often given the revolutionary movements forward-looking theoretical impulses, but conversely have also led to catastrophic mistakes and misjudgements. This also applies to Latin America and the "focus theory".

The problem is exacerbated by the fact that the analyses and propagation of certain revolutionary options by one and the same revolutionary are often contradictory and/or lead to serious misunderstandings.

Many revolutionaries were well aware of this, as Leon Trotsky writes in Permanent Revolution: "The most remote, and, it might seem, quite 'abstract' differences of opinion, if they are thought through to the end, must sooner or later express themselves in practice, and this does not leave a single theoretical error unpunished". (Trotsky, 1981: 7)

This thesis of Trotsky, first commander of the Red Army, is also borne out by a critical reading of the writings of a revolutionary of political and personal integrity like Ernesto Che Guevara: The "difference of opinion" between the **initial** Guevarist thesis that the guerrillas could only be successful if they were directed against an "illegal" government and Guevara's **later** claim that the guerrillas could and must be everywhere in Latin America, **regardless of the political form of** the government, these "differences of opinion" in the writings of one and the same author were almost as fundamental and had similar catastrophic consequences as the "differences of opinion" between Stalin and Trotsky, to which the latter alludes in the above quote.

As we have seen, the overly uncritical adoption of Che Guevara's tacitly revised thesis on the necessary socio-political preconditions for guerrillas has often had disastrous consequences for Latin American liberation movements: The crushing of the Venezuelan, Peruvian and Bolivian guerrilla fronts, which acted against at least halfway democratically elected populist governments with a mass base - in contrast to the Cuban and later Nicaraguan guerrillas, who fought against a generally hated dictator - **makes it clear how elementary an analysis of concrete social conditions and developments is for revolutionary action, and moreover how important a genuine social anchoring in the people is. Economic statistics say nothing**

about the existence of an actual pre-revolutionary or revolutionary situation...!

Fernando Gebeira, a leading member of the Brazilian urban guerrilla MR-8 - a parallel organisation to **Carlos Marighela's ALN** - also points out the **theoretical deficits of the guerrillas** in his political autobiography: "...**the organisations were incapable of formulating theoretical goals.** Apart from the demands of everyday life, there were no theoretical tasks at all. Apart from the fact that **the theoretical level was generally very low,** the organisations were very suspicious of theory. None of us had read Capital, **none of us really knew about the revolutionary experiences in other countries, none of us questioned certain aspects of Marxism, let alone familiarised ourselves with new material. We had a rather narrow conception of the movement, and many thought that action was everything.**" (Gabeira, 1982: 117)

An overly mechanistic transfer of unsuitable revolutionary concepts in conjunction with an often inadequate analytical, i.e. theoretical, examination of the concrete social totality has undoubtedly been a significant handicap of the Latin American revolutionary movements.

I have tried to show that even in Latin America petty war was **only** a promising revolutionary method and will probably only be so in the future **if it arises from the context of political-economic-social and not least cultural processes, but cannot replace them - petty war without this prerequisite is simply terrorism by a small minority and will rightly fail!**

Small-scale war as a "revolutionary method of intervention" can only be successful if it comes "from the depths of the social and economic space".

Both the Cuban and Nicaraguan examples show that, **under certain historical conditions,** a small armed group can succeed in defeating a well-trained and numerically superior regular army; **however, these examples also make it clear that these initially very small armed groups must be groups that are anchored in the revolutionary movement of the people and have emerged from it.**

The failure of the Castristian-Guevarist guerrilla concept in the course of the sixties, especially the failure of the Bolivian guerrillas under such a distinguished, experienced and talented guerrilla leader as Ernesto Che Guevara, makes this particularly clear: Guerrillas as a people's war, as a more or less significant component of a revolution emanating from the people, are a sharp weapon against a regular army that is already hated by the people; **however, as a substitutionalist method of social and anti-imperialist**

revolution by the armed avant-garde, guerrillas have also been unsuccessful in Latin America and, in my opinion, will continue to be so. and will continue to be so in the future.

What is said here also applies analogously to the Latin American concept of the urban guerrilla, but there is a fundamental difference here: While rural guerrillas, especially in the initial phase, are constituted in a redoubt that is difficult or impossible for government troops to control and have the opportunity to build up a political, social and sometimes even economic "counter-power", in which, in the best case, elements of the desired new social system can be anticipated and the guerrillas' political target groups can at least be **given a** rudimentary **example of** a social alternative, urban guerrillas are relegated to permanent mobility, which, in contrast to rural guerrillas, is usually defensive in nature and causes wear and tear.

The permanent compulsion to move house, living underground and, in general, the conspiratorial way of life can only poorly and imperfectly replace the redoubt of the rural guerrilla, and the necessary conspiracy is not exactly conducive to continuous political work.

The fact recognised by Carlos Marighela that the urban guerrillas operate under conditions of "strategic encirclement" is expressed concretely in their conspiratorial character, which, however, as experience has shown, can never be conspiratorial enough not to be infiltrated sooner or later by informers and agents of the security organs.

The fact that the urban guerrilla must by its very nature be a conspiratorial "avant-garde organisation", i.e. a relatively very small group of revolutionary cadres, means that under the conditions of an open dictatorship it is initially more likely to escape the grasp of state repressive forces - in this respect Marighela is right, Marighela is right when he says that the mass parties are "the death of revolutionaries", but it is precisely this initial strength that makes it easier for a state apparatus determined to do anything to isolate the urban guerrillas politically, to discredit them as a criminal gang and, once there is a crack in the conspiratorial network, to smash them completely.

However, whether urban or rural guerrillas, **success ultimately depends on non-military factors that can only be controlled by the guerrillas to a limited extent**: These include not only the presence of appropriate social explosives, but also the willingness of large sections of the population to support the guerrillas even at the risk of their lives.

"Two, three, many Vietnams" (Guevara) also require corresponding social potential, which is by no means always available...

Even in Brazil, where not only the "objective" economic and social conditions suggested the existence of a revolutionary situation, but also a brutal, dictatorial military junta had seized power, neither the land guerrillas nor the ALN nor the MR-8 succeeded in motivating the mass of the population to take active action, despite their spectacular actions.

If state repression exceeds a certain level, experience shows that only a few take the risk of torture and death...

However, things are quite different at the height of an objectively and subjectively revolutionary situation in which the masses are not on the defensive but on the offensive and are already on the brink of an armed uprising. In such a situation, however, an armed revolutionary vanguard that resolutely makes a start and assumes a leading role may play an elementary role.

This leads us to another aspect of the development that is very detrimental to both rural and urban guerrillas: the perfection of the state "counterguerrilla" and "counterinsurgency".

After the victory of the "26 July Movement" in Cuba, the USA began to provide massive support for the modernisation of the national Latin American armies and to restructure and train them with regard to their suitability as a counter-revolutionary instrument. The US secret service, the CIA, played a particularly important role in this process.

Although such military measures should not be fetishised - the Vietnam War and other battles have shown how relatively ineffective the use of so-called elite units has been - this should not be underestimated: A popular revolution that has started rolling can hardly be stopped by such measures - state terror usually has the opposite effect. However, as we have seen, this is different in the case of a numerically small guerrilla cadre, which is more or less alienated from the masses due to its predominantly intellectual and conspiratorial structure: the use of more or less selective repression, especially in conjunction with reforms or sham reforms, has led to the destruction of most guerrilla fronts before they have even emerged from their initial stage.

Finally, **the importance of the "time" factor** should be emphasised: The more time passes without the guerrillas succeeding in constantly increasing their number of members and, above all, their radius of action, the more initially spectacular forms of action wear out, the better the state gradually succeeds in adapting to the initially completely unfamiliar way of fighting and thus at least constantly driving up the price of successful guerrilla actions.

Experience with Latin American urban guerrillas in particular shows that the state apparatuses sooner or later learn to adapt and act relatively unscrupulously against most revolutionary groups: Above all, the paramilitary right-wing radical terror groups set up almost everywhere by the Latin American security services with advice from the CIA, which, covered and financed by the secret service and parts of the oligarchy, hunted down all democratic and left-wing forces and did not even shy away from the public murder of a generally revered bishop during a mass - as happened in El Salvador - have become a factor that can hardly be underestimated.

Chapter 19 Urban guerrillas in the Federal Republic of Germany

Preliminary remark:

As the chapter on the Chinese People's War made clear, this resulted from the political and economic conditions of a predominantly agrarian, semi-feudal and semi-colonial social structure, as well as from the Chinese Communist Party's ability to reflect on these social conditions and to develop a revolutionary strategy from these concrete circumstances that actually turned the existing revolutionary potential into a socially transformative force.

The same can certainly be said for the Vietnamese People's War, which has not been dealt with here: In both cases, these were people's wars based on the poor rural population and subsistence farming.

The possibility of creating liberated territories was rightly understood by Mao Tse Tung and later, under modified conditions, also by the Vietnamese and Cuban leadership as the sine qua non of the revolutionary war.

If liberated territories were a prerequisite for ultimately successful guerrillas, this possibility of establishing liberated territories as a guerrilla redoubt resulted from the specific socio-economic and geographical-demographic conditions of the respective country: Only an archaic subsistence economy in the countryside, largely independent of modern technology, combined with large areas with little access to transport, made the necessary "counter-economy" possible, i.e. a largely self-sufficient economy that was more or less detached from the rest of the national economic cycle.

This is characterised by "positional thinking" even for such masters of the war of movement as Mao: although Mao always emphasised that the Red Army must never lose its ability to "move away", i.e. to completely clear liberated areas if necessary, the very existence of liberated areas has a point of contact with regular war, which is about asserting and gaining territory: There are also limits to the guerrillas in terms of mobility if they do not want to degenerate into a "roving bunch of rebels", something Mao repeatedly and resolutely opposed.

It is quite logical for Mao's strategic conception to include positional warfare, but only in a phase where the guerrilla army is already superior to that of the enemy, i.e. in the "strategic offensive": In this phase, war of movement, i.e. offensive advances into areas controlled by the enemy, and war of position, i.e. the defence of liberated areas, must complement each other.

The conditions are completely different in an industrially structured, complex society with an extreme division of labour: here - quite apart from the military circumstances, i.e. the ability of the state in densely populated industrialised countries to **concentrate huge contingents of troops in almost any part of the country within a very short space of time if necessary** - there can be no "liberated areas" simply because of the complex interrelationships between all areas of social production: A "liberated Hamburg" or a "liberated Black Forest" would be an absurdity for purely economic reasons.

This alone renders the "victory in a people's war" often propagated by the RAF meaningless. Adopting the concept of people's war along Chinese, Vietnamese or Cuban lines in a metropolitan revolutionary concept would therefore simply be absurd. (See also Haffner, 1966: 27ff; Müller-Borchert, 1973: 103 ff)

As we have seen, Mao himself **rejected** his people's war as an **unsuitable means** for the industrialised nations and propagated the usual approach of the communist parties at the time, namely agitation and propaganda, organisation of strikes and demonstrations, workers' control and only then armed insurrection, and Ernesto Che Guevara also initially only gave the guerrillas a chance where they were based on appropriate political and economic conditions and were directed against a system that had illegally seized power.

If, despite the multiple failures of the Castristian-Guevarist orientated guerrillas in Latin America - not to mention the Maoists, who, with the exception of "Sendero Luminoso" (Shining Path) in Peru, have hardly got a foot on the ground anywhere in Latin America - and despite the failure of the urban guerrillas in Brazil, Uruguay, Venezuela, Argentina, etc. Despite the failure of urban guerrillas in Brazil, Uruguay, Venezuela, Argentina, etc., the concept of revolutionary state creation with the help of urban guerrillas also had such appeal for small sections of the left in industrialised countries, this must be seen not least in the context of the development of the left in these countries:

A large part of the left, as the RAF rightly stated in this case, has long since "bet on a different horse" and no longer sees its task as advancing the social revolution, but rather as reform-oriented politics within the framework of the laws of parliamentarism. The long-term goals may still be the realisation of socialism, but the methods now concentrate on forms of action that are both legally compliant and at least partially capable of winning a majority.

The traditional communist parties in Europe - i.e. in the Federal Republic of Germany at the time primarily the GDR-orientated **DKP** - also relied less on revolutionary extra-parliamentary mass action and no longer strove for the "dictatorship of the proletariat" analogous to the classic Bolshevik strategy, but instead oriented themselves towards parliamentarism and attempted in this way - with varying degrees of success, but nowhere with resounding success - to participate in political power. This applies not only to Germany, but also to Britain, France, Italy and Spain.

The RAF rejected this orientation as "revisionist" and derived its "urban guerrilla concept" from Lenin's theses on the "labour aristocracy" (see Lenin, Imperialismus, 1970: 763)

In fact, it is quite true that the majority of the "working class" did not and does not have the proletarian, revolutionary and internationalist consciousness that not only characterised significant sections of the Russian proletariat at the time of the October Revolution around 1917, but was also characteristic of large sections of early German social democracy: **the modern proletariat predominantly identifies with the existing status quo**.

Marx's paradigm that genuine social revolutions ultimately result from the **contradictions of material production** can be verified on the basis of Germany's post-war development in particular. **To date, the working class has ultimately participated in economic development on a European**

scale; for the wage-dependent population there was generally no material hardship in the post-war decades, so the most important prerequisite for large-scale social unrest or even a pre-revolutionary situation was missing.

When the RAF concludes that due to the totality of capitalist relations, i.e. the fact that "with the introduction of the 8-hour day (...) the 24-hour day of the domination of the system over the worker has begun its triumphal march", and that it follows from this that the "revolutionary subject is anyone who frees himself from these constraints and refuses to participate in the crimes of the system" (RAF, 1983: 431), this expresses not only an elementary revision of fundamental Marxist categories - remarkable for a group that is so fond of polemicising with the term "revisionism" - but also, in my. The RAF's assumption that it would be possible to "free oneself from the constraints of the system" and "refuse to participate in the crimes of the system" completely contradicts the Marxist concept of totality: the characteristic feature of complex capitalist society is precisely the fact that everyone is forced to "join in", or, as Theodor W. Adorno puts it: "There is no individual emancipation without that of society."

The RAF thus acts in a highly "**un-Marxist**" way: it individualises collective constraints which, according to Marx, can only be eliminated collectively, i.e. by the organised working class as the historical "revolutionary subject", to which managers and workers alike are subject; **the social revolution thus tends no longer to be understood as a historically necessary product of an economically, socially and politically antagonistic development, but becomes a moral-philosophical category - this has little to do with Marxism...**

The "revolutionary subject" that "frees itself from the constraints of the system and denies its participation in the crimes of the system" is unlikely to refer to the social potential that Marx once labelled the "lumpenproletariat" and which cannot be described as a "revolutionary subject" either in accordance with Marxist theory or due to the real situation: The socially marginalised population is supported by the state and has hardly appeared anywhere as revolutionary.

In our opinion, there is a decisive difference here compared to the Latin American countries: Here, the "marginales", above all peasants and rural labourers who had migrated to the cities and had to eke out a living in miserable conditions under more or less authoritarian political conditions, actually formed a certain revolutionary potential - these "marginales" were always a social potential from which the revolutionary movements in Latin America could draw.

Under the heading "Poverty in the Federal Republic", the RAF concretises the revolutionary potential (RAF: 392): According to this, around 14 million people live in poverty in West Germany, but after a detailed list of these particularly underprivileged groups, the RAF rightly states, "The actuality of poverty is not identical with the actuality of revolution. The poor are not revolutionary, not suddenly, not of their own accord." (RAF: 394)

In order for these groups to become the revolutionary subject, the RAF believes that revolutionary action is needed, and for the RAF revolutionary action means the concept of urban guerrilla!

The revolutionary conception of the RAF therefore proves to be extremely **voluntaristic** - not to say idealistic - **because it makes the social revolution dependent on a single concrete form of action, namely the urban guerrilla of a tiny "avant-garde".**

At least verbally, the RAF also professed its commitment to factory work and the like, although in practice this was at odds with its strategy and priorities.

The frequent use of quotations from Mao makes it clear that the RAF also refers to this "classic of Marxism-Leninism", although it is extremely **selective** in its approach: Mao's motto that the party commands the guns must fall completely by the wayside in RAF practice, since the RAF is neither a party nor the armed arm of a party, let alone the armed arm of a party with a mass base, as was true not only of the Chinese Communist Party, but also of ETA (Herri Bartasuna in the Basque Country) or the IRA (Sinn Fein) in Ireland.

Mao's statement **that one should not begin armed struggle if the objective and subjective conditions for it are not present is resolved by the RAF in a succinct statement:**

"We maintain that the organisation of armed resistance groups at this time in the Federal Republic and in West Berlin is right, possible and justified. That it is right, possible and justified to organise urban guerrillas here and now. That the armed struggle as "the highest form of Marxism-Leninism" (Mao) can and must be started now, that without it there is no anti-imperialist struggle in the metropolises." (RAF, 1983: 342).

However, the RAF fails to provide us with concrete proof of this bold assertion; we search in vain for a derivation from the social, political and economic conditions and realities...

The armed struggle as "the highest form of Marxism-Leninism", which according to the classical Marxist paradigm represents the culmination point and the final phase of a revolutionary mass movement, is thus simply placed at the beginning by the RAF.

Mind you, this is not happening in a situation of extreme state repression, where other forms of political debate would not be possible, **but in a situation of freedom, freedom also for public discussion and articulation.**

For the RAF, armed struggle is no longer, as it was for Lenin or Mao - to whom the RAF likes to refer - and even as it was for the early Che Guevara or Fidel Castro shortly after the seizure of power by the 26th July Movement in Cuba - the result of a more or less lengthy process of mass politicisation and radicalisation. July in Cuba - **the result of** a more or less protracted process of politicisation and radicalisation of the masses, but **a substitute for** this, it is the revolutionary intervention method of a numerically very small "avant-garde" that hopes to initiate a revolutionary mass movement - parallels to the Focus theory in the later writings of Che Guevara and Regis Debray with the idea that the small motor of a cadre guerrilla drives the large motor of the revolution are therefore by no means coincidental.

The RAF itself expresses an awareness of the fact that the **concept of urban guerrilla is basically the product of a non-revolutionary situation** when it says: "The concept of urban guerrilla comes from Latin America. It is there what it can only be here: **The revolutionary intervention method of altogether weak revolutionary forces."** (RAF, 1983: 356, emphasis mine.)

In order to collect the "rivulets and drops of popular agitation"(1) and channel them into a broad stream, the RAF believes that "the practical revolutionary intervention of the avant-garde" is required, which must begin with armed struggle "here and now" and end with "victory in the people's war".

For the RAF, urban guerrillas had the strategic function of tearing the democratic mask off imperialism's face and exposing it once and for all. This is where the **"unmasking theory"** reappears, as it was also the basis of **the concept of the Tupamaros**, which the RAF also refers to expressis verbis and which in turn is linked to Che Guevara's later writings and views.

Since the RAF already considers the situation in the metropolises of capitalism to be **potentially revolutionary** due to the immanent contradictions of the capitalist-imperialist system (cf. RAF,1983: 351 ff), and only the ideological superstructure, i.e. the mass media, led by the Springer press, and the state "repressive apparatus" prevent the revolutionary outbreak of the masses, it is logical for the RAF to orientate itself towards "destroying the state apparatus of rule at individual points, partially overriding it, destroying the myth of the omnipresence of the system and its invulnerability". (RAF, 1983: 356).

Here it becomes clear how **contradictory and unrealistic** the assessment of the social and political situation in Germany in the 1970s and 1980s is.

On the one hand, the RAF rightly recognises that the political consciousness of the German "working class" is reformist at best, **on the other hand it assumes that its terrorist actions could generate revolutionary consciousness: However, not only every historical experience, but also the manifold examples in this work show that this is pure wishful thinking - fortunately!**

If we can draw one **lesson from historical experience,** from the **narodniki** in Tsarist Russia (see Chapter 6) to the urban guerrillas in Latin America, the left-wing terrorist groups in Italy, etc., it is this: **Social revolutions have many preconditions, which is why they are special historical events. It takes a more or less prolonged phase of politicisation and radicalisation of broad masses of people based on their concrete everyday experiences, it takes a prolonged period of dissatisfaction not only in the economic distribution struggle, but also deep dissatisfaction with the ruling elites and the organs of the**

state, before broad sections of the population see the appropriate means in revolt or social revolution...

Only when the economic situation appears unbearable, when the confrontation with the state has led to great frustration among the population and the dissatisfaction has also spread to parts of the army and police, **can** a revolutionary situation arise.

As long as our democratic system allows for different political currents and gives them the opportunity to articulate and co-determine, the state is not really discredited and any form of armed struggle or "resistance" will rightly meet with widespread rejection among large sections of the population.

It therefore takes a longer phase of confrontation with state violence before not only isolated social outsiders such as the members of the RAF, but also the population itself "lights the fire of revolution" (Mao), i.e. sees the only way out in armed resistance.

The realisation formulated by Friedrich Engels that "the times are finally over **when small minorities make the revolution**, but the revolutionary people themselves step onto the political stage" (see Chapter 3) is confirmed by the history of revolutions, especially in the 20th century. **The** examples discussed in this work also clearly demonstrate this.

The RAF's belief that a tiny avant-garde of social outsiders, if only they were determined enough, could "destroy West German imperialism at individual points" has, in my opinion, ideological points of contact with the prevailing opinion that the revolutions in Russia, China, Cuba etc. were ultimately the product of small demagogic and terrorist communist conspiratorial circles which, when they came to power, showed their true colours.

Things are more complex: it is true that the revolutions mentioned would probably not have taken place without their leaders, and it is also true that the leaders of these revolutions usually became despots and, in the long term, did not bring society as far as was perhaps once intended.

On the other hand, these examples also show that most revolutions could certainly not have taken place **without** a corresponding mass basis, above all **without** an overall crisis-ridden development of all areas of society.

Despite many different positions in the global communist movement, most Marxists share common theoretical premises, not least of which is the realisation that genuine social revolutions are never the work of small minorities, but in abstract/general terms are the **result of extremely antagonistic social processes.**

Despite their situational and temporal differences, all victorious social revolutions had at least one thing in common: they were rooted in and emerged from the revolutionary mass movement of the people. The historical and social examples presented here prove this once again!

But precisely this decisive condition of armed revolutionary struggle *does not exist* **in the Federal Republic of Germany, as the RAF itself emphasised***!*

What also applies to the Brazilian urban guerrillas and the Tupamaros in Uruguay is therefore increasingly true for the urban guerrillas in the Federal Republic: the urban guerrillas operate under the conditions of "strategic encirclement", without it being possible to recruit a significant number of underground cadres, without whom even a pure cadre guerrilla cannot achieve effective results in "destroying the state apparatus of rule at individual points" (RAF).

How a cadre guerrilla, relegated to the underground, is supposed to succeed in winning over the masses for the "victory in the people's war" repeatedly propagated by the RAF is incomprehensible, especially when it is taken into account that the mass disposition for revolutionary violence - if at all - can occasionally become effective in a revolutionary situation, but not in a situation characterised by a pronounced weakness of the revolutionary movement, as the RAF itself admits when it says that the concept of urban guerrillas is "the revolutionary intervention method of weak revolutionary forces as a whole."

Terrorism versus people's war

As we have tried to show, there is **a big difference between a people's war, in which broad sections of the population are involved because they see no other way of secure existence, and terrorist groups that wage a proxy war against establishment institutions in the name of (socialist) or anti-imperialist liberation as the "vanguard". Such terrorist groups are rightly rejected by the vast majority of the population - they have neither a democratically legitimised mandate nor do they visibly represent the real interests of the population.**

It should therefore come as no surprise that identification is almost always with the raison d'état and almost never with the terrorists. Terrorist groups are often people who, due to their personal biographies, have little overlap with the majority of the population, i.e. who therefore also appear as **outsiders. This makes it even easier to stigmatise and**

isolate them as a group - which is the most important step in rendering these groups harmless.

The more the state organs succeed in further isolating the terrorist group socially, the easier it is to infiltrate and disband it.

The methods of smashing terrorist groups were already successfully used against the Social Revolutionaries during the Tsarist era (see Chapter 6 p. 55 ff)), and the methods are still applicable and used today, albeit usually more subtly and skilfully.

As long as the democratic state does not overshoot the mark and does not overreact, but consistently emphasises the special interest of the terrorist group and the state succeeds in largely preserving the rule of law, terrorist groups will not achieve their political goals - the more the state can preserve the trust of the population, the more terrorist groups are condemned to remain marginal groups that need to be eliminated as effectively as possible...

Afterword by the author

I originally wrote this thesis as part of my diploma course in social sciences at the Carl von Ossietzky University of Oldenburg in autumn 1986.

I have refrained from adding to it or revising it substantially, merely correcting a few grammatical and spelling mistakes and the odd stylistic flourish.

The temptation to update and supplement the work was great, but the developments since the completion of this work at the end of 1986 are so extensive - one need only think of **Islamist extremism and terrorism - that a supplement to the content that included this topic would have gone far beyond the scope of the work....**

This work, originally published in 1986, undoubtedly has weaknesses, the most important of which is its **topicality**: **unfortunately,** it has to be said, a lot has happened in the field of small-scale wars and terrorism since 1986, so **none** of this has been included here.

Why not? The question is easy to answer: the innovations relate to Islamist terrorism, which played a barely recognised role at the time this work was written, although it already had serious consequences back then and still does today: the small-scale war of the mujahideen, now **the Taliban**, in Afghanistan was already a topic among experts at the time, and I was of course also aware of it, but I refrained from taking it up thematically in this work at the time because it did not really fit in with the topic and the sources were also relatively poor, and I also lacked and still lack the religious-historical expertise!

It was also known that the Mujahideen or Taliban were at least partly the result of geopolitical, global interests of the Soviet Union and later the USA as sponsors in Afghanistan at the time: They gained their importance not least because of the massive financial support they received from the USA...the devil that was summoned at the time was then never got rid of, so that later US troops fought against those who had once made them great - not the only irony in the history of US foreign policy...

But back to the topic: this work deals with the social and theoretical history of important small-scale war events in history using the examples I have selected: This always includes an arbitrary moment, because the topic naturally requires a **selection** and **limitation** of the war events and the theories of the respective protagonists about them.

I have taken a comparatively simple path here: I was guided by the question of **historical significance** on the one hand and the **existence of formulated theories of the protagonists and the availability of sources on the other**: I think this was right, at least from my point of view! The Frankfurt School's realisation that all theories **are subject-**

bound, i.e. also the **result of the protagonists' respective personal experiences,** is also evident in this presentation!

But in some places the realisation becomes particularly clear that these subjective experiences occasionally tempt the actors to **generalise** their **subjective** experiences, which are due to a **historically specific situation**, and to **transfer** them to **other**, socially and historically **completely different cases.**

Ernesto 'Che' Guevara's attempt to transfer the Cuban revolutionary model to other countries such as the Congo or Bolivia is a particularly good example of how this can sometimes be a **serious mistake: Here I have taken a particularly critical look at this and also used the history of theory to show how a narrowing of the perspective led to serious social and political misjudgements...**

In conclusion, I would now like to briefly touch on the question of the **meaningfulness** of the small-scale wars described here, as these violent conflicts have in some cases cost almost unimaginable numbers of human lives: Experts estimate that many millions of people died in the Kuomintang's small-scale wars with the Communists, whether as a result of direct war events or related disasters: Displacement and famine.

Here the question must definitely be asked whether such a high number of victims can be justified by **anything** at all, my personal opinion has not changed here either: Today I think that the question of **peaceful solutions** should be much more in the foreground, even if they are **more arduous and protracted**...

We find a particularly positive example of this in our own peaceful recent history: an extremely peaceful revolution led to the fall of the wall between the two German states, followed by a not always painless reorganisation and reunification of Germany without a shot having to be fired - **yet the revolutionaries were neither cowardly nor opportunistic, on the contrary!**

This is not just about the question of the loss of human life, but also about the question of what continued violence does to the people who carry it out and survive...!

This is not the place to answer these questions exhaustively, but it is clear that a violent change of power would not exactly facilitate peaceful coexistence in the future....

From this perspective, revolutionaries such as the **Philippine national hero Dr Jose Rizal**, the Indian freedom hero **Mahatma Gandhi** or the leader of the peaceful Portuguese Carnation Revolution **Otelo Saraiva de Carvalho** are much closer to me personally today than Mao Tse Tung or Ernesto Che Guevara - but that is of course a question of perspective and perhaps also of personal maturity and development....

It is certainly true that it is morally justifiable to use terrorist methods to help and eliminate inhumans like Hitler, as **Colonel Claus Schenk Graf Stauffenberg** tried, unfortunately unsuccessfully, to do.

Only "democratic eunuchs" - to use a term used in this context by Leon Trotsky (in his work "Terrorism and Communism") - will raise their moral index finger here...other, politically-minded people will undoubtedly see this form of terrorism in its **historical context** and view, judge and evaluate it in a correspondingly differentiated way!

Nevertheless, I would like to take up a question here that has been somewhat neglected in this work: the question of permissible means, of a morally and politically justified political option that regards and utilises small-scale war and terrorism as legitimate means...

So the question is: **does the end justify all means?** Hardly! Unfortunately, a correct answer is all too often only found **posthumously, i.e. in retrospect** of the events and their **consequences**: Only here does it become clear whether, in retrospect, violent courses of action can be regarded as legitimate and sensible or not!

But it is not easy to give a very clear answer here, because you always have to consider the **alternatives**: what would have become of Cuba if the revolutionaries of the 27 July Movement **had not** seized power?

The answers to these questions remain as much a matter of speculation as the question of what would have happened if the Communists under Mao's leadership had **not** fought the Kuomintang in China. **Would there have been fewer casualties, would China today be a country with Western-style democracy and human rights?**

All speculation and not scientifically provable!

Finally, the question arises **as to what conclusions can be drawn from this work:** For me, it is quite clear that social events such as the small wars of history **were always particularly successful when the protagonists' and actors' desire for freedom was the primary driving force behind the processes,** when the war against invaders or a political system that was perceived as bad **was born from the depths of the social space, i.e. from the people themselves!**

Nevertheless, as I have also shown here, certain other factors play a role in success or failure that should not be underestimated: the role of the **"leaning power"** and the role of the **foreign and/or own army**, i.e. the question of how well the revolutionary or anti-imperialist subject succeeds in undermining the morale of the enemy and attracting **parts of the armed state organs to its own side**, etc., and so on. All these questions have at least been touched upon, presented and analysed by me in this social and theoretical history of small-scale wars and terrorism, and reading this work has answered these and other questions in an argumentative way, as it is **not just** a matter of presenting **facts and theories**, but also of **evaluating** them and drawing conclusions **in order to clearly work out the inner bond that visibly links these historical processes across time and space. I think this has become clear from reading the book: It is the wishes and strategies of the people for a better future, but it is also the theories about time and space on the subject of terror, guerrillas, small-scale war and people's war, it is the will to freedom, but sometimes also simply the will to power!**

Erich B. Ries, October 2024

LITERATURE

Allemann, Fritz R.: Power and powerlessness of the guerrillas

    Munich 1974

Alves, Mario M.: Break up the islands of prosperity? In:

    "Smash the islands of prosperity of the

    Third World" Hamburg 1971

Arendt, Hanna: Reflections on Violence in:

    Mercury, 1, : 5 ff 1970

Bartelheimer, P. /

Moneta, J. That can't be all there is to it

    The fight for 35 hours in Frankfurt

    a.M. 1984

Berner, Wolfgang: The Evangelist of Castroism-Guevarism. Regis Debray and his Guerrilla Doctrine Bingen 1969

Boger, Jan (Pseudonym for David Theodor Schiller) : Snipers and their weapons In: German Weapons Journal (DWJ) 2/1983, 166 ff

Bondarev, Juri: Hot Snow Berlin East, 1975

Bonwetsch, B.: Soviet partisans 1941 - 1944 Legend and reality of the "general people's war" in: G. Schulz (ed.): Partisans and

People's War Göttingen 1985

Borcke, Astrid von: Violence and terror in revolutionary Narodnicestvo: The party "Narodnaja Volja" (1879 - 1883) in: Mommsen/Hirschfeld (see under Mommsen/Hirschfeld)

Borges, Thomas: Interview with the "taz" in: taz-journal No. 2 o. year Berlin: 43 ff

McClure, Brooks: Russia's Hidden Army in: The war from the darkness (see Osanka)

Calley, William: "I loved being in Vietnam" - Lieutenant Calley reports Frankfurt a. M. 1972

Cartier, Raymund: The Second World War Vol. 1 (1939 - 1939)

1942), vol. 2 (1942 - 1945)

Munich/Zurich 1977

Claessens/Klönne/

Tschoepe: Social studies of the Federal Republic of Germany

8th A. Düsseldorf/Cologne 1978

Clausewitz, Carl von: On War German Literature Vol. 12

Rowohlt Classics 138 1963

The same Political Writings and Letters quoted

From: "Guerilleros, partisans"

See Schickel

Conley, Michael: Protests, subversion and Urban guerrilla
In: Contributions to Conflict Research Vol. 3, 1974

Dach, Hans von: The total resistance Biel 1966

Detrez, Conrad: Carlos Marighela in the succession Che Guevara in: "Smash the Islands of prosperity in the Third World" : 26 ff

Detrez, C. / **Marighela**, C. Interview on the "Revolutionary War" in: "Smash the

Islands of prosperity in the Third World"

94 ff

Deutscher, Isaak: Trotsky - The Armed Prophet

Stuttgart 1972

Dinegar, W. W.: The "Long March" as an extended

Guerrilla warfare in: The war from the

Dark (see Osanka)

Dohnany, Ernst von: Fight against Soviet guerrillas

In: The war from the darkness

(see Osanka)

Ebeling/Engelbrecht: Fighting and getting through -

The lone fighter - close to war

Training for offside behaviour

of the troop Koblenz/Bonn 1981

Engels, Friedrich (a): Preußische Franctireurs in:

Engels/Lenin: Military policy

Writings (see Wollenberg)

The same (b): Principles of Communism in:

Marx/Engels Works (MEW)

Berlin East 1980, 361 ff

The same (c) :   Mr Eugen Dühring's revolution of the

Science ("Anti-Dühring") in:

MEW 20, 171 ff

The same(d) :   Introduction to Marx "The

Class Struggles in France" in:

Engels/Lenin s. Wollenberg

Derselbe (e): Die Reichsverfassungskampagne in:

Engels/Lenin (see Wollenberg)

The same(f): Address of the Central Authority to the

Bund in: Wollenberg op. cit.

Fetscher, Iring/

Rohrmoser, Günther: Ideologies and Strategies.

Analyses of terrorism vol. 1

Opladen 1981

Frank, Piere: History of the Communist Party

International Vol. 1 and Vol. 2

Frankfurt a. M. 1981

Frederick William III: Decree on the Landsturm in:

    Guerilleros, partisans (see Schickel):
72

Fichtner, Hans: Brazil from 1930 - 1980 Vom

    Populism into dictatorship in:

    Gabeira, The guerrillas are tired (p.

    Gabeira)

Gabeira, Fernando: The guerrillas are tired (Biography)

    Frankfurt a. M. 1982

Galeano, Eduardo: The open veins of Latin America

    Wuppertal 1983

Gneisenau, N. von: Plan for the preparation of a Popular uprising in: Guerilleros, Partisans (S. Schickel)

Guevara, Ernesto: Guerrilla Warfare: A Method in The same: Guerrilla - Theory and Method Berlin 1972

Same: What is a guerrilla? In derselbe: Guerilla - Theory and Method Berlin 1972

The same: Venceremos - we will win! In the same: Guerrilla - Theory and Method

The same: The guerrilla war in: Guevara, Guerrilla - Theory and method

Guldimann, Tim: Latin America. The development of the Underdevelopment Munich 1975

Haffner, Sebastian: Introduction to Mao Tse-Tung: Theory of the guerrilla war Reinbek 1966

Hahlweg, Werner: Guerrilla - War without fronts Stuttgart 1966

The same: Stadtguerilla in: Allgemeine Schweizer Military Journal Vol. 139, 1973, No. 11 580 ff

Hanrahan, G. Z.: The Red Chinese Army and the Guerrilla warfare in: The war from the Dark (see Osanka)

Heideking, J.: American secret services and Resistance movements in the Second World War II in: Partisans and People's War (see Schulz, G.)

Hildemeier, M.: On the terrorist strategy of the Social Revolutionary Party of Russia (1900 - 1918)

Hobsbawm, E. J. : Political Violence and "Political Murder" in: Social protest, violence, terror (see Mommsen/Hirschfeld)

Hubermann/ **Sweezy** (ed.): Focus and Free Space Berlin 1979

Hübner, S. F.: S. A. S. - Who dares, wins!

International Weapons Review 1/1983: 41 ff

Jacobs, W. D.: Irregular warfare and the Soviets
In: The war from the darkness
(see Osanka)

Kieler, R. E.: Guerrilla and Revolution Bonn 1975

Knipping, Franz: Military conceptions of the French Resistance in the 2nd World War World War II in: Partisans and People's War
(see Schulz, G.)

Kutger, J. P.: Irregular warfare in the Changing times in: The war from the

Dark (see Osanka)

Lenin, V. I.: The Fall of Port Arthur in Lenin/Engels

(S. Wollenberg) 43 ff

The same (b): State and Revolution in: Lenin,

Selected works in 3 vols. vol. 2,

Berlin East 1970

The same (c): The partisan war in:

Lenin, Works Vol. 11 Berlin East 1974

The same (d): The military programme of the

proletarian revolution in:

Selected works vol. 1

Berlin East 1970

The same (e): Two tactics of social democracy

in the democratic revolution in: Selected Works Vol. 1 Berlin East 1970

The same (f): Marxism and Insurrection in: Selected Works Vol. 2 Berlin East 1970

The same (g): The lessons of the Moscow Uprising in: Lenin, Selected Works Vol. 1 Berlin East 1970

The same (h): Advice from an outsider in: Selected Works Vol. 2 Berlin East 1970

Lenin, V. I.: Letter to the Central Committee (1917) in: Selected

    Works Vol. 2 Berlin East 1970

Lusso, Emilio: Theory of insurrection (pirated edition

    without place and year)

Mandel, Ernest: The Marxian Theory of

    Original accumulation and the

    Industrialisation of the Third World in:

    Consequences of a theory

    (collective of authors) Frankfurt a. M. 1972

Mao Tse-Tung: Military Writings Beijing 1969

Mao Tse-Tung (a): On the rectification of wrong

    Views in the Party (1929) in: Mao

Tse-Tung: Military writings

Mao (b): On the protracted war in:

Mao: Military Writings 223 ff

Mao (c): Strategic problems of the guerrilla warfare against the Japanese Aggression (1938) In: Mao, Military Writings 179 ff

Mao (d): Strategic problems of the revolutionary war in China in: Mao, Military Writings 87 ff

Mao (e): Problems of war and strategy

In: Mao, op. cit. 327 ff

Mao (f): The conclusion of the defence of the second

Communist Campaign in: op. cit, 347 ff

Mao (g): Bringing the Revolution to a Close (1948)

Mao, op. cit., 453 ff

Mao (h): Why can the Chinese Red Power

exist? In: Mao, op. cit. 5 ff

Mao (i): The Battle in the Djinggang Mountains in:

Mao, op. cit. 17 ff

Mao (j): Announcement of the Chinese

People's Liberation Army in: Mao, op. cit.

479 ff

Mao (k): Strategic course for the second year of the War of Liberation in: Mao, op. cit. 393 ff

Mao (l): A spark can turn into a tumbleweed fire Mao, op. cit. 71 ff

Marek, Franz: Philosophy of the World Revolution Vienna 1966

Marighela, Carlos: Letter to Fidel Castro in: "Smash the Islands of prosperity in the Third World"

The same (a): Letter to the Executive Committee of the Communist Party of Brazil in: Smash the islands of prosperity ....

The same (b): Handbook of the urban guerrilla

(pirated) 6th edition 1983

Marx, Karl: Das Kapital Vol. 1 Marx Engels Works

MEW 23 Berlin East 1979

Derselbe Zur Kritik der Politischen Ökonomie

Foreword MEW 13 Berlin East 1975

Marx/Engels: Manifesto of the Communist Party

In: MEW 4 Berlin East 1980 493 ff

McAffee Brown, R.: Of the Just Revolution -

Revolution and violence

Stuttgart 1982

Mires, Fernando: Cuba - The revolution is not an island

Berlin 1978

M.N.L.

Tupamaros: We, the Tupamaros Berlin 1974

Mommsen/

Hirschfeld : Social protest, violence, terror

Stuttgart 1982

Moneta, Jakob: The strikes of IG Metall Frankfurt 1984

Müller-Borchert,

Hans-Joachim: Guerrilla in the industrialised state Hamburg 1973

Nohlen, D. (ed.): Lexikon Dritte Welt Reinbek 1984

Osanka, Frank M.: The War from the Darkness - 20 Years of Communist Guerrilla Fighting Around the World Cologne 1963

Perrie, Maureen: Political and economic terror

as a tactical weapon in the Russian

Social Revolutionary Party before 1914

In: Mommsen/Hirschfeld see Mommsen

Piekalkiewiciz,

Janusz: Spies, Agents, Soldiers Secret Commandos in the 2nd World War Frankfurt a.

M. 1972

The same: S.O.E. - London trains saboteurs

op. cit. 22ff

The same: Russia's Forest Army op. cit.

The same: Prague, 27 May 1942 op. cit.

Radetzky of Radetz,

Johann Joseph Wenzel: Field Instruction for the Infantry,

Cavalry and artillery Olomouc:

New builder 1847

RAF - Red Texts Revised and updated

Army faction edition 1983 (without location, not

(Collective) in bookshops

Reed, John: Ten days that shook the world

>Berlin East 1982

The Reibert The Soldier's Handbook

>Herford

>Army edition 1981

Rosenberg, Alfred: History of Bolshevism

>Frankfurt a. M. 1966

Rossi, Carlo: Stalinism in Latin America

>In: Rote Hefte No. 6 (ed. GIM)

>Frankfurt a. M. n.d.

Sanguinetti,

Gianfranco: On terrorism and the state

>Hamburg 1981

Schulz, Gerhard: The Irregulars in: Schulz, G. (ed.)

    Partisans and people's war

    Göttingen 1985

The same: Partisans and People's War Göttingen

    1985

Schulz, H. - J.: The Secret International - on the

    History and function of the

    Secret services Frankfurt a. M. 1982

Der Spiegel Munich V-man - Just a confused man

    Lone offender? 14 July 1986: 75 ff

Sun-Tse: The 13 Commandments of the Art of War

(Passages series) Munich 1972

Tophoven, R. /

Becker, H.: Terrorism and guerrillas

Düsseldorf 1979

Torres, S./

Aronde, J.: Debray and the Cuban

Experience in: Focus and free space

Berlin 1979

Trotsky, Leon: Their morality and ours in: Trotsky,

Memo 386 ff

Trotsky, Leo: Terrorism and Communism -

Anti-Kautsky Dortmund 1978

The same: Denkzettel Politische Erfahrungen im

The age of permanent revolution

(Essays) Frankfurt a. M. 1981

The same: History of the Russian Revolution

Vol. 1, Vol. 2.1 and Vol. 2.2

Frankfurt a. M. 1982

Trotsky, Leo: The Permanent Revolution Frankfurt a. m.

1982

The same: The young Lenin Frankfurt a. M. 1982

Vorwerck, E.: Tupamaros in: Wehrkunde 20. vol,

Issue 8, 1971, 403 ff

Wallach, Jehuda: Theories of War Frankfurt a. M. 1972

Wilkins, Frederick: Guerrilla Warfare in: Osanaka op. cit.

Wollenberg, E.: Engels/Lenin: Military-political writings Offenbach Frankfurt 1952

Zentner, Christian: ...the dagger in the garment. Political Murders through two millennia Munich 1968

Ed.: Duve, Fr. : "Smash the islands of prosperity of the Third World!" Hamburg 1971

Expert opinion and table of contents for this thesis by Prof. Dr Fernando Mires (then still a private lecturer).

Prof Dr Fernando Mires, then Faculty 3, Institute of Sociology at the CvO University of Oldenburg, is a proven expert on the subject, especially Latin America and Cuba in particular.

"The work being assessed here is not a thesis in the usual sense.

Because of its scope, the range of the topic, as well as the topic itself, it is more suitable for a dissertation. Erich Bernhard Ries has proven that he is capable of undertaking global analyses, comparing different historical situations and yet not losing the thread of logical continuity.

The work can be seen as a comparative historical analysis. The subject matter is not questions of violence and terror in general, but the specific theory and practice of so-called petty warfare. Although the author distances himself radically from any stylisation of violence as a political method, he does not overlook the fact that it is a permanent historical fact and thus has a place in social-scientific and political theory from Neidhardt von Gneisenau to Clausewitz and Che Guevara.

E. B. Ries confirms very carefully that the primacy of politics over war can be found in almost all 19th century theories of small-scale warfare. Despite understandable differences between a Clausewitz and an Engels, one finds an inseparable link between political and military theories in the thematisation of the two. The author devotes special attention to the subject of the Russian revolutionary movement of the 19th century (chapter 6)

Such analyses show very clearly that the idea of small-scale war cannot be separated from the intention to "change the world", i.e. from the principles of the ideologies of the Enlightenment period. Small-scale war as a historical mandate?

However, the practice of small-scale warfare during the 20th century is more differentiated than that of the 19th century. The author presents us with a whole range of experiences. He emphasises military support for social processes (Russia, China) and defensive small-scale warfare (Soviet Russian partisan warfare against the German Wehrmacht, anti-fascist liberation in Europe, Sino-Japanese war).

For Erich B. Ries emphasises the theory and practice of Latin American guerrillas (chapters 12, 13, 14, 15, 16). The reasons are obvious. Latin America was highly stylised as a continent of guerrilla movements in the 1960s and 1970s. According to

E. B. Ries' analysis, however, it emerges that the Latin American guerrillas were also based on a false self-conception, namely that the Cuban revolution had proven the maturity of the "continental revolution". As the author points out, this serves a false and over-idiologised interpretation of the Cuban Revolution.

Despite a few passages that are characterised by a positivist style, I consider this thesis to be one of the most interesting and informative contributions that have been written on questions of violence in recent times.

As a result of the above judgement, I propose a grade of one (1) for this thesis."

Dr Fernando Mires

Expert opinion and table of contents for this thesis by Prof. Dr Shapour Ravasani.

Prof Dr Shapour Ravasani was an expert in social economics and international politics in Department 3, Institute of Sociology

"Mr Ries' initially very broad and abstract topic of "small-scale war - people's war" is concretised by him using a number of different examples.

Firstly, he looks at various terms such as terrorism, people's war, small-scale war, guerrilla war, etc. and develops definitions.

From Clausewitz - despite generally recognised differences of opinion - to Engels, Trotsky, Che Guevara and Mao Zedong, war and small-scale war are described as the "continuation of politics by other means". Politics is given primacy over the means of war, of violence. However, the content of this "politics by other means" depends on which class takes the lead within the (small-scale) war and for what purpose it is waged.

The "means", or its strategy and tactics, is in turn dependent on the objective.

Mr Ries states that "...such political options, which all result from antagonistic political interests,...can only be discussed in the context of the very political purposes to which they owe their origin...". And he sets himself the task of presenting people's wars as: "options whose morality or immorality, sense or nonsense can only become clear in their social context"

Accordingly, Mr Ries analyses the topic in detail on a historical and theoretical level, with particular attention to the problems of strategy and tactics of small-scale warfare.

Throughout the work, he succeeds in maintaining a close link between historical and theoretical analysis. This enables the reader to form their own judgement on the causes and developmental conditions of small-scale wars.

In the historical part of the work, Mr Ries proves that he has broad and well-founded knowledge in this area; he evaluates the historical material in a very differentiated and precise manner.

He examines the conditions under which small wars arose and developed in the 18th, 19th and 20th centuries within various continents and countries. The spectrum ranges from selective examples from the 18th century to the Spanish People's War, the Napoleonic invasion army (1807 - 1814), the Franco-Prussian War (1870/71), Russian small-scale war tactics in the 19th century, the Russian revolutions of 1905 and 1917, the Soviet partisan war and the wars between the Soviet Union and Russia. The book covers everything from the 19th century, the Russian revolutions of 1905 and 1917, the Soviet partisan war against the German Wehrmacht (1941) to the Chinese War of Liberation, guerrilla movements in Latin America after the Second World War (Cuba, Brazil, Uruguay) and the prospects for guerrilla tactics in industrialised nations.

Mr Ries' above-average ability to present and evaluate causes, consequences and contexts is convincingly demonstrated in this section. On the one hand, he succeeds in working out the common basic conditions and contexts of the emergence of small-scale wars, while on the other hand he always takes into account the specific national or epoch-bound preconditions and conditions when analysing the concrete case.

The question of strategy and tactics, success or failure in small wars is directly dependent on the concrete analysis, which takes into account the specific circumstances of a society in every respect.

In this context, Mr Ries makes it clear that the significance and effect of the exogenous factor, colonialism and imperialism, plays an ever-increasing role within the *underdeveloped countries. An anti-colonial or anti-imperialist small war within underdeveloped countries is at the same time class struggle against the ruling class cooperating and intertwined with foreign countries. And vice versa, a struggle against oppression and exploitation by this class is basically an anti-colonial or anti-imperialist struggle.*

In order to recognise and evaluate these connections, an above-average knowledge of history and theory is necessary. Mr Ries proves with his work that he has this knowledge.

When analysing social theories and the theory of small-scale warfare, he works as carefully as he does critically and predominantly uses primary literature. In this context, criticism does not mean strict rejection, but rather a creative and constructive debate.

One of the advantages of this work is that it always sticks to concrete analyses and does not slip into abstract considerations that are detached from practice.

Mr Ries also takes a clear and firm position on the core issue of violence. This includes the thesis "Violence has played a decidedly reactionary role in the majority of historical events..." as well as the previous statement: "People's wars are therefore, insofar as they are directed towards the goal of establishing popular sovereignty, part of democratic movements..."

Although I disagree with Mr Ries on some of his political assessments, his above-average historical and theoretical knowledge has enabled him to convincingly present a stringent, well-founded analysis of a complex topic. I therefore award the thesis the grade

Very good (- 1 -)

Prof Dr Shapour Ravasani

Milton Keynes UK
Ingram Content Group UK Ltd.
UKHW032015161124
451262UK00019B/604